Livingstone's Labour

LIVINGSTONE'S LABOUR
A Programme for the Nineties

Ken Livingstone

UNWIN
PAPERBACKS

LONDON SYDNEY WELLINGTON

First published in Great Britain by the Trade Division
of Unwin Hyman Limited, 1989
Reprinted 1989

First published in Unwin ℝ Paperbacks in 1990

UNWIN HYMAN LIMITED
15-17 Broadwick Street, London W1V 1FP, UK

Allen & Unwin (Australia) Pty Ltd,
8 Napier Street, North Sydney, NSW 2060, Australia

Allen & Unwin (New Zealand) Pty Ltd in association with the
Port Nicholson Press Ltd,
Compusales Building, 75 Ghuznee Street, Wellington 1,
New Zealand

British Library Cataloguing in Publication Data

Livingstone, Ken, *1945–*
   Livingstone's Labour. A Programme for the Nineties
   1. Great Britain. Political parties. Labour Party
   (Great Britain). Policies
   1. Title
   324 24107
   ISBN 004 440 7327

Typeset in Garamond and printed in Finland by
Werner Söderström O.Y.

Contents

v

for Kate Allen

Preface

The idea for this book originated in the aftermath of Mrs Thatcher's third election victory whilst a wave of defeatism was sweeping through the parliamentary Labour Party. Many of the party's most senior figures were convinced that Labour could never again win a general election and were beginning to argue that the only way back to power was by accepting many of the changes the Tories had made to the British economy and state. As I listened to my colleagues debating the merits of wider share ownership or the need for Labour to accept a large part of the Tories' Education Act, I realised there was a real need for a book that evidenced the continuing strength of the Labour and socialist movement, setting out the policies and the basic underlying principles which should form the basis for the first term of a Labour government.

We need to start by looking at the major and completely unforeseen changes in our society which have transformed Britain in the last three decades. At the beginning of that period, in October 1956, Tony Crosland's *The Future of Socialism* was published and rapidly became the Bible and route map for the social democrats who dominated the 1964 and 1974 Labour governments. But the end result of those years was failure, defeat for Labour and the triumph of Thatcherism. Therefore, before we can begin any lasting reconstruction of the Labour Party, we must understand why Labour failed in the past and how that failure was inextricably linked with the continuing failure of the British economy.

This book is not meant to be a shopping list of worthy policies about which most of us would agree anyway – that would be profoundly boring and mean covering a range of subjects so wide that none could be looked at in depth. There is no point in writing several thousand words proving that the Tories have been nasty to the National Health Service and that Labour will spend more because everyone knows this – it is a battle we have won and Labour already occupies the high ground in the area of health policy. Instead, I have concentrated on those more difficult areas where Labour has failed in the past and continues to be confused and uncertain in the present – the economy and the trade unions, defence and international relations, the undemocratic nature of the British state, the rights of women, the environment, Third World debt, racism, and Ireland.

The book is deliberately limited to what I believe would be an achievable package of modernising reforms capable of being carried out in the lifetime of one Parliament. However, in examining the problems a Labour government would face, I have invariably taken a long historical view of their origins because I find it is easier to understand a current situation and arrive at a solution if it is studied from a historical perspective rather than in the heat and confusion of current political squabbles. The drawback to this approach is that in covering such a wide area of policy one is inevitably forced to be highly selective in deciding which historical events have the greatest relevance to understanding current problems. Virtually all the chapters could be expanded to become a book in their own right but such a project would take me well beyond the next election, completely losing any relevance to the current debates about the way forward for the Labour Party.

I have, of course, been assisted by many people in the production of this book and because of the wholly inadequate nature of research assistance available to MPs, almost all that help has been voluntary and unrewarded (indeed when I started I was still operating without even a desk or a telephone in the House of Commons). As a member of both Labour's National Executive Committee and the Policy Review Committee, dealing with the economy, I have had access to all the papers and debates of those two bodies. I have incorporated into this book many of the ideas and facts considered by those two committees and would like to thank those who unwittingly assisted me in this way. For similar reasons, I must also thank the Ariel Road Group. This is a small group of radical economists who meet monthly to discuss modern economic problems and I have been privileged to be invited to take part. They kindly devoted an evening to discussing my labours and I will repay this by not mentioning them by name, as some of them work for employers who would not approve of the company they keep!

I specifically wish to thank John Ross, who assembled both the economic data base I have used in this book and also much of the material for the chapters dealing with international relations. Jacques

Peretti also assisted in these two areas. Robin Ramsey kindly read and corrected the section on MI5 and MI6. Geoff Mulgan provided comprehensive and valuable guidance on the vital question of fibre optic cable systems. Neil Grant (who also suffers the mixed blessing of being the Chair of Brent East Labour Party) did a massive amount of original research on the dirty war in Ireland and the abuses of power by MI5 and MI6. Colin Wallace and Fred Holroyd both provided valuable information about the intelligence services (much of which it has not been possible to use because of the restrictive libel laws in Britain). Sheila Rowbotham and Hermione Harris gave detailed and lengthy lists of criticisms and corrections to the chapter on women, as well as being prepared to devote hours of their time to debating them with me. I have also been lucky to have access to the work of Chris Knight whose radical and controversial research on early civilisations will be published within the year. Vital in ensuring that I found the time to write this book whilst not neglecting my other duties was Maureen Charleson, my secretary/PA at the House of Commons, who against all the odds has still retained a sense of humour after ten years of working for Labour MPs.

I particularly want to record my appreciation for my agent, Anne McDermid, who went looking for someone to publish my humble efforts, and Michael Pountney of Unwin Hyman who came to my rescue, stepping in when Collins backed out of publishing the book on the grounds that it was offensive to Rupert Murdoch. Finally, to Janet Clayton, my editor, who tolerated my six-month delay in completing the manuscript without ever once losing her temper, I promise to do better next time.

1

Losing Badly

Labour's 1987 general election defeat was more unexpected, systematically comprehensive and demoralising than anyone could have anticipated. Within the Labour Party, both locally and nationally, the sheer professionalism of our campaign had convinced us all that even if we could not defeat Thatcher this time around, we could at least close the gap so that victory was an obvious possibility at the following election. It certainly looked as though we would finally dispose of the ridiculous claims of the centre parties that they were the real alternative to Thatcher, and we might even reduce the Tory majority in the Commons to the point where Tory rebels would be able to block the more unpopular Thatcherite policies.

These hopes were not based on daydreams. During the election itself there was an overwhelming consensus in the media that Labour had run the best campaign and there were obvious signs of panic in the Tory camp during the last weekend before polling day. Whatever doubts party activists may have had about the obvious concentration on the personality of the leader at the expense of explaining our policies, the cynical asides about 'Kinnock – the video' faded away as the opinion polls showed Labour closing the gap on the Tories. The Harris poll in *The Observer* on 17 May was the first to show the Tory lead dropping into single figures with the gap closing to just 6 per cent. In the days that followed there were another nineteen polls in which the Tory lead was under 8 per cent, of which four were down to 4 per cent. The final week of the campaign started with the now notorious Newsnight poll showing the Tory lead reduced to just 3 per cent which, if accurate, would have meant a hung Parliament and the eviction of Mrs Thatcher from 10 Downing Street.

In addition, most people assumed that the 1983 general election had been a freak result which was so bad for Labour that we had nowhere to go but up. In that year the Labour Party had run what was by common consent the worst campaign of any major political party in a Western democracy in the post-war world. The party's 1983 manifesto had been attacked by an array of former leading figures from the Labour movement and was almost completely ignored by most Shadow Cabinet spokespeople (who were privately rubbishing it in off the record briefings to the media). The defence policy was savagely attacked by former Labour Prime Minister James Callaghan and its interpretation was argued over throughout the campaign by Michael Foot, the leader of the party, and Denis Healey, the deputy leader. Michael Foot himself, although one of the most decent and sincere people ever to rise to a position of leadership in the party, was completely lacking in the less savoury skills required of a party leader – a fact that was painfully apparent to the public throughout the length of the campaign. In running its campaign, the party completely ignored polling and advertising until the last minute, thus helping to create the impression of a party incapable of governing itself let alone the country.

Against the background of this shambles the slick efficiency (and cost) of the Tory campaign was painful to behold. The economy was booming (following the usual pre-election government induced spending spree) and Britain was still basking in the post-victory glow of the Falklands War (in which, after thirty-seven years of post-war decline, Britain had finally been able to beat the hell out of a country smaller, weaker and even worse governed than we were).

It is not surprising, therefore, that there was considerable optimism about Labour's chances both nationally and in the various local campaigns. In my own constituency of Brent East, where we were defending a majority of 12.4 per cent over the Tories, an independent opinion poll conducted for the *London Daily News* a week before election day showed the majority increasing to 19 per cent. Other polls carried out in Bernie Grant's Tottenham and Mrs Thatcher's Finchley showed similar swings to Labour. The Brent poll merely confirmed the general mood I encountered on the streets and the findings of our canvassers on the doorstep.

The only small clouds on the horizon concerned taxation and lesbian and gay rights. Some voters were clearly worried by the confusion over Labour's taxation policy and feared that their taxes would rise under a Labour government. Others had been taken in by the campaign run by Norman Tebbit and the worst elements of the Tory press which alleged that some Labour councils were encouraging children to become homosexuals. Sadly, the Labour leadership chose not to explain or defend what Labour councils were doing, so the case for the defence went by default and many voters took Labour's stereophonic silence on the issue to be an admission of guilt. The result was that I encountered life-long Labour voters who were 'not voting this time because of all this lesbianism being taught in the schools'. But still the response on the doorstep was overwhelmingly favourable and it was only the final canvassing returns from the last days of the campaign that showed a small decline of 2 per cent in the vote promised to Labour. On election day itself many of my local party workers felt confident enough to go off and get out the vote in Westminster North.

It was only after 10 p.m. when the polling booths closed and the ITN exit poll initially predicted a Tory lead of 9 per cent that it was obvious that Labour had again lost very badly indeed. The final Tory lead over Labour in Great Britain was 11.8 per cent, a swing to Labour of only 1.7 per cent. The Labour vote had crept up by just 3.2 per cent (at the expense of the centre parties) whilst the Tory vote had declined by only 0.2 per cent!

These raw figures concealed a pattern that actually made this a worse election result than that of 1983. Then, we had many excuses for doing so badly. None of these applied in 1987. There was a grim warning here for Labour in the way in which our vote was actually continuing to decline in the more prosperous areas of Britain where the population was growing whilst increasing in areas of poverty and population decline – with the obvious exception of Scotland which needs to be looked at separately. Thus although we were winning seats in the North we were actually losing seats in southern England, including three in London.

At the count in Brent East the increase in the majority promised by the opinion poll failed to materialise and the majority was actually reduced from 12.4 to 4.2 per cent. There was no way to avoid the conclusion that we had been badly damaged in that last week by the confusion over our taxation policies.

As the news gradually came through from the rest of the country my gloom increased. I suspected that rather than conduct a rational, academic analysis of the reasons for our defeat, the leadership of the party would look at the superficial pattern of the results and simply blame it all on the left wing and in particular on the London Labour Party, as they had done in the aftermath of the Greenwich by-election defeat at the beginning of 1987. It was only a matter of hours before my suspicions were confirmed. That weekend the papers were filled with planted stories from Neil Kinnock's office announcing that he intended to crack down on the 'loony left' by changing the way in which local Labour parties selected their candidates. It was predicted that this would reduce the number of left-wingers selected. There were also the first leaks hinting that the party would have to dump its policy of unilateral nuclear disarmament, as well as accepting many of the economic changes that had taken place under the Tories – such as privatisation, wider share ownership and anti-trade union laws – as permanent.

Soon, there followed a series of articles from academics and former Marxists announcing that the working class had shrunk to the point where Labour could never hope to win another election. Leading members of Labour's Shadow Cabinet began to talk of the need for an electoral pact with the centre parties as the only way of defeating Thatcher. All this defeatism was gleefully taken up by the media and rapidly became the perceived wisdom of the day. Needless to say, those of us arguing a different case were largely ignored by the media who, having trumpeted that 'Mr Kinnock had a good campaign', could not now report the claims of the left that Labour's campaign had been fundamentally flawed from start to finish.

Every election study of recent times, both here and in the USA, has demonstrated that the single most important factor in determining the outcome of an election is economic policy. This economic factor comprises several different but related issues: whether or not people have had an increase in their standard of living in the months preceding an election; whether they think the economy will improve or deteriorate under the incumbent government; whether they feel the opposition's policies would be better or worse for the economy; and what they remember of the state of the economy the last time the opposition was in power.

Given the ability of the government of the day to manipulate the economy to increase the feeling of economic well-being in the run-up to an election, any opposition starts at a disadvantage. On top of that, most voters in Britain still have a vivid recollection of the disastrous economic policies of the last two Labour governments of 1964 and

1974 – so any Labour opposition campaign starts from a doubly disadvantaged position. Thus in order to win any opposition needs to capture the economic high ground from the government of the day. If it does that then no other issue, however ruthlessly exploited by the government, is going to cost it the election. For this reason, the leadership's obsession with the idea that Labour would have won had it not been committed to the removal of nuclear weapons is a diversion. Undoubtedly, the party's defence policy is a mass of contradictions, but as Ron Todd explained to the 1988 Labour Party Conference, if it was the case that it cost us the election then how was it that Labour's vote increased in the North and Scotland? Surely, no one is going to suggest that it is only people in the South who are concerned with the issue of defence.

Unfortunately, the leadership did not seem to realise that our need to capture the high ground on the economy and iron out the contradictions in our defence policy meant that we should concentrate the bulk of our campaigning work on these issues. Instead, they spent much of the four years before the election campaigning on 'soft' issues such as the National Health Service, where we already have massive popular support for our policies.

Indeed, throughout his leadership Neil Kinnock gave the impression that rather than concentrating on the political enemy outside, most of his time was being spent on internal party battles around the issues of the miners' strike and the Militant tendency. Many people contrasted the strength of his vigorous denunciation of Derek Hatton with the weakness of his attack on Mrs Thatcher during the Westland debate in the House of Commons. The same question of priorities was raised again at the time of the leak of the notorious letter from his press officer, Patricia Hewitt, which complained that it was the handling of the issue of lesbian and gay rights and other 'loony left' issues which had cost us the Greenwich by-election. As he became embroiled in this further party dispute, the leaders of Britain's two largest unions, (John Edmonds of the General and Municipal and Ron Todd of the Transport and General) publicly criticised the fact that he was giving so much of his time and energy to these internal party rows.

Yet whatever the public image, the reality was that Neil Kinnock was more firmly in charge of the Labour Party than any previous leader since Harold Wilson, in the early 1960s. He had a commanding majority on Labour's elected National Executive Committee which he downgraded as he transferred power to the Shadow Cabinet and his own coterie of advisers. Labour's standing in the polls had jumped by 10 per cent following his election as leader and this had restored morale inside the Parliamentary Labour Party although there was some continuing criticism of his lack of 'weight', or success, in the twice weekly ritual clashes with Mrs Thatcher at Prime Minister's Question Time. His influence over the party conference was such that he had been able to persuade it to drop the Labour Party's opposition to both council house sales and the Common Market.

Given his strong control of the party, it is even more difficult to understand why he did not launch an early, vigorous campaign on the issue of the economy. Soon after becoming leader he came out with the clear idea that Labour had to be a party that was strongly identified with expanding Britain's productive capacity rather than simply redistributing existing wealth, but it was not until January 1987, just five months before the election, that the party's economic policy statement was issued. By that time the resurgent Tory lead in the opinion polls had created a deep sense of demoralisation inside the party headquarters and despair in the leader's immediate group of advisers.

MORI, the Labour Party's pollsters, had already circulated a confidential memorandum in August 1986 warning that although Labour still had a lead in the opinion polls, this would disappear when people were asked which party had the best policies generally. It also showed that the leader was seen as 'lacking in strength' and pointed out that 'people want a party that they can trust, that will keep its promises, that has a concern for the interests of the people and that can best improve their standard of living'. MORI advised the party that it had to recover the voters who had been captured by the Tories from amongst skilled and unskilled workers, as well as trade unionists, but that in the key marginal seats that Labour needed to win there were above average numbers of white-collar workers and home owners.

By the time MORI again reported confidentially to the party in April 1987, the Tories had surged ahead in the polls and Labour had been through the disasters of the Greenwich by-election, the bungled handling of the Zircon spy satellite affair, and Neil Kinnock's inept and humiliating trip to Washington to try to explain Labour's defence policy to President Reagan. The MORI report was shattering. Amongst voters, 69 per cent felt Labour's leaders were 'poor', 69 per cent felt the party was 'too extreme' and 55 per cent felt the economy would worsen under Labour.

The April Gallup poll delivered a further blow when it reported that only 26 per cent thought Neil Kinnock was doing a good job as opposed to 63 per cent who thought he was doing badly. Mrs Thatcher's rating was 30 per cent better. Although Neil Kinnock's 26 per cent rating compared unfavourably with Harold Wilson's 58 per cent shortly before he became Prime Minister in 1964, it was almost identical to Edward Heath's 28 per cent shortly before he won the 1970 election. Before that election Heath had spent five years attacking the economic record of the Labour government, and during the election campaign he had taken on and decisively won the economic argument against Labour.

The message of the polls was clear. Labour's only chance of defeating the Tories was to win the economic argument, but the lack of attention to developing a coherent economic policy and campaigning for it in the preceding four years had left the party fatally weakened in this area. As early as 1985, the party's private polls had reported that the public perceived 'Labour as a party that cares ... but that does not know how to generate wealth and that prints money to solve economic problems'. Given the weakness of Labour's position on the economy, the leadership decided to con-centrate on the social issues where Labour was in tune with public thinking and to emphasise the positive qualities in Neil Kinnock's personality. It was in this panicky atmosphere that the detailed tables showing how the Labour Party's proposed tax changes would affect different groups of taxpayers failed to get the serious study that was needed.

In line with the new election strategy, the party's research depart-ment was told to produce a short manifesto which avoided detail. Unlike the 1983 manifesto, the final draft did not include commit-ments to withdraw from the Common Market, abolish the Lords or take over private hospitals. The defence policy was watered down by ignoring the party's policy of getting rid of US nuclear bases and saying that cruise missiles would be retained whilst US–USSR disarmament talks continued.

Once the election was under way, the lack of clear economic and defence policies rapidly became apparent. A survey (Butler and Kava-nagh, *The British General Election of 1987* (1988)) of one-sixth of all local election addresses showed that Labour candidates reflected the lack of leadership on these issues. Although 89 per cent mentioned unemployment, 56 per cent public spending, 35 per cent manufacturing industry and 25 per cent the minimum wage only 18 per cent dealt with income tax, 1 per cent with inflation and 0 per cent with growth! In contrast with 1964 when 75 per cent of our candidates mentioned the modernisation of the economy, a mere 6 per cent dealt with new technology in 1987 – a clear indication of how much Labour had lost the initiative in the debate about the future of the British economy. Things were little better on the issue of nuclear weapons with only 38 per cent mentioning the issue, in contrast with 58 per cent in 1964.

Although the policy content of Labour's campaign was fatally weak, the techniques of presentation were so professional that initially they attracted more attention and comment than our policies. For the first time in living memory it was the Labour machine which won so convincingly that even the Tories accepted they had lost the media battle.

Arising from the disaster of the 1983 campaign, the Labour Party went back to square one and spent much of the time between the elections completely rethinking its attitude to modern polling, advertising and marketing techniques. It was profoundly influenced by the trail blazed by the GLC in its campaign against abolition, and when the party saw the impact that campaign had had it rapidly decided that the time had come to join the twentieth century. The party could not spend on anything like the scale of the GLC between elections, but funds were set aside so that during the vital few weeks of the election campaign it would be able to spend about half as much as the Tories.

What the Labour leadership overlooked, however, was the fact that the GLC used glossy packaging in order to sell radical, socialist policies. It was ridiculous to assume that during the heat and debate of an election campaign the glossy packaging could be used to obscure the lack of modern, relevant policies.

In the first week, the intense concentration on the frenetic pace of Neil Kinnock around the country held the media's attention. It also established a pattern which meant that by the end of the campaign Neil Kinnock had been quoted 481 times on television and radio as opposed to Mrs Thatcher's 421 appearances, Dr Owen's 384, David Steel's 287 and Norman Tebbit's 139. The only other figures from the Labour Party to be quoted more than Denis Healey's 40 times were Brian Gould at 72 and Roy Hattersley at 95.

When the Labour Party used another senior party figure to issue a policy statement on subjects such as women or science and technology, it was often the case that coverage was swamped by that day's photo-opportunity with Neil Kinnock.

The first televised Labour Party political broadcast on 21 May (directed by Hugh Hudson, whose work included 'Chariots of Fire') carried this approach to an extreme. After what was undoubtedly the most effective and evocative item of political propaganda ever seen in Britain, Neil Kinnock's ratings in the polls jumped briefly by 16 per cent. As a project of selling Neil Kinnock it had succeeded temporarily, but the very fact that it did not deal with any specific policy and ended with the word 'Kinnock' on the screen, rather than the usual appeal to vote Labour, only served to remind people of their doubts about Labour's readiness to govern. In *The British General Election of 1987*, Martin Harrison describes it as

> a stunning invocation of the Labourism of the 1940s by the media techniques of the 1980s. For all its technical brilliance, though, its implicit defensiveness was revealing of the party's underlying weakness. To focus so deliberately on an internal dispute [with Derek Hatton] smacked of desperation as well as audacity. And its single-minded promotion of the leader at such cost to Labour tradition spoke volumes about the failure to establish him securely over the three preceding years, and about the party's vulnerability on policy.

It was not possible, however, to distract attention from policy for long. Four days later the Tories claimed that Labour's spending plans would increase income tax to 58 per cent or VAT to 50 per cent. Brian Gould and Roy Hattersley promised that no one earning under £500 a week would be hurt by Labour's tax changes but Neil Kinnock admitted that some would be losers. Immediately, the press moved on to the attack and Brian Gould was forced to announce that only the richest 5 per cent of people would pay more, but by now the damage had been done. Like other candidates I was now as confused about our policy as our leaders were. Fortunately, I always managed to get a laugh out of the problem, when asked at public meetings what our tax policy was, by replying that I was 'totally opposed to any tax increase on the sort of people in the audience tonight'.

The private MORI polls for the Labour leadership continued to make depressing reading. Although Labour scored well on its traditional issues such as health and education, the party continued to register terrible ratings on the economy. Most people thought we would handle the economy, particularly inflation, badly. A total of 56 per cent believed there would be an economic crisis if Labour won. During the campaign those who thought we would handle defence well fell from 31 to 24 per cent. By the end of the election, for each person being swung towards Labour by our campaign two were moving away. The only good news was that in the personality ratings Neil Kinnock had closed the gap on Mrs Thatcher to 8 per cent.

Unfortunately, though, votes are determined on the key issue of the economy and when the ITN exit poll asked voters for the one most important issue which decided their vote, only 6 per cent mentioned any party leader. After all the effort that went into the selling of Neil Kinnock, the final Gallup analysis must have made bitter reading for those who had devised the strategy. Asked which leader had performed most impressively in the campaign 43 per cent chose the Labour leader compared with just 20 per cent for Mrs Thatcher. But when the same sample was asked who would make the best Prime Minister 42 per cent chose Mrs Thatcher to just 28 per cent for Neil Kinnock. Of all the party leaders Neil remained the one with the highest negative rating – 44 per cent of voters saying he would make the worst Prime Minister. All the massive effort of the previous month had lifted Neil's ratings by just 6 per cent and reduced the Prime Minister's by 4 per cent. The gap on policy remained as wide as ever.

In the detailed election analysis published by John Curtice and Michael Steed in *The British General Election of 1987*, they come to various conclusions:

1 Whilst former Alliance voters in the North switched mainly to Labour, in the South they split equally between the two main parties.
2 'At almost every election since 1959 Labour have done better in the North of Britain than in the South, while the opposite has been true of the Conservatives. This pattern was particularly marked in 1979 and 1983. The geography of voting changes in 1987 in general terms continues this well established divergence ... We conclude that a large part of the geography of voting in 1987 must reflect such fundamental changes as the long-term decline

of the North's economic base and the social processes, such as middle-class migration, which that has produced.'
3   Labour's ethnic minority candidates do not necessarily suffer from discrimination in voting.
4   'There is no evidence of a general unwillingness to vote for left-wing Labour candidates.'
5   Labour faces the danger of becoming a permanent minority party unless it can reverse the Tory advance in southern urban England.

In retrospect, it can be seen that Labour ran a very professional campaign with a very traditional message that was already beginning to lose its appeal thirty years ago. It seemed we had little to say to attract back those who had been alienated by our economic incompetence in the past and did not even begin to understand those who work in the new technological industries, or whose main concern is with the new issues of the environment, gender, race or leisure. We appealed successfully to our traditional supporters but failed to break out of that declining ghetto. Our private polls showed that the key uncommitted voters we needed to win in the South were worried that we would damage their standard of living. Although many of them disliked the radical right-wing policies of Mrs Thatcher, the issue of the standard of living overrode any other consideration.

How Labour should respond to that situation is the subject of the following chapter.

2

The Fall of Hindhead

Every Tuesday and Thursday afternoon when Parliament is in session the benches of the House of Commons are packed for the spectacle of Prime Minister's Question Time in which anyone from the Leader of the Opposition down to the newest backbencher gets the chance to throw a question at the Prime Minister. Hours of work go into devising the nastiest imaginable questions and no doubt in No 10 even more hours of work are devoted to anticipating the supplementary questions which will follow the Prime Minister's answer. Unfortunately, the rules of the House only guarantee a member the right to ask a question – they lay down no restrictions on what may pass for an answer and there are frequent appeals to the Speaker to rule that the question has not really been answered at all. Many answers are evasive and sometimes there is a point blank refusal to answer – as in the case of any inquiries about the security services. But the answers which are most commonly given, and cause the most anger and uproar, are those which simply dismiss any criticism of the present government's record by reciting some old statistic from the period of the last Labour government which, it is claimed, demonstrates that the particular problem was even worse then. Whilst as a technique it is quite effective at squashing former Labour Cabinet ministers it is, of course, particularly galling to those opposition MPs who were still in secondary school at the time of the last Labour government.

It is no good them simply complaining that Mrs Thatcher does not answer the question. The vast majority of politicians have always behaved that way and there is no doubt that the vast majority of the population find it both childish and very boring. It can also be very confusing. No one who listens to politicians swapping statistics about which party has the worst record on inflation or productivity or investment can come to any conclusion other than that they are all telling the truth and therefore have all been appallingly incompetent.

Listening to this twice weekly ritual of abusive statistic swapping made me realise that Labour's inability to escape from its record of economic failure could mean we would never again win office – unless we can come up with an economic policy more credible than those we had on offer at the last three elections. I therefore volunteered to go on the Labour Party's Economic Policy Review Group and make that my major area of study and research during my first two years on Labour's NEC.

As I ploughed through the piles of documents produced by Labour's economic advisers and several historical analyses and monetarist tomes, slowly absorbing the various arguments about who was responsible for Britain's economic problems, it became apparent that our long historic decline can be dated from the 1840s. Although it might seem ridiculous to pinpoint the start of Britain's current economic problems at the time when Sir Robert Peel was Prime Minister (he has after all been dead since 1850), unless we understand the importance of the shift in national economic priorities that took place during the period of his government between 1841 and 1846, we will never understand just how deeply ingrained in British institutions and thinking are the causes of our economic decline.

The truth is that the key decisions which shaped British economic development were taken in the mid-nineteenth century. Britain emerged from the Napoleonic Wars as the undisputed winner. Its early lead in the Industrial Revolution, coupled with its vast and expanding empire, meant that Britain's GNP increased at twice the rate of its population growth. Between 1815 and 1850 average real wages increased by between 15 and 25 per cent. In 1750, Britain had been a minor player in European politics but by 1800 it had already overhauled all other nations in its level of industrialisation and by 1860 it controlled 40–45 per cent of the entire industrial capacity of the world.

Peel, however, came to power in 1841 at a time of recession and industrial and political unrest. The political upheavals surrounding the Great Reform Bill of 1832 had converted Peel into a classic and early example of a 'one nation' consensus Tory. He believed that Britain's industrial lead and imperial wealth allowed it to make concessions to the domestic working class which its major competitors could not afford to make. By repealing the Corn Laws he produced cheap bread for the masses and opened the way for British industrial capital to set about creating an international free trade system. Peel's great compromise thus defused any revolutionary potential in the British working class and gave it a shared interest in the preservation of empire with financial capital, the most powerful section of the British ruling class. As the rest of Europe was convulsed by the revolutions of 1848, Peel remained convinced that Britain's rulers had only avoided a similar fate because of the historic compromise he had engineered.

Of itself, the struggle to create an international free trade system via the repeal of the Corn Laws would not necessarily have led to a decline of the British economy – on the contrary, it might have led to intensified development of the domestic economy in order to engage in international competition. What was decisive was that British capital was concentrated in investment overseas instead of building up the domestic economy.

Investment abroad increased from £6 million a year in the early 1820s to £75 million a year in the early 1870s. By that time the £50 million annual profit on these overseas investments was also being largely invested abroad, on a scale not matched by any rival power. This becomes clear if Britain is compared with the two countries which overtook it in the latter part of the nineteenth century – the United States and Germany. The United States was a net importer of finance capital throughout the latter part of the nineteenth century and German investments abroad remained tiny compared to domestic investment.

Table 2.1 Germany and the United Kingdom: Foreign Investment as a Percentage of Total Net Capital Formation at Current Prices

	Germany	UK
1851/5–1861/5	2.2	29.1
1861/5–1871/5	12.9	40.1
1871/5–1881/5	14.1	28.9
1881/5–1891/5	19.9	51.1
1891/5–1901/5	9.7	29.7
1901/5–1911/13	5.7	52.9

Source   David S. Landes, *Unbound Prometheus* (1969).

As can be seen in Table 2.1, the pattern of British and German investment was totally different. German overseas investment never rose above 20 per cent of total investment and was frequently below 10 per cent, domestic investment always accounting for at least 80 per cent of the total. At the other extreme, British foreign investment never fell below 28 per cent of total investment and by the eve of the First World War was nearly 53 per cent. Germany pursued a pattern of economic growth with investment concentrated in the domestic economy; Britain pursued a pattern of growth in which investment took place abroad and not in the domestic economy. With such a pattern of investment the far higher rate of growth of the German and US economies is completely logical.

Britain's decline was not immediately obvious. Although industrial production grew at an annual rate of 4 per cent a year between 1820 and 1840, it declined to 3 per cent between 1840 and 1870 and only 1.5 per cent a year between 1875 and 1894. Britain's share of world manufacturing output dropped from 22.9 per cent in 1880 to just 13.6 per cent in 1913. The USA and Germany soared past Britain and by the start of the First World War Britain was third in the industrial stakes and still going down whilst owning 43 per cent of the world's foreign investments.

Such a pattern of overseas investment was self-reinforcing – a negative spiral of decline. The profits from overseas investments took the pressure off British industry to be competitive because, unlike Germany, the balance of payments could be balanced *without* a competitive domestic economy. It also allowed the British establishment to avoid many of the conflicts with organised labour which would have arisen if British workers had been forced to match the increasing productivity of foreign workers.

Without such competitive pressure, and with a far lower proportion of investment going into the domestic economy, it was unnecessary to adopt the latest techniques or produce a highly skilled workforce – as did the United States and Germany – requiring, as they do, high levels of direct and infrastructure investment. Administering and safeguarding British overseas assets, however, eventually called for high military spending and a premium on quite different skills from those of the rapidly progressing technologically based US and German economies.

This distortion of the skills required for the British economy worked through at every level from the top to the bottom. In Britain in 1902, for example, there were only about 300 teaching posts for scientists in British universities, a further 250 posts in government laboratories, and perhaps 180–230 posts in British industry. This contrasts with Germany where the chemical industry alone employed over 1,500 scientists.

In Britain, the highest paid occupations were not those involved in building up manufacturing industry but those managing its foreign investments. In 1914, the salary of a university lecturer varied between £150 and £250 compared with the average salary of a dentist of £368, a barrister of £478, and a Treasury civil servant (principal grade) of £855. In Britain, apart from the scholarships awarded under the 1851 Great Exhibition there were only 214 full-time postgraduate research awards anywhere in the country. By 1872 there were eleven technical and twenty other universities in Germany and in the United States well over seventy universities. In both the United States and Germany systematic organisation of postgraduate scientific research was introduced; in contrast there were only four universities in England and a further four in Scotland.

In the late nineteenth century, Germany was establishing universal primary education and an unparalleled system of technical and engineering education. Future British Tory Prime Minister Lord Salisbury was not impressed. He characterised the attempt to establish primary education in Britain as 'pumping learning into louts'. By 1900, the average German worker had spent 32 hours a week for 9 years in school and then a further 5 hours a week for 2 to 4 years in part-time education; whereas the average English worker received 2 years less in school, with only two-thirds of the hours each week, and with no part-time education afterwards. The technology gap represented by such figures is devastating. Britain was already trapped in a low investment, low skill economy ninety years before Nigel Lawson coined the phrase.

As foreign investments were the main priority and concern of the financial institutions of the City of London, this inevitably led to the subordination of domestic manufacturing to the international operations of the City. The result was a frequently overvalued pound which in turn further weakened the already relatively feeble domestic manufacturing base of the British economy.

Following the First World War, the situation rapidly deteriorated. The war had cost Britain 23 billion dollars (40 per cent of the entire cost to the allied powers) and this had necessitated the liquidation of much of this country's foreign investment. Britain's leaders now set out to try to regain its former power just at the time when a savage recession cut world manufacturing production by 7 per cent. The appalling wreckage of the domestic economy during the 1920s was caused mainly by an overvalued pound, demanded by City financial institutions eager to resume investment overseas and restore pre-war exchange rates based on a return to the gold standard. The upshot was that although world manufacturing production returned to pre-war levels by the end of 1922, it took Britain until the late 1920s to achieve the same position – the worst record of any of the major powers.

Following the Second World War, the same mentality and policies dominated the economic strategies of both Labour and Tory governments throughout the post-war period up until the election of the Thatcher government in 1979. Faced with a further massive liquidation of Britain's overseas assets in order to finance the war, successive governments tried to close the resulting trade gap with the rest of the world by a series of exhortations to British workers to work harder. When these failed governments resorted to wage freezes and recessions in order to 'shake out surplus labour'. These policies were constantly undermined, however, by the desire to pretend that Britain was a still a major power, by artificially high defence spending that flowed from this, and as governments struggled to maintain an artificially high pound this meant a constant erosion of our industrial base.

In contrast, the post-war Japanese and West German governments produced their economic miracles by ridiculously undervalued currencies, by concentrating on domestic and not foreign investment, and by domestic policies which ensured that the interests of the financial sectors of their economies were subordinate to the needs of industry. They undoubtedly found this easier to achieve because of the relative weakness of the financial institutions in Japan and West Germany after the destruction of the Second World War and by the elimination of their foreign investment.

In Britain, of course, the constant erosion of our industrial base only increased the influence of the financial institutions within the economy and governments became ever more sensitive to 'City opinion' in devising their economic policies.

It would be possible to go on at length about the particular failures of each government, but to little point. The same underlying pattern of British financial institutions, preferring to invest abroad rather than modernise and expand our own industrial base, has been in evidence for nearly 150 years with devastating consequences for our industrial performance. On its own, this neglect of our domestic economy would have been bad enough to cope with, but it had a further damaging effect in terms of the influence of the policy of overseas investment on British defence strategy and levels of defence spending.

A national economic strategy based on foreign investment demanded immense military expenditure to protect those overseas investments. In the fifty years that followed the end of the Napoleonic Wars, in 1815, Britain was so unchallenged as the world superpower that military spending could be kept to under 3 per cent of GNP. By the late nineteenth century, however, the growing power of Germany and the USA forced a massive increase in defence spending as Britain struggled to ensure that its fleet remained the most technologically advanced military force in the world.

As Paul Kennedy demonstrates in *The Rise and Fall of the Great Powers* (1988), there is a recurring pattern of low levels of military spending as a nation rises to become an economic superpower. As each rose to predominance in its turn, first Britain between 1820 and 1860, the USA up until 1940, and Japan between 1945 and the present day, defence spending never rose above 3 per cent of GNP and was usually kept below 2 per cent. There is also a clear link between increasing levels of defence spending and loss of economic dynamism as a larger and larger proportion of the national wealth is consumed in escalating armaments programmes.

The consequences of this for Britain as it struggled to keep up with the USA and the USSR in the period following the Second World War are well documented. The nonsense of maintaining a British presence east of Suez was ruinous for the balance of payments. It is the case that between 1950 and 1970 the British balance of payments would have been in surplus for all but three years if overseas military spending had been curtailed. Thus those twenty years of wasted stop–go economic policies could have been avoided if Britain had refused to play the role of policing the world on behalf of the USA.

The second impact of excessive defence spending on the British economy was the disproportionate consumption of our scarce scientific and technical resources by the military. When we wonder why it is that we do not produce the same proportion of new techniques, products and processes in our domestic economy as do Germany and Japan, it is because over half our scientists are working on military projects. Half the scientists in Western Europe working on defence projects are in Britain!

These problems continue to the present day. The British economy still spends a higher proportion of GDP on military spending (Table 2.2) than any other major state in NATO (except for the United States) – in general two per cent higher than West Germany. If Britain was to reduce its defence spending to the same proportion of its GDP as France and West Germany, it would release an average of £9 billion a year for investment in the modernisation of our industry or the reconstruction of our welfare state.

Table 2.2   Military Spending as a Proportion of GDP

	1970	1973	1975	1977	1978	1981	1982	1984
USA	7.4	6.1	5.9	6.0	5.1	5.8	7.2	6.4
Britain	4.9	4.9	3.7	5.0	4.6	5.0	5.1	5.5
W. Germany	3.3	3.4	3.9	3.4	4.2	3.4	4.3	3.3
France	3.7	3.5	2.6	3.6	4.0	4.2	4.1	4.1
Japan	0.8	0.9	0.9	0.9	0.9	1.0	1.0	1.0

Source   International Institute for Strategic Studies

These then are the endemic problems of the British economy and political success or failure for the Labour Party depends on its ability to tackle them. Unfortunately, any impartial analysis of the five periods of Labour government reveals a record of failure and broken promises which is so bad as to have become a major barrier which the Labour Party must overcome if it is ever to have a chance of winning another election.

The classic pattern of Labour governments is one in which the party comes to power at a time of economic crisis, promising to rebuild our industrial base and redistribute wealth more fairly within society. The redistribution of wealth (usually in the form of increased spending on health, education and housing) takes place rapidly, but the various incentives and national plans aimed at increasing investment in our industrial base fail to have much of an impact and the economic position stubbornly refuses to improve. After two or three years an economic crisis, usually emanating from the financial institutions in the City of London, causes a collapse of confidence in the pound. The Labour government, in its desire to restore financial orthodoxy, is forced to cut back the welfare state and increase taxes on ordinary working-class families. Not surprisingly, many disgusted Labour voters then abstain at the next election and the Tories win.

Although the record of the 1945 Attlee government is much the best of the five (especially on the redistribution of wealth), this pattern has recurred in the last four and would no doubt have occurred in the first if it had survived a little longer. In particular, the last two periods of Labour government under Wilson from 1964 to 1970 and Wilson/Callaghan from 1974 to 1979 fit that depressing pattern perfectly.

It is the memory of the economic incompetence of those two governments which lies at the heart of Labour's electoral decline since 1966 and opened the way for the Thatcher experiment. The incomes policies of the last Labour government reduced the value of real wages by 10 per cent as well as introducing massive cuts across the whole range of welfare state services. It is little wonder that Labour lost the 1979 election or that many voters still doubt our economic competence.

Mrs Thatcher arrived at No 10 determined to reverse the decline of Britain which she believed to have been caused by post-war consensus across the political parties. She had no doubt where her loyalties lay and pursued policies which ensured that the rapidly increasing oil revenues funded a massive programme of investment abroad, and thus tried to rebuild the traditional pattern of Britain as a rentier nation.

Her policies of high interest rates, an overvalued pound and the doubling of VAT were in the direct interests of the most powerful groups of British capital. The great multinational companies, banking, oil, retail and property groups boomed as never before and more than £46 billion of foreign investment flowed out of Britain in the first four years of the Thatcher government. By 1987, the eighth year of the Thatcher government, the total outflow of direct and portfolio investment had reached £139 billion. After decades of decline Britain's share of world foreign investments began to rise again – increasing from 11.2 per cent in 1975 to 14.5 per cent in 1980. This development, coupled with the privatisation of new boom sectors of the economy such as telecommunications, aerospace and oil, helped to reinforce the already dominant position of finance capital within the economy.

The deep recession of 1979 to 1981, which had been triggered by the new government's policies, had a devastating effect on British manufacturing whose output fell by 17 per cent during those two years. But if a few, smaller sectors in domestic manufacturing industry had to go to the wall that was simply the normal process of recession, weeding out the weakest and most subordinate areas of the economy.

From the government's viewpoint the other benefit of this policy was to create a pool of 3 million unemployed who could be used to undermine the wages and conditions that trade union organisations had been able to achieve. The unions themselves were weakened. They lost a quarter of their members following the dramatic contraction of the highly unionised sectors of manufacturing industry. In those areas of the economy where new jobs were being created there was often only rudimentary or non-existent trade union organisation. Thus Thatcher was able to preside over a huge shift of power and wealth from workers to employers.

She also succeeded significantly in shifting the distribution of income within the working class. A combination of mass unemployment, tax changes, public sector pay restraint and cuts in benefits was used to widen income and other differentials within the working class. The effect of these shifts even in purely electoral terms was evident in the deepening divisions between different regions of the country – the 'North–South divide' which has become such a favourite topic of discussion among electoral commentators. The South of England was and is by every measure the most prosperous part of Britain with the highest wages, lowest unemployment, lowest child mortality. The Tories vote held up well there. But in the North, which was increasingly hit by the economic crisis, Tory support fell sharply, even compared with the decline which had already taken place in the 1960s and 1970s. The rapid increase in unevenness and differentials within the working class produced by Thatcher's policies accentuated that process.

The severely increasing differentials within the working class were also reflected in studies of the social base of the Tory vote. Tory support in virtually every single section of the population declined between 1970 and 1979, except among skilled and therefore higher paid workers where it actually increased by more than 4 per cent. It was this shift among skilled manual workers that maintained Thatcher's support in recent elections but despite this the Tory vote did not rise above 42 per cent.

In short, she reinforced the international positions of British capital. She used this to mount a massive offensive against the Labour movement, a major part of that drive being to split the working class and win the loyalty of its better-off sections to the continuing Thatcher experiment.

In retrospect, we can see that Thatcher has maintained Britain's economic role of the last 150 years as an international financier, to the continuing detriment of our industrial base. By 1988 Britain had overtaken the USA and was second only to Japan in the scale of its overseas investment balance. As a proportion of its economy, it has the highest foreign investments of any major country. Thatcher had calculated that the increased flow of profits returning from overseas investments would cover the growing trade gap that arose from the withering of our manufacturing base. We can now see from the size of the trade deficit that she miscalculated.

From the viewpoint of her supporters there is a logic and coherence to Thatcher's strategy – provided they are prepared to live with the consequences and the casualties, although for the Labour Party it could never be acceptable. Not only should we find the individual poverty and the destitution of whole regions immoral but Labour has to be a party based on the productive sectors of the economy, not those of finance capital or foreign investment.

Therefore, it is all the more surprising that in the past Labour has been so feeble in imposing its will on the City of London's financial institutions or multinational companies to ensure that adequate investment takes place in the domestic economy. Nor is this problem of underinvestment in industry improving. Even today, after the six years of growth in the economy which have followed the 1979–81 recession, the Bank of England estimates that the service life of equipment in British manufacturing industry is twenty-eight years compared with eleven in Japan and eighteen in the USA.

Looked at objectively, Labour's past economic policies have been a series of gimmicks and diversions acting as substitutes for any serious attempt to impose national priorities on our domestic financial institutions. We have watched the attempts of both the Wilson and Callaghan governments to co-operate with the private sector in various National Plans and Planning Agreements fail. It is instructive to read the diaries of Tony Benn (*Office Without Power*, 1988) on this point as he was an industry minister throughout the period of both governments. He says of the first Wilson government:

As Minister of Technology my departmental responsibilities extended to the aircraft, shipbuilding, motor, machine tool, computer and nuclear industries, as well as to regional policy. All of this presented me with the immensely complicated problems of trying to sustain and rejuvenate our manufacturing base and check the downward drift towards deindustrialisation. It became clear that these problems could not be solved by the policies that the Cabinet had accepted, and which I had worked so hard to implement . . . all my efforts in the period [1968–70] to bribe and bully businessmen into co-operating with us, while following the demands of market forces, had simply not produced the results we had hoped they would.

Tony Benn's response to this failure was to review policy. He won commitments that the next Labour government would seek a major extension of public ownership and have compulsory planning agreements for each sector of the economy. But as soon as Labour won the 1974 election Harold Wilson began undermining the policy, he vetoed the concept of compulsory planning agreements and responded to pressure from the City of London by replacing Benn with the pliant Eric Varley. Wilson then fell back on the usual policies of wage restraint and public spending cuts leading to the inevitable lost election in 1979.

Back in opposition the feeling that we had a good policy but that it had been sabotaged by Wilson and Callaghan helped to swing the party to the left. Activists now concentrated on trying to make MPs accountable to their local Labour parties so as to prevent further betrayals in the future, but in so doing overlooked the fact that we were defending a policy (the Alternative Economic Strategy) which had been assembled during the early 1970s at the end of a 25-year-long world economic boom. Those easy days had gone, perhaps for a generation, and policy needed to be reviewed in the way that the Tories had done in the aftermath of Mrs Thatcher's seizure of the Tory leadership from Edward Heath.

It is only possible to admire the speed with which the Tories adjusted to the end of the post-war boom. Whilst Labour struggled to try to find a way to return to the happy days of the fifties and sixties, the Tories found a tougher, anti-consensus leader and decided their priorities in terms of what must be protected (defence and the foreign investment of capital) and what could be sacrificed (full employment and the welfare state).

In painful contrast, the right-wingers, who won a majority on Labour's NEC in 1982, rethought nothing and fought the 1983 and 1987 elections on an incoherent mishmash of watered down and warmed-up leftovers from the policy rows of fifteen years earlier. To make matters worse, the Shadow Cabinet remained dominated by the old-time failures from the Wilson–Callaghan era who did not believe a word of the policies for which they were campaigning – and it showed.

Nowhere was the bankruptcy of ideas more apparent than on the issue of the economy. Night after night during the 1983 election the public saw Peter Shore (Shadow Chancellor) trying to explain that Labour would rebuild the economy by borrowing £11 billion, thus reinforcing the general public's perception that Labour would once again stoke up inflation and cripple the nation with a vast burden of debt. This might well have been unfair, but then politics often is.

The early period of Neil Kinnock's leadership actually saw some interesting new thinking on the question of the economy. There was an acceptance that Labour had to become a party of production and some discussion of higher taxes being imposed on those companies which refused to invest in the domestic economy. But instead of campaigning on these issues in the four years before the 1987 election, Neil devoted most of his time to leading internal party battles against Arthur Scargill and Derek Hatton. By the time the election arrived it was too late to set the agenda on Labour's terms and the whole debate focused around the issue of which taxes Labour would increase and who would be hit by this. Labour failed completely to set the pace with a discussion concerning the need to rebuild our industrial base, and the tax debate only served to remind ordinary middle-income people that they had been severely penalised by the tax policies of the last two Labour governments.

If Labour is to win next time then it must break with the failed policies of the past and face up to the fundamental challenge which it has so far ducked throughout its eighty-eight years of existence. To rebuild our industrial base we must intervene to redirect the flow of private investment into industry. If we go into the next election without such a commitment then the voters will know that a Labour government will inevitably end up increasing taxes on ordinary middle-income earners in order to pay for the reconstruction of our industry. Not surprisingly, Labour voters do not see why they, who have not been the cause of our industrial decline, should now bare the burden of reversing it.

Even if a Labour government could be elected without a commitment to impose public priorities on the City of London's pattern of investment, it could never increase taxes enough to pay for the creation of all the jobs we need. At the GLC the few thousand jobs that were created or saved under our industry and employment policy cost about £10,000 each, which was very much cheaper than the £100,000 plus per job it has cost the government in the London docklands. But even if we could create the 3 million new jobs needed to return to full employment at the lower GLC costs, it would still add up to £30 billion. No government that increased taxes on the scale required could survive. There is no alternative for Labour – it has to intervene in the direction of private investment.

To be credible with the electorate the Labour Party needs to demonstrate that it has learnt the lessons of the past and will not repeat them. We need to admit that the monetarists are right when they say that increasing the money supply more rapidly than we increase the real wealth of the economy does indeed lead to increased inflation (although this can find its outlet in house prices or the stock market as well as the retail price index). Control of the money supply is just one of many economic tools that we can use to control the economy.

The mistake of the Thatcher government was to elevate it to the level of a religious creed at the beginning of its administration and then virtually ignore it afterwards. This meant that the recession of 1979–81 was made worse and then it helped to fuel the stock market and house price booms of the late 1980s. It has also meant a rate of inflation in the RPI which has been consistently worse than that of our major trading competitors, contributing to a further loss of foreign markets and the widening trade gap. We should answer Mrs Thatcher's claims to have reduced inflation by pointing out that this is simply because, largely due to international factors, inflation is down all over the world. Britain still has the worst record of the Western industrial economies on inflation and it continues to erode our trading position. These days, if Mrs Thatcher dared to claim that she was a monetarist, it is likely that Milton Friedman would have to sue on the grounds of misrepresentation.

In contrast to this sorry record, Labour should become a party of 'sound money' for it is our supporters who are worst hit by inflation – although we would control inflation by very different means from Mrs Thatcher. Labour's potential supporters are not able to switch their assets around on the international currency markets in order to protect their position. Instead they see their wages and their pensions eroded. Workers in industry find their jobs less secure as higher domestic inflation causes instability in the exchange rate. This usually leads to higher interest rates which reduce the chance of industrial expansion and the prospect of new jobs for the unemployed.

This does not mean that there will not be times when an increase in the money supply above that justified by the increase in national wealth is called for, but it will feature as part of a planned strategy of industrial reconstruction. It cannot act as a substitute for the need to direct capital into the reconstruction of our manufacturing base.

Much the same arguments apply on the issue of borrowing. Like monetarism, the Keynesian theory is a useful economic tool but it is no substitute or replacement for intervention within the capital markets to ensure the investment we need. In the same way that the monetarists have seen their theories abused by politicians, so too with the teaching of Keynes. He basically advocated that when the economy is in recession the government of the day should borrow money in order to restart the sluggish economic engine. But he also insisted that those debts should be repaid when the economy was booming – a part of his theory politicians conveniently tend to forget once in power. However, Keynes could never solve the problem of investment – the basic flaw of his policies.

The effect of Labour's mismanagement whilst in office, plus the consistent and often dishonest Tory propaganda, has left a strong suspicion amongst the voters that Labour cannot manage the economy. The opinion polls show that even when the Tories are clearly seen to be mismanaging the economy, the vast majority of people polled still think that Labour would only make matters worse. When an election comes along the constant Labour emphasis on spending more on health and education only reinforces the doubts in people's minds about where the money is coming from to pay for all these promises. The lack of a clear answer reawakens all the old doubts about swingeing tax increases.

The only way out of this dilemma is if Labour can establish in the public mind a much sharper perception of a distinct and coherent set of economic policies. With the memory of the last election still painfully sharp, we need to start with taxes.

Labour must make it quite clear that it will never again adopt the tactic of increasing taxes on the middle third of earners in order to pay for its programme. The government has won the allegiance of many people in this middle-income bracket because of its very successful propaganda *vis-à-vis* the cut in the rates of income tax. However, like all but the rich they are still paying more to the state than when Thatcher first came to power. The trick has been to take the same amount of money in different ways: by doubling the rate of VAT we end up paying twice the tax we used to on the taxed items we buy; by cutting state subsidies to the former nationalised industries she has forced them to increase prices; by cutting government grants to local councils she has forced up rates and council rents.

When Thatcher came to power in 1979 the married man with two children on average earnings was paying 35.1 per cent of his earnings to the state in the form of income tax, national insurance, rates, VAT and other indirect taxes. By 1988–9, the same worker on average earnings (now £254 a week) paid 37.3 per cent of that wage to the state and yet it is Labour that is seen as the party of high taxes! Someone earning twenty times as much (£5,080 a week) has seen their total tax bill cut from 74.3 per cent to 38.5 per cent – only 1.2 per cent more than the average worker. In contrast, a married man with two children earning only half the average wage (£127 a week) has seen his tax bill rise from 2.5 to 7.1 per cent under Thatcher!

Average taxpayers in Britain are not vicious capitalist exploiters of the poor. Very often these are exactly the people who, with help from the welfare state, have been able to lift themselves and their families out of poverty during the space of a generation. The fact that they can afford to buy their own homes and take foreign holidays does not mean they are rich or enemies of the poor. Often they face a real struggle to maintain their standards of living and a tax increase, even if imposed by a Labour government, is a painful blow against it.

The Labour Party must accept that the average earner is now paying more in taxes than ever before and give a completely unqualified pledge that the bottom two-thirds of earners in Britain will pay no greater percentage of their income in total taxes to the state than they are at present. This would still allow the government to shift the balance between one tax and another and to cut the tax burden on the poor by increasing taxes on the top third of earners, but it would prevent the Tories from being able to raise the tax scare yet again. Such a statement has the advantage of simplicity and would avoid a repetition of the confusion on the issue which cost us so many votes in the closing days of the 1987 election.

Of course, it is equally important to be absolutely straight with the electorate that Labour will maintain its opposition to any form of wage restraint policy. There is no evidence that any of the wage freeze policies of previous Labour or Tory governments led to a revival of the British economy. But there is plenty to show that the reduction in living standards for ordinary families, caused when previous Labour governments introduced such policies, leads to such a loss of electoral support that no Labour government that has introduced a wages policy has ever won a working majority in Parliament in the subsequent election. Furthermore, the entire issue of incomes policy is, economically, a diversion from the task of tackling the real distortions of the British economy.

Labour's programme must be paid for in other ways. In the first instance, we need to challenge the successful Thatcher propaganda that claims we cannot as a nation any longer afford the proper provision of housing, education and health care that are the norm in most of the other Western European countries. We need to remind the people of Britain that we remain the sixth most powerful economy in the world. Only the USA, USSR, Japan, West Germany and France have greater wealth at their disposal. It is not that we cannot afford the provision of these fundamental human economic rights, it is simply that the present government does not consider them a priority. Increasingly, as people from Britain travel in countries such as West Germany, the Netherlands, Denmark, Sweden and Norway, they are shocked to discover just how shabby and run down Britain appears by comparison.

Britain has the wealth at its disposal to tackle these problems if it is prepared to change its priorities. First and foremost amongst these is the need to reduce the exorbitant amount of British defence spending to the same levels as those of our European allies. In 1987, France spent 3.9 per cent of its GNP on defence, West Germany spent 3.1 per cent and the average figure for all NATO countries excluding the USA was 3.3 per cent. Why then did Britain spend 5.4 per cent? Why are we now spending 20 per cent more in real terms on defence than when Mrs Thatcher first came to power in 1979? Does anyone seriously believe that we are 20 per cent more likely to find ourselves at war with Gorbachev than we were with Brezhnev? One only has to ask the question to realise how implausible the prospect sounds.

More than anyone, other than Reagan himself, Mrs Thatcher has been obsessed with increasing arms spending, even to the point where it seriously distorts and damages our domestic economy and welfare state. And now, after four years of Gorbachev's unilateral disarmament initiatives, when even Reagan finally had to respond positively by signing the INF Treaty, Thatcher remains the most reluctant of all Western leaders to reduce arms spending.

Labour should respond to the changed international situation by planning a phased reduction of our defence budget over five years to reach the same proportion of GNP spent on defence as West Germany. This would release £9 billion to be spent on other priorities and allow time to ensure that workers in defence industries could be retrained and their factories retooled to produce more socially useful products. Such a strategy would actually increase the number of jobs available overall because defence spending is the least labour intensive form of public spending.

The reallocation of defence spending, together with policies designed to ensure that a greater proportion of British capital was invested in the UK than is at present the case, increased taxes on the top third of earners and the most profitable sectors of the economy, plus a limited and short-term increase in borrowing for capital investment in a major public works programme, should be the basis on which a Labour government begins the rebuilding of our economy.

The reconstruction would have three overlapping phases. Initially, it must be led by a major programme of public works in the classic Keynesian pattern. Throughout Britain the infrastructure of our society is disintegrating. Homes, schools, hospitals, roads, railways and the environment need massive repair and reconstruction merely to catch up with the standards of the best in the rest of northern Europe. Education and training need to be expanded on a massive scale. We need the provision of a universal pre-school childcare system so that the parent with childcare responsibility (90 per cent of whom are women) can be free to work or further develop their skills via higher education. It is a scandal that we do not have adequate local authority care for the elderly. All these would not only improve the quality of life in Britain dramatically but they are all labour intensive and would massively increase the number of jobs available.

The government's own figures demonstrate that each unemployed person who resumes work saves the country £7,000 a year, thus releasing more funds to continue the public works programme. Furthermore, those that are put back to work and earn a decent wage begin purchasing goods and services which in turn creates work for other people. It is also the case that the goods and services bought by the previously unemployed are much more likely to have been produced in the UK than abroad. Thus putting people back to work, implementing a national minimum wage or increasing the pathetic level of state pensions and benefits all has a much better impact on the balance of payments than using the same amount of money to reduce taxes for the rich, who tend to spend the extra money in ways which suck expensive imported goods into the economy.

Perhaps the most important aspect of the first phase of reconstruction would be to begin to tackle the crisis of Nigel Lawson's 'low skill, low tech' economy which as we have seen was already apparent in the last century. Raising the school leaving age to 18 and at least trebling the numbers of our young people who go on to higher education would be a beginning, but we also have to recognise that technology is now developing so fast that most people really need to return to education two or three times during their working lives and the universities should be adapted and expanded to accommodate this need.

Paralleling this expansion of education must be a vast increase in research and development. In 1988, British Aerospace commissioned a report from PA Consultants on the state of research and development in UK industry. They concluded that it was only in Britain that the number of people working in R&D was declining. They also pointed out that since Mrs Thatcher came to power UK manufacturing had grown by only 0.1 per cent compared with Japan's growth of 6.1 per cent over the same period, and that only 20 per cent of our manufacturing industries was 'successful and dynamic', as opposed to the other 80 per cent which was 'stagnating'. The result was that Britain's share of new Western European patents had dropped from 26 per cent in 1963 to 16 per cent in 1985, whilst West German patents had increased from 34 to 42 per cent over the same period. Throughout the Thatcher years government funded R&D has been systematically cut back in every field except defence projects. If we were to invest the same proportion of our national wealth in training and research as is the case in West Germany, we would be spending £6,000 more per worker or £20,000 more if we chose to match Japan. As well as increasing the overall level of R&D, we must also tackle the imbalance within the distribution of the R&D budget so as to reduce the proportion of our scientific talent consumed in armaments research, switching them to more socially and economically productive projects. As long as over half our scientists are working on armaments we will continue to fall behind Japan and West Germany in the development of new technology.

The second phase of our economic reconstruction must be to tackle the growing balance of payments problem by producing in Britain more of the high quality manufactured goods that we are currently importing. Under Mrs Thatcher one-fifth of our manufacturing industry closed with devastating effects in vast areas of the country and now with equally devastating effects on our balance of payments. In order to reverse this decline a Labour government must impose national priorities on the pattern of investment by our financial institutions. Because of the high interest rates and overvalued pound which have been recurring features of the Thatcher years, it has usually been in the short-term interests of financiers to invest abroad in property or currency speculation rather than expand the productive sector of our own economy. Even successful companies have found that they can get a better return on their profits by investing on the stock markets or in property rather than expanding their own factories.

We should not be surprised at this state of affairs for individual financiers, faced with an investment decision, must take a view based on what is in the best short-term interest for themselves or their clients. Not to do so would often be illegal which is why so many trade unions and Labour councils have found themselves blocked when trying to invest in local industries or more socially acceptable projects rather than investing abroad. It has never been the responsibility of individual financiers to create a sound national economy – that is the job of government and in West Germany, France and Japan it has happened.

One of the reasons why it has been easier for the governments of those three countries to achieve better manufacturing growth is that, unlike Britain, they have not been subject to the dominance of finance capital. In West Germany and Japan, the banking systems were smashed by the Second World War and both governments were able to ensure that as their economies were reconstructed the banks made it their top priority to finance the growth of a modern and dynamic manufacturing base. In France, finance capital was weakened dramatically because in the period before the First World War the government invested massively in Russia and lost the lot in the revolution. Between the wars, French financiers then decided, with breathtaking optimism, that the best place to invest was in Eastern Europe between Hitler and Stalin, promptly losing it all again in the Second World War. Thus in the aftermath of the Algerian War when de Gaulle decided to modernise the French economy, the banks were not strong enough to resist even if they had wanted to.

The contrast between these countries and Britain is stunning. Again and again, new products and processes invented in Britain are ignored by our own banks and end up being developed abroad and imported back into the UK with some other country making the profits and jobs that could have been ours. These priorities are reflected within the career structure of each bank with the best and brightest of their staff attracted to the departments dealing with overseas investment whilst the domestic investment departments are considered a backwater.

Furthermore, the whole basis of company law in Britain prioritises the interests of finance capital over those of industry. In West Germany, company law makes it almost impossible for a successful manufacturing company to be the subject of a hostile takeover bid, whereas in the UK managing directors often have to spend vast resources of time and money fighting off some squalid little asset stripper who has no concern for the national interest, let alone the rights of the workers in that firm. A Labour government must change the law so that the balance of power shifts in favour of productive industry.

Britain's financial institutions are not practising some form of economic treason when they fail to invest in our manufacturing base, they are simply following a pattern of investing abroad which has dominated their thinking since the middle of the nineteenth century! The real guilt lies with those politicians who have never been prepared to impose a new set of priorities on the City of London.

The sums of money involved in the flow of investment abroad cannot be sustained without damage to the economy, and there is public unease about a policy that has seen British financiers buying up £60 billion worth of assets in the USA alone while domestic manufacturing continues to decline. There would be overwhelming public support for a government prepared to insist that our domestic financial institutions bring some of that money back to fund a modernisation programme of our existing industries, thus providing our own workforce with equipment the equivalent of that in Japan and West Germany. That programme should also include the creation of new plants and factories to produce many of the high tech products that Britain is currently importing. To achieve this end there must be an interventionist industrial policy which does not 'leave it to the market' in the way now being advocated by the Labour leadership.

The modernisation of our industry is not something that can be run from London; a different strategy should be devised for each region of the country and for each industry. To be really effective this will require the input of local knowledge rather than conformity to a plan devised in Whitehall.

Given the problems that previous Labour governments have had with our financial institutions, the question that is paramount is will the City of London cooperate?

I believe that if a government was confident, built popular support for its policies and was clearly committed to a long-term modernisation of the economy, it could not be resisted by the City. If it was, then the very act of economic disloyalty would itself create a public backlash, allowing the government to impose its will on any domestic financial institution either via an imaginative policy of punitive taxation or by controls which allowed the government to direct investment into Regional Enterprise Boards. For any Labour government to succeed and have any chance of being re-elected it has to break the pattern of past investment and impose its will on the City.

Once the idea of intervention is accepted, the question is how should it be done? No one in their right mind would wish to repeat the mistakes of previous forms of public ownership in Britain in which vast, remote, undemocratic, Morrisonian bureaucracies alienated the groups they were supposed to serve. Nor do we want some state-owned investment bank based in London and managed by a few well-meaning City bankers who have at sometime in the past been known to vote Labour in a good year. It would be a great mistake to recreate in our new system the inherent failings of the present centralised metropolitan financial system.

We must ensure that what Labour creates is based in the different regions of Britain and is inherently participatory and democratic. If we can create an investment system which involves the workforce on an industry by industry, company by company, and plant by plant basis, it would not only be very difficult to abolish following a change of government but it would usher in economic rights for the individual citizen in addition to our traditional electoral rights.

I have no doubt that people in the future will look back at the present time and express amazement that private investors and accountants could intervene to contract and close firms based solely on a short-term financial decision, whilst the people and sometimes whole communities who had given their lives to that firm had no rights except to draw the dole.

It will no doubt come as a shock to those who wield power and influence at the top of great bureaucracies and corporations to suggest that their workforce should have control over the investment programme of their company, but in the long term they are the people who have the greatest stake in the success or failure of the firm. Instead of the investment decisions being taken solely by a firm's directors and accountants, who are so often only interested in the quickest short-term return and therefore decide to invest the company profits in stock market or property speculation rather than expanding production or developing new products, we should give the workforce in each firm a power of veto over all investment plans and the power to initiate an alternative strategy. The workforce would require access to all the relevant information about the firm or industry concerned, plus adequate research resources for it to take part in any debate about future prospects. The most obvious way to provide such resources is on a regional basis and this would be the most important function of elected regional authorities, discussed in the next chapter.

All the evidence from other parts of the world, and the more limited experience of Britain in this field, shows that workers in a firm take a much more long-term, strategic view, if for no other reason than their jobs depend on the survival and success of the company concerned. I have no doubt that had such economic rights and responsibilities been introduced by the post-war Labour government under Attlee, then the British economy would by now be a lot closer to that of West Germany in strength and size.

These sentiments will seem alarming here in Britain where the class system is still so much more of a barrier to judging individuals on their merits than in the other more modern Western democracies. Indeed, there is no doubt that these reactionary and arrogant attitudes have been strengthened during the Thatcher premiership with the constant emphasis on the theme that 'managers must be free to manage'. Given the gross mismanagement of the economy by our 'managers' over the past decades, there is little empirical evidence to suggest that British managers' ability to run the economy is such that the rest of us should simply do as we are told whilst fervently hoping that their success rate improves.

The Kinnock–Hattersley 'Aims and Values' document endorsed at the 1988 party conference was appalling on this issue of democratic rights within the economy. It failed to assert the fundamental principle that those who devote their labour and their lives to the work of a company or industry have a greater right to determine its activities and priorities than those who merely contribute money. Moreover, the document implicitly, and in some cases explicitly, asserted that those who contribute their labour and lives have barely equivalent or even less rights than those who provided capital. This led to a fundamentally undemocratic policy document – a position unacceptable to a democratic socialist party.

These undemocratic attitudes related directly to the section on markets – in which it should have been asserted unequivocally that in conditions where the interests of democracy and markets clash the Labour Party unhesitatingly upholds democracy against the market. The document appeared to state the opposite. It also confused the issue of markets as a means of wholesale and retail distribution – in most sectors of the economy this will continue indefinitely – and their role in investment and labour where, as this book demonstrates, the workings of the market have failed to give us the industrial and skills base we need.

In fact the whole weakness of Labour's review of economic policy is that it has been too concerned with the desire of the leadership to pander to the media and present a 'respectable' image to the City of London by watering down Labour's commitment to bring back into public ownership those sections of the economy that have been privatised. This has meant that the more important fundamental economic issues have been given inadequate weight. Instead the Labour leadership has set up a pointless debate about whether the next Labour government could find the £80 billion necessary to buy back privatised industries at their full stock market value and anyone who challenges the premise of the question is denounced as proposing renationalisation without compensation. As compensation would consume over half the first Budget of the government, it would obviously not be possible simply to buy back these industries at market value, and as the trade unions would not vote for nationalisation without compensation, the leadership's logic leads inevitably to dropping the present policy.

The choice posed by the leadership is, however, a false one. Previous nationalisations were paid for by the Labour government issuing bonds to former shareholders on which it paid interest and there is no reason why such a policy could not be used again with part of the profits of the renationalised industries providing the interest repayments. But the Labour leadership is now opposed to such a policy, not for any economic reason but because the number of shareholders has trebled since 1979 to 9 million today and there are also 11 million members of occupational pension schemes which have purchased stakes in the privatised industries. It is the fear of losing these voters rather than any issue of principle or economic efficiency which is behind Neil Kinnock's drive to change our policy.

Yet because the leadership is trying to devise a policy based on vote catching rather than on economic coherence, it is building into the policy all sorts of inconsistencies and contradictions. Thus they pledge not to renationalise public utilities for fear of offending shareholders but recognise that British Telecom has to be an exception because of its central importance to the economy. They accept that the water industry, which is of central importance to the quality of the environment, cannot be left in private hands. But are not the other public utilities such as gas and electricity almost as important as water?

To resolve this problem the leadership proposes to designate all the privatised utilities as Public Interest Companies (PICs), each of which would be subject to regulation by three PIC Commissioners appointed by the government but thereafter 'independent of the industry and the government'. Their powers would be to set pricing policy, performance and investment targets. They would have powers of investigation and be able to impose penalties such as refunds to consumers or other 'sanctions' against the company.

When this proposal was made to the Economic Policy Review Group, I asked why it was if the PIC Commissioners were thought to be adequate to ensure dynamic and efficient public utilities we were not proposing them for all British industry. Surely it is just as important to make sure that the other sectors of the economy have proper performance and investment targets, yet any such suggestion was rejected on the basis that the market is an adequate mechanism to achieve these ends. There was no answer when I pointed out that the 'market' has consistently failed to achieve these ends for over a hundred years.

My own view is that we should approach the 6 million people who have become new shareholders during the Thatcher years in the same way that we should treat middle-income taxpayers. They are not an enemy that needs to be punished nor are they fools who can be seduced by a slick election slogan. In the main, they are people who are natural allies of a Labour Party which wants to modernise Britain via investment led growth.

In the last twenty-five years, the proportion of UK shares owned by individuals has declined from 58 to just 20 per cent. During this time the proportion of shares owned by institutions has risen to 80 per cent and it is estimated that these institutions are managed by 300 City fund managers. It is over this vast accumulation of unaccountable and undemocratic power that a Labour government must assert itself, not the private shareholders, 59 per cent of whom now own shares in only one company.

If we examine the structure of share ownership in British Telecom, we will see that 98 per cent of the shareholders own only 10.3 per cent of the shares. I can see no reason why these 1,285,078 small shareholders cannot simply be allowed to keep their shares. Indeed, they could be a very positive influence on the board of BT in maintaining standards to consumers and ensuring that investment policies are farsighted. To regain control of BT a Labour government should issue bonds in exchange for the shares held by the 344 financial institutions which control 33 per cent of BT, structuring the interest payments on those bonds so that it guarantees the return required for pension funds and insurance companies, thus protecting the interests of the 11 million members of occupational pension schemes.

If a Labour government took this approach to public ownership then it becomes possible to reverse the damage done by privatisation without alienating millions of ordinary people or bankrupting the government's budget.

The Keynesian programme of public works and the expansion of investment in our manufacturing base that I have dealt with so far are only part of the answer to ending Britain's economic decline. There is no way that these two areas could be enough on their own to fill the breach in our economy caused as the oil runs out and the balance of payments gap returns to dominate the political debate. To create an economy capable of supporting our needs, we must identify and invest in those industries which will dominate the developed economies at the turn of the century. That should be the third phase of our economic reconstruction and the shortsightedness of the Thatcher government has opened a wonderful opportunity for Labour to seize the initiative.

The history of the Industrial Revolution has always been linked to the question of mobility and communications. Britain's early dominance was intertwined with its establishment of canals which opened up the waterways as a commercial network and consolidated by our massive investment in the first national system of railways. The more recent ascendancy of the USA was assisted and strengthened by its overwhelming superiority, first, in the field of motorways and car production and, secondly, in the arena of aviation and aircraft production. Previous advances in industrial economies have been closely linked to the increasing mobility of people and products, however, the next steps forward will come not from further advances in the physical movement of goods and people but in the rapid transmission of information. It is those nations that lead in information technology which are assuming a new supremacy.

Communication infrastructures such as telephone networks, data networks, networks for transmitting orders, for transferring funds, for collaborative research, videotex and electronic publishing are rapidly changing the competitive advantages between and within nations. Already 75 per cent of value added services in telecommunications are based in the south-east of Britain and the BT rival, Mercury, has built its fibre optic grid to cover just the major cities (and only included Glasgow under pressure). Most of Britain is being left behind in this new revolution and there is a real danger that whole regions will miss out on the new opportunities in communications, computing in manufacturing, distribution, retail, design and research.

Already Japan is planning the investment of $120 billion over the next eleven years in order to create a fibre optic cable system which will link up the whole nation. After a slow start the USA is now expecting to spend similar sums and recently announced plans to create a 'data superhighway' of fibre optic cable costing $400 million which will link dozens of supercomputers, enabling 3 billion items of data to be transmitted each second. In France and West Germany, the modernisation of networks has been used as a tool of regional policy backed by $1 billion from the Common Market.

By contrast, in Britain it is the same old story. In December 1988, the government appointed team which had spent nearly two years examining the problem recommended against following the other leading industrial nations down the path of establishing a national fibre optic grid. Although the report showed that the grid would create an extra 700,000 'job years' and generate over £3 billion a year in extra revenue from new services, it recommended against going ahead on the grounds that 'market forces' should determine the emerging pattern, and a fibre optic system would reinforce BT's dominant position within the telecommunications industry.

Optical fibres pulse laser light through minute strands of pure glass and just two strands have the capacity to carry 30,000 phone calls or thirty television channels simultaneously. It would cost somewhere between £20 and £30 billion to link up every home, factory, office, school and university in the UK by cable, and would have enormous spin-offs for numerous industries such as equipment manufacture, cable laying and construction, the creation of new services, teleworking, teleshopping and television itself.

As the earlier history of the Industrial Revolution shows, the availability of a new infrastructure creates new demands and new markets and meets old demands in new ways. It would allow a Scottish crofter to work directly with partners in Brixton and Plymouth without ever needing to meet in the flesh as they created and sold their product. The French Minitel videotex system created a new network and gave free terminals to subscribers. This in turn created 6,000 new services to meet the demand. A fibre optic grid could foster the decentralisation of economic activity and the revitalisation of new regions but it would put enormous power in the hands of the network owners and would conversely accelerate decline in those regions that the 'market' wrote off.

Government policy was spelled out in 1982 when the then Minister for Information Technology, Kenneth Baker, claimed that the UK would eventually get its fibre optic grid as more and more people acquired cable television. Unfortunately for the government, people in Britain seem to feel that four indifferent television channels are enough and have been unprepared to pay through the nose for thirty more.

This total lack of imagination on the part of the Tories opens the way for Labour to take the lead in the whole area of information technology, with a commitment to provide a fully cabled nation in which no region is excluded and people and companies have access to the grid as of right. The obvious vehicle to carry out this programme is a renationalised British Telecom which could establish the common standards and long-term investment that are vital to the growth of communications industries. The all-party House of Commons Trade and Industry Committee has already condemned government complacency and called for the construction of a national electronic grid. There is no way that the private sector will achieve this alone given the vast sums of money involved, indeed the former technical director of BT was a member of the government's investigation team.

Britain is already a world leader in fibre optic technology, through BT's laboratories in Martlesham where an optical building block (the soliton) was recently developed, but under Mrs Thatcher's leadership we have turned into a net importer of information technology. Labour must make its top investment priority the provision of a fully cabled economy by the end of the century or preside over our continued decline into a low skill, low tech backwater of the world economy.

Although there is universal acknowledgement amongst economists that information technology is already the most important sector of the economy in all the developed industrial nations, there is no such agreement about the likely importance of biotechnology, even though it is certain to rival information technology as a source of profits within the next twenty-five years. Perhaps because there is still too much of a science fiction atmosphere in the reporting of this new area of investment and employment, many people fail to take it seriously.

Newspaper stories at the end of 1988 are typical of the problem concerning what is involved and what is at stake. In the month of December alone there were three major biotechnology stories reported. First, we were told that Dr David Rees of the Medical Research Council had announced that the first human gene transplant to correct defects which cause inherited diseases such as haemophilia will be carried out in the next few years. This news was followed by the statement that doctors at the Hammersmith Hospital will shortly start screening two-day-old human embryos for genetic defects such as cystic fibrosis and muscular dystrophy. This involves laboratory fertilisation of the mother's egg using the standard test-tube baby technique and only implanting the embryo in the mother's womb once it is certain that it does not carry an inherited disease. Finally, in his presidential address to the Royal Society, the Nobel prize winner, Professor Sir George Porter, warned that biotechnology could 'insidiously' change the human species. He said that how far scientists should manipulate evolution was the most pressing and ominous question: 'In areas of applied biology and medicine things are already happening rapidly enough to frighten people – transgenic animals, transgenic implants of organs, rewriting the human genetic code. We are no longer pawns in the game of evolution, we are not even the kings and queens. We are the players.'

The coincidence of these three news stories led Melanie Phillips of *The Guardian* to ask what will happen when we can

> screen out embryos that are not themselves damaged but which are carriers of disease. Take a condition like hypercholesterolemia, which predisposes a person to early heart attacks. It is not too far-fetched to imagine a future government deciding that since the cost of heart surgery is prohibitive, all embryonic carriers of hypercholesterolemia should be eradicated.

Ms Phillips then asked why it was that the government still had not legislated to deal with this area of research although five years had passed since the Warnock Committee urged that embryo research should be allowed, provided it was licensed by a statutory authority and took place within the first fourteen days of gestation. The simple answer is that one half of the government still does not understand what the issue is all about, the other half recognises the economic importance of biotechnology but fears that on the promised free vote public worry and confusion about the moral problems involved could lead to MPs banning any future research in this field. Therefore, the government has let the matter drift on rather than take a decision one way or the other.

However, the giant international corporations are well aware of what is at stake and, as *The Economist* revealed in a major survey in May 1988, are beginning to invest billions of dollars in preparing for the biotechnology revolution. New drugs, diagnostic tests, fertilisers, crops and pesticides have already been developed and are being marketed. By 1987 sales had reached $700 million and Genentech's drug TPA, which can stop heart attacks immediately, is now available in 85 per cent of US hospitals. Drugs to combat haemophilia, anaemia, dwarfism, diabetes, and general anti-cancer agents are not far behind. Bioengineered hormones to accelerate wound-healing and nerve regeneration, as well as antibodies to destroy poisons, could each reach sales of $1 billion in the early 1990s.

This scale of likely profits has made the multinational corporations much quicker to respond than governments. Chemical companies have spent $10 billion acquiring seed firms in the past ten years. The US chemical giant Monsanto has almost completely committed its research department to biotechnology, as has the drug giant Schering-Plough. Eli Lilly and Bristol-Myers have both taken over biotechnology firms, Eastman Kodak has acquired Sterling Drug in order to develop a biotechnology capacity, and ICI, Ciba-Geigy and Sandoz have committed a third of their research budgets to biotechnology. The Japanese government, alarmed that it is falling behind in this field, has decided to target biotechnology as a major growth area.

Given this scale of financial commitment from what are some of the most dynamic multinationals, it is sobering to recall that it was only as recently as the early 1970s that the first gene transplant took place, and only in 1982 that the first animal gene transplant took place when the addition of a rat gene to a mouse created a supermouse twice the normal size. Since 1970 we have seen the formation of over 600 (mainly US) biotechnology firms of which 98 per cent have survived. By 1982 genetically engineered insulin became the first such product to reach the market and this has been followed by five others. For example, Genentech's hormone Relaxin relaxes the cervix during labour thus offering a hope that Caesarean births could soon become almost obsolete. Over 150 similar drugs are now undergoing clinical trials. The Monsanto company has produced a genetically engineered super-tomato which can resist both tobacco hornworm and the tobacco mosaic virus, thus increasing yields by over 20 per cent and in Cambridge the merging of sheep and goat genes has produced the academically interesting but economically useless 'geep'. At the time of writing there are seventeen applications to patent 'new' animals pending in the US Patents Office.

Over the next ten years we will see the marketing of genetically engineered seeds which will render many, if not most, pesticides redundant (which is why chemical companies have spent $10 billion acquiring seed firms) and genetically engineered bacteria which will protect plants from frost and increase the ability of plants to extract nitrogen from the soil, thus reducing the need for environmentally devastating nitrate fertilisers to be added to the soil. The first biotechnology product to hit the market in a big way will be the hormone bovine somatotropin (BST) which can increase milk production by up to 24 per cent and will be available by 1990. This will be followed in 1991 by PST which can reduce back fat in pigs by 70 per cent and reduce feed costs by 25 per cent.

According to *The Economist* survey, the top twenty US biotechnology firms will reach $2.5 billion worth of bio-drug sales by 1990 – a fivefold increase in just two years, and by the year 2000 US sales alone of genetically engineered crops will reach $65 billion, with livestock adding another $25 billion. Already the biotechnology firms are targeting the world market for farm fertilisers, chemicals, seeds and drugs which is currently worth $62 billion.

The massive potential of the developing biotechnology industry has already alerted environmentalists to the probability of terrifying dangers if there is not the strictest regulation and most careful testing and preparation before each new product is released on to the market or into the environment. The decision to release a genetically engineered organism into the environment can never be reversed and the consequences can never be wholly foreseen. So far we have been lucky and the twenty 'new' organisms released into the environment have caused no trouble. The examples of ecological destruction that have been caused across the globe by the actions of previous generations of settlers in transporting plants and animals across the face of the planet is too well documented to need repeating here, but they serve to demonstrate the need for the most rigorous control by new national and international agencies. There is also the very real danger that because the 'new' animals and plants that will be genetically engineered over the next decade will be patented, this will reduce the farmer to a licensee and concentrate power over food production in fewer and fewer and very unaccountable hands.

There is now no chance of stopping the development of biotechnology. Too much has already been invested and even if one country decided to ban all such work, it would simply continue in neighbouring nations whose successful experiments would eventually have to be imported and paid for by those who had taken no part in it.

Whilst there will no doubt be many people in all societies who wish to stop genetic engineering on moral or religious grounds, I believe that we should see it as a logical and inevitable development of our civilisation and science. Dr David Paisley of the University of Illinois has estimated that 70 per cent of the increase in corn yields in the USA since 1930 has been caused by genetic improvements achieved by selective breeding. Genetic engineering rapidly accelerates that process and it began at the dawn of civilisation with the first farmers. It is 10,000 years too late to decide that genetic manipulation is a bad thing. Never again will it be possible for humankind to live in a natural balance with the Earth as we once did; this planet could only support a few million humans in such a state not the 5,000 million who inhabit it now. If properly controlled and democratically accountable biotechnology gives us the chance to devise a carefully controlled science which will allow us to compensate for the detrimental changes that the human species has already wrought on the face of the planet. If genetic engineering means we can produce plants that need less of the environmentally damaging insecticides and fertilisers which are rapidly poisoning our soil, then this is an acceptable lesser of two evils. If the increased yields from genetically engineered plants and animals allow us to return some of our farmlands to a natural state, this can compensate for the destruction of the rain forests and assist in reducing the greenhouse effect.

We need to see the development of biotechnology in the context of natural evolution. Over the 4 billion years that life has existed on Earth, the rigid Darwinian law of the survival of the fittest has ensured the increasing sophistication and complexity of all species. For the first 3 billion years progress was slow because change within species was slow. Asexual reproduction meant that each organism grew and divided and any mutation occurring in that organism would be restricted to its descendants. The vast majority of mutations are harmful or of no use and die out but if the environment changes in a way beneficial to an organism with a particular mutation then the rest of the species would die out leaving the mutated organisms as the survivors. With the evolution of sexual reproduction about one billion years ago the pace of change rapidly increased but still rested on the survival of the fittest. Sexual reproduction meant that the exchange of genes which took place with every mating tested the strength of one set of genes against another, as well as spreading a useful mutation much more rapidly throughout the whole population. But in recent times the impact of humankind on the environment has led to a level of pollution which is changing our surroundings at such a rate that no biologically complex species could hope to adapt naturally. The death of seals in the North Sea in 1988 is a particularly striking example of this process at work.

We should see genetic manipulation as the logical development that followed, and is required, once we had intervened in the progress of evolution to modify the process of natural selection by the survival of the fittest.

Nowhere will the debate about genetic engineering be more bitter than on the issue of how we apply its techniques to our own species. Already 300 of the 50,000 to 100,000 human genes have been duplicated and are now being mass produced, and the first map of the human gene chain has been produced by the Collaborative Research Company of Massachusetts. As the full detail of the map is developed, it will allow the diagnosis not just of genetically inherited disease but also the identification and correction of inherited susceptibility to diseases such as cancer and heart disorders. It will also be possible to engineer improvements such as the strengthening of our immune system in order to resist both disease and environmental pollution. Indeed, we may develop the ability to eradicate horrors such as AIDS by strengthening our immune system long before we are ever able to devise a cure for the disease itself.

Given that one child in twenty is born with a genetic disorder, it will inevitably follow that parental pressure will cause us to develop the capacity to counteract this. Already work is proceeding on correcting Severe Combined Immune Deficiency disease (SCID) whereby babies are born with immune systems too weak to resist even the mildest infections, and the fatal blood disorder beta-thalassemia. If Britain were to ban genetic engineering it would not stop this work continuing in other countries, and British couples who could afford it would go abroad to buy the treatment guaranteeing that their children would be born healthy. Poorer parents would, of course, be denied the right to do the same from lack of funds.

I have written at length on biotechnology to demonstrate how little governments seem to be aware of the scale of change which this new industry will bring about within the next ten years. Before another twenty-five years has passed bioengineering will have affected almost every aspect of our lives and become the largest and most profitable industry in the history of the world. It represents a potential power that dwarfs anything exercised by either the giant multinational companies of today or governments and it must therefore be subject to the strictest environmental and democratic controls.

It is only necessary to have read the brief account above to realise that there is no way that any nation will be able to sit out or ignore the biotechnology revolution without condemning itself to massive economic decline. For Britain in particular the opportunities are enormous for although it is the USA which is already well in the lead in biotechnology, the UK is still in second place in this emerging science. Our educational bias towards the biological sciences (which has been an economic disadvantage over the last hundred years) now offers us the chance to consolidate our position as the world's number two in the field. Unfortunately, to do this will require massive government intervention to fund research and establish the new companies to develop and market the products and techniques of biotechnology – something that is contrary to the whole philosophy and practice of this government.

As with the government's failure in the race to be the first country to create a national fibre optic telecommunications grid, so their failure to intervene to create a strong biotechnology industry gives Labour its opportunity to become the party that advocates a modern and dynamic economy. If we have the foresight to seize that initiative Labour could find itself in government for a generation or more.

3

Glasnost UK

In the summer of 1988 socialists all over the country became addicted to the Channel 4 adaptation of Chris Mullins' book *A Very British Coup*. Although it was widely rubbished by Labour right-winger Roy Hattersley, it became one of the television successes of 1988 with its gripping account of how the British establishment, ably assisted by the White House, tries one ploy after another to destabilise the radical socialist government of Prime Minister Harry Perkins. First, there is a run on the pound by the City of London with the press raking over the private lives of ministers in search of scandal. When those fail the electricians union leader uses a strike to try to force the replacement of Perkins with the right-wing Chancellor of the Exchequer who works for MI5. Then MI5 kill the government's main anti-nuclear weapons adviser and try to blackmail the Prime Minister about a former lover. Perkins calls another election in order to expose what has been going on and when it becomes clear that Labour is heading for re-election there is a military coup backed by the King. This story revealed much regarding the undemocratic nature of British government. So also did the extraordinary train of events surrounding the *Spycatcher* and other scandals.

Much has been written about Peter Wright's *Spycatcher* (1986) and the attempt to destabilise the 1974 Wilson government, and everyone now accepts as proven the long list of governments destabilised and overthrown by the USA – some violently as in Chile, others such as the Australian Labour government of Gough Whitlam without physical violence. The knowledge of what has happened in the past means that socialists often find themselves debating the question: what if a genuinely socialist government were elected in Britain – could it survive? In the face of all the evidence, the Labour leadership still claims that such speculation is simply the product of a paranoid imagination and

46

ridicules anyone who raises the issue. Yet having lived through the sustained assault that was mounted against the GLC I do not share the leadership's naivety on this issue. When we consider all the attacks that were directed against just one socialist council, I have no doubt that a radical, socialist government would face attempts to destabilise it from several quarters.

There is no better point from which to start than the security services themselves. When Tony Benn and myself raised the issue of MI5's past interventions in the Labour movement at a meeting of Labour's NEC in late 1988, we were shouted down. When the government presented its Security Services Bill to Parliament the Labour attack was muted. Unlike other controversial government legislation that is always subject to a three-line whip by the Labour leadership, this Bill was often only opposed with a two-line whip which meant that many members did not bother to turn up to vote against it.

The venom of Roy Hattersley's attack on *A Very British Coup* suggests that the issues of disloyalty, destabilisation and treason by the establishment against an elected government are issues which the Labour leaders do not wish to acknowledge. This is certainly confirmed by their behaviour in Parliament where no one on Labour's front-bench ever raises the recent abuses of power by the intelligence services and backbenchers who do are interviewed by senior party figures and told to stop. The result is that it is left to independent-minded backbenchers to pursue these cases, but they can never command the media attention that would be the case if the issues were raised by the party leadership. Yet if it were taken up by the front-bench, the exposure of the destabilisation campaign against Wilson would do massive damage to the Thatcher administration because of the involvement of her closest friend in that campaign.

The question of treason by MI5 is nothing new. The Zinoviev letter which led to the downfall of the first Labour government in 1924 was a forgery. Now believed to have been produced by two Russian émigrés working in Berlin it was passed to MI5 by one of their former officers, Donald im Thurn. Once in the hands of MI5, senior officials realised that its lurid details of a communist plot to take over Britain, via the subversion of the army, would be a devastating blow to the Labour government in the closing days of the election. They leaked it to the Tory MP and former intelligence officer Sir Reginald (Blinker) Hall, Tory Central Office and the *Daily Mail*, which obligingly ran the story on the front page. Given its own complicity in the affair, the incoming

Tory government did not conduct an enquiry into the matter and when the files came to be checked in the mid-1960s, the forged letter had disappeared.

In the run-up to the 1929 election the head of MI5's Investigation Branch, Major Joseph Ball, was employed by Conservative Central Office to run agents inside the Labour Party. After the election Ball was rewarded with the directorship of the Tories Research Department.

What has changed since these MI5 plots to bring down Labour governments in the 1920s is the rapid post-war growth of MI5 and MI6, the increasing interference in Britain by the CIA and to a lesser degree the South African intelligence service BOSS (Bureau of State Security).

It was during the Attlee government at the start of the cold war that the expansion of the domestic surveillance activities of MI5 began to expand in a big way. There was also the establishment, in 1946, of operational links between the intelligence services of the old white commonwealth and the USA. Yet whilst it is highly unlikely that any officers in MI5 or MI6 actually voted Labour in 1945 they could scarcely have been unhappy with the strength of the Labour leadership's commitment to the cold war. It was after all Foreign Secretary Ernest Bevin who, in 1947, signed a treaty with the United States to divide up the world into British and US intelligence zones, pooling all the information gained by electronic spying operations from stations such as GCHQ in Britain and Fort Meade in Maryland. Much of this work was delegated to the BBC's station at Caversham and involved BBC employees working directly for the CIA which had an office there.

Attlee agreed, in 1948, to a major expansion of MI6 and the establishment of the Information Research Department (IRD), a 'black' propaganda unit aimed at destabilising the communists at home and abroad. It was set up by Christopher Mayhew, a Labour MP and former intelligence officer who eventually defected to the Liberals. The Foreign Office forced the BBC to broadcast IRD propaganda and it partially funded *The Observer* news service and Reuters. As late as 1962, the IRD was still supplying right-wing trade unionists and Labour MPs with confidential information about left-wingers which was used by the Labour leadership for expelling them from the party.

Labour also assembled various military units involving former SAS officers for use in Palestine. This was done at the behest of Ernest Bevin whose anti-Semitism led him to believe that the new Israeli state would become a Soviet puppet. Working against Jewish partisans, they rapidly gained a reputation for torture, murder and kidnapping. Without any authority from Parliament Bevin also authorised raids into Soviet territory using guerrilla bands who were expected to 'set the Soviet Union ablaze'. As well as these parachuted invasions into the Ukraine, Caucasus, Black Sea and Latvian regions of the USSR, Albania was also covertly invaded. According to international law these were acts of war.

The attitude of MI5 and MI6 to Third World countries was contemptuous and racist. George Young, the director of MI6's Middle East operations, who worked with the CIA to organise the overthrow of the Mossadeq government in Iran, wrote: 'The non-European world still looks to us as the master culture.' Young also tried to overthrow both the Syrian regime and Nasser. When these moves failed the then Tory Prime Minister, Anthony Eden, authorised an assassination attempt against Nasser using nerve gas.

Although there was a massive pro-Tory bias inside MI5 and MI6 it would be wrong to assume that the intelligence services were not well connected with leading members of the Labour Party. Hugh Dalton, the first post-war Labour Chancellor, had been in charge of 'black' propaganda activities of British intelligence in the war and two of the new Labour MPs, Hugh Gaitskell and Christopher Mayhew, had worked in the SOE (Special Operations Executive). In addition, another new Labour MP, Kenneth Younger, had been a director in MI5 and Tom Driberg, an MP who was also a member of Labour's NEC, was an active agent for MI5 (although the effect was somewhat spoiled by the fact that he was also working for the KGB).

One new MP who was most definitely not on good terms with MI5 was Harold Wilson. As the minister responsible for trade, his attempts to increase exports constantly ran up against US government opposition towards any growth in trade with the USSR. Like many people since, Wilson felt that the USA used the hysteria of the cold war to prevent Britain from increasing trade with the USSR and thus building its economic independence from the United States. This was not a position which was likely to be viewed with favour in MI5 or MI6 and there was near hysteria when Wilson was sent to the USSR to negotiate the sale of twenty advanced jet engines.

Wilson was only a junior minister carrying out a Cabinet decision but from that point on he was viewed with concern by MI5. Matters became worse after Labour went into opposition and Wilson went on almost annual visits to the USSR to try to encourage trade between the Soviets and private firms with whom he was on good terms. Had MI5 known that the Russians had photographed Wilson in the company of one of the women on his staff hoping to use this as blackmail, Wilson's career would have been over. As it was, this perfectly innocent photograph did not fall into the hands of MI6 until just before Wilson retired.

MI5 had no such doubts about Gaitskell or George Brown when they became leader and deputy leader of the Labour Party. Brown was regularly in touch with MI5 asking them to investigate left-wing Labour MPs and candidates. But when the unexpected death of Gaitskell led to the election of Wilson, MI5 immediately tried to recruit his campaign manager, George Caunt, to spy on the new leader.

Wilson's election as Prime Minister came at a difficult time for MI5. He had a vague idea that MI5 viewed him with suspicion and they in turn feared that he would take any opportunity to curb their powers. Shortly before the 1964 election the FBI told MI5 that they had discovered a KGB mole who had been operating inside MI5 in the key post-war period. The fact that Sir Anthony Blunt was a KGB agent, and had close connections with the Queen was certain to create a spy scandal as damaging as that of Kim Philby. Even worse for MI5 was the knowledge that they had been tipped off about Blunt's spying over a decade earlier and had taken no action. They now feared that Wilson would use the opportunity of this scandal to dismember their organisation. Sir Roger Hollis, Director-General of MI5, and Arthur Martin, head of the counter-espionage department, decided on a cover-up and did not even tell the outgoing Tory Prime Minister, Harold Macmillan. Instead Blunt was to be granted immunity and interrogated by Peter Wright who makes the position clear in *Spycatcher*: 'We had strict orders from successive Director-Generals to do nothing that might provoke Blunt to go public.' Blunt then proceeded to waste eight years of Wright's time at 'interrogations' where he revealed nothing whilst consuming large quantities of gin. All this was concealed from Wilson who was also not told when Hollis and his deputy, Graham Mitchell, eventually came under investigation as KGB moles themselves.

Other news was kept from Wilson. In 1961, Anatoli Golitsin, a KGB defector, had arrived in the USA with all sorts of wild allegations, few of which yielded anything of substance except the identity of the Admiralty spy, John Vassall. By coincidence, shortly after Wilson's election as leader of the opposition, Golitsin was sent to Britain to be interviewed by MI5. His agreed 'fee' was £10,000 a month (£70,000 at today's prices), a considerable incentive to keep the interest of his MI5 hosts. Although he had made no mention of it during his two year interrogation in the USA, he now announced that he had heard of a KGB plot to kill the leader of a West European political party so that 'their' man could take over.

This was all Peter Wright and other extreme right-wingers inside MI5 needed to confirm the suspicions that had been hanging around since the jet engine trade deal and Wilson's annual visits to the USSR. They believed that the 'assassinated' party leader had to be Gaitskell, who had died unexpectedly and whose cause of death was not clear. In fact Gaitskell had died on 18 January 1963 following a complete collapse of his immune system. But in 1963 the workings of the immune system were nothing like as well researched as is now the case and this ignorance allowed Wright's fevered imagination to indulge in endless speculation. His favourite theory was that Gaitskell had been given a cup of coffee containing a slow acting poison whilst on a visit to the Soviet consulate in December 1962, or perhaps an even slower acting poison whilst on a visit to Poland in August 1962!

By the time, the now substantially richer, Golitsin returned to the CIA his memory had become much clearer and he was able to assure them that Wilson was indeed a Soviet agent. CIA director John McCone warned President Kennedy and James Jesus Angleton, the head of the CIA counter-intelligence branch. Angleton, a paranoid alcoholic, who was eventually to be sacked because of his illegal mail intercept programme, took over the case. Angleton was a reactionary who had even been a fan of the pro-Nazi poet Ezra Pound. He was convinced that along with Wilson both the West German Chancellor, Willi Brandt and the Australian Prime Minister, Gough Whitlam were threats to Western security and devoted a considerable amount of his time to trying to remove all three from office.

Oblivious to the suspicions of MI5 and the CIA, the new Labour Prime Minister issued instructions that MI5 was to stop tapping the phones of MPs, although it never occurred to him that MI5 could continue to get access to the information gleaned from any taps run by the CIA or GCHQ. He also instructed that MI5 should stop using MPs as agents without knowing that one Tory MP, Captain Henry Kerby, had been used by MI5 to ingratiate himself with Wilson's Shadow Cabinet colleague George Wigg by spying on the Tory party for Wigg.

These instructions caused deep resentment inside MI5 where some officers retaliated by leaking damaging bits of gossip about members of Wilson's government from MI5 files to the press. This was, of course, a breach of the Official Secrets Act but no one has ever been prosecuted.

MI5 believed that seven members of Wilson's government and three other Labour MPs were either spies or at the very least security risks. Only one of these ten, the not very bright Will Owen, MP for Morpeth, eventually turned out to be guilty. He had been taking £500 a month from Czech intelligence in exchange for low-grade information which they could most probably have got more cheaply from reading Hansard and the quality press.

All the other names on MI5's list were completely innocent but this did not stop the hounding of them by Wright and others. Bernard Floud, who had been devastated by the death of his wife, was pursued until he finally committed suicide in a moment of despair. And when Treasury Minister Niall MacDermot had his promotion to the Cabinet blocked following MI5 pressure on Wilson, he resigned from politics in disgust and went to live abroad.

The other seven people on MI5's list were John Diamond, Tom Driberg, Judith Hart, Stephen Swingler, John Stonehouse, Barnet Stross and, of course, Wilson himself.

The MI5-inspired rumours about Wilson eventually reached the ears of former Prime Minister and Leader of the Opposition Sir Alec Douglas-Home. He asked James Scott Hopkins, yet another former MI6 officer who had become a Tory MP, to conduct his own investigation to see if there was any danger of Wilson being blackmailed.

Whilst MI5 had all the time in the world to spread rumours about the Wilson government, they did not seem to be able to prevent BOSS, the South African intelligence service, running an agent inside the Cabinet Office. Helen Keenan was finally uncovered not by MI5 or MI6 but by Special Branch after passing Cabinet minutes to a BOSS agent who forwarded them to the illegal Smith regime. Of course, not everyone in MI5 and MI6 felt that BOSS was the enemy. In particular Maurice Oldfield, who was destined to become head of MI6, could often be found at the home of Bruce Mackenzie, who had helped Oldfield set up the Kenyan intelligence service, partying with agents from both BOSS and SAVAK (the Iranian secret police). Oldfield's favourite party piece was to keep everyone entertained with details of particularly brutal interrogations he had conducted.

As the economy disintegrated under Wilson's mismanagement, there began to be talk of the need for a change of government or even a coalition of the great and the good drawn from the British establishment. In the summer of 1967, the CIA, the FBI, MI5, MI6, and the Australian and New Zealand security services met in secret in Melbourne, Australia. They were addressed by Golitsin about his Wilson allegations and Wright presented information which he claimed raised the question of the loyalty of Willi Brandt. This meeting was followed by a visit to MI5 by Angleton who claimed to have confirmation from another source, whom he claimed could not be named, that Wilson was indeed a Soviet agent.

Matters began to hot up when the press baron Cecil King, a long-standing MI5 agent, began to discuss the need for a coup against Wilson. He informed Peter Wright that the *Mirror* would publish any damaging anti-Wilson leaks that MI5 wanted aired, and at a meeting with Lord Mountbatten and the government's Chief Scientific Adviser, Solly Zuckerman, King urged Mountbatten to become the leader of a government of National Salvation. Zuckerman pointed out that this was treason and left the meeting which came to nothing due to Mountbatten's reluctance to act.

Whilst all this seems quite eccentric in the cold light of day, it is important to remember that the Greek colonels had just taken power (with US backing) in a coup aimed at preventing the election of the Greek Social Democratic party. There were also strong rumours that a military coup against the Italian government had been actively considered. Certainly, one army intelligence officer admitted that contingency planning took place to identify a suitable site for internees in the Shetland Islands.

Much of this feverish paranoia involved former MI5 and MI6 officers who had kept their intelligence links since retiring from the service. One such was George Young, the former number two in MI6. He outlined his thinking in *Subversion and the British Riposte* (1984), a book published some years later:

> a security counter-action need cover no more than 5,000 persons, including some 40 MPs, not all of them Labour; several hundred journalists and media employees, plus their supporting academics and clerics; the full-time members and main activists of the Communist Party and the Socialist Workers Party; and the directing elements of the 30 or 40 bodies affecting concern and compassion for youth, age, civil liberties, social research and minority grievances. The

total internment could easily be accommodated in a lesser 'Gaelic Archipelago' off the West Highlands.

Although this reads like something out of a Frederick Forsyth novel, we should remember that the author would have been a strong contender for the post of head of MI6, had he not retired early in order to further his business interests. He was eventually to stand for Parliament in 1974 as the Tory candidate in Brent East.

In the end, all the talk of a coup came to nothing. The devaluation of 1967 eventually produced a balance of payments surplus, no one inside the Labour Party was prepared to move against Wilson and it was expected that Labour would lose the forthcoming general election anyhow. Wilson's supporters hit back and the increasingly unreliable King was removed from his post at the *Mirror* newspaper group. (King's behaviour became ever more erratic and in 1974 he urged a group of officers at Sandhurst to take power in a military coup. They thought he was mad.)

The defeat of Wilson at the 1970 general election did nothing to reduce the hysteria inside MI5. In the first place, because of his ill-concealed contempt for the fantasies of the more extreme elements in MI5, Heath was considered unreliable. Heath's attitude to MI5 was revealed in a debate in Parliament in 1988:

> I ... met people in the security services who talked the most ridiculous nonsense, and whose whole philosophy was ridiculous nonsense. If some of them were on a Tube and saw someone reading the *Daily Mirror*, they would say 'Get after him, that is dangerous. We must find out where he bought it.'

In MI5 the contempt was reciprocated. The Tory MP Captain Henry Kerby – the MI5 agent who had ingratiated himself with George Wigg – was used, whilst Heath was still in opposition, to spread rumours that Heath was a homosexual who had had an affair with a Swedish diplomat. I suspect that for some in MI5 being a Swedish diplomat and homosexuality were virtually synonymous anyway!

These doubts about Heath were not confined to the more extreme elements who naturally clustered around Peter Wright. The newly appointed head of MI5, 'Jumbo' Hanley, decided not to inform Heath that there were now investigations to try to determine whether or not Sir Roger Hollis had been a KGB agent. He certainly did not inform him about MI5's doubts about Wilson or reveal the contents of the file on Wilson which he had inherited from his predecessor, Furnival Jones. This was kept in the safe of the director and filed under the name Henry Worthington.

The second factor that increased MI5's alarm was the rise in working-class militancy which expressed itself as a wave of strikes and demonstrations against Heath's anti-union laws. This also had an effect on the Labour Party where opinion began to swing to the left.

This swing was accentuated by the third factor which was Heath's determination to take Britain into the EEC – thus splitting the right-wing coalition of MPs and trade union leaders which had dominated the Labour Party since the Second World War. The right-wing MPs clustered around Roy Jenkins intended to break the party whip and vote with Heath to take Britain into the EEC, whereas the right-wing trade union leaders were mainly anti-market. In the past, the right wing of the Parliamentary Labour Party had been able to rely on the trade union block vote to give it control of both the Labour Party Conference and the TUC. As this old coalition fell apart many right-wingers on the Labour Party NEC and the TUC General Council lost their seats to the left wing which, for the first time, gained a tenuous majority on both bodies.

For many in MI5 it seemed as though Britain was on the slippery slope to a Marxist dictatorship. Retired, gin-sodden generals began to set up 'secret' armies of 'patriots'. George Young pondered about the point at which treason against the government of the day might become justified or as he was to put it in later years 'the officers of . . . the security service may feel that the only course of action is to grab their Top Secret files and head . . . for the United States embassy'.

In London there were anxious discussions late into the night at the Special Forces Club, the City Golf Club and the Carlton Club, as former and serving intelligence officers discussed the 'desperate' measures that might be necessary to save democracy from the 'enemy within'.

Any pretext that MI5 existed to catch Russian spies now became rather thin and from 1972 onwards there was a vast growth of those sections in MI5 which involved domestic surveillance. Trade unionists, peace campaigners, Cabinet ministers and political activists in their tens of thousands became the object of illegal phone taps and letter intercepts. The recruitment of agents on a scale not even considered necessary at the height of the cold war meant that by the mid-1970s even a small group of half a dozen left-wingers, meeting to discuss some local campaign, would be likely to have one of their number reporting to MI5 on their activities. Before long 2 million British citizens had acquired confidential security files.

With the Heath government's poll ratings falling MI5 redoubled their efforts to remove Wilson. Peter Wright began flying over regularly to see James Angleton at the CIA to try to learn the identity of the alleged informant who could confirm that Wilson was a Soviet agent. Although he was unsuccessful, the meetings between these two believers in the theory of the omnipotent red menace could only have increased the paranoia inside both organisations. Angleton decided that the CIA should organise the publication of the allegations of the Czech defector Josef Frolik. These would repeat the old allegations about the 'spies' in Wilson's Cabinet and, he hoped, damage the chances of Labour at the next election.

The story that Gaitskell had been murdered by the KGB was given to the press and a constant drip of innuendos about Wilson's loyalty was fed to *Private Eye*, which could be relied upon to take bigger risks with the libel laws than Fleet Street.

One of the main sources of leaks to *Private Eye* was David Candler who had moved from Labour Party headquarters to work for Wilson at No 10 as a political aide, between 1967 and 1970. Candler had been in contact with MI5 on another matter and remained friendly with Michael Halls, the liaison officer between No 10 and MI5. Halls considered Marcia Williams to be a security risk and funnelled damaging smears about Wilson and Williams to *Private Eye* via Candler. As luck would have it Candler eventually came to work as head of the GLC Labour Group office where his conspiratorial and ingratiating manner made his tenure a short one.

Wright and Angleton must have been annoyed when Heath called an early election before the Frolik book could be published. They must have been horrified when, against all the expectations, Wilson won the election. As far as these two men were concerned, the KGB now had its man back in Downing Street and any measures would be justified to remove him. As Wright put it: 'most people in MI5 didn't have a duty to Parliament. They have a duty to the Queen ... It's up to us to stop Russians getting control of the British government.' Angleton started visiting Britain regularly to urge MI5 to take firm action to remove this threat to Western security. He authorised the use of many new CIA agents to penetrate British trade unions and a big expansion of the Forum World Features news agency, a CIA front with close links to the 'black' propaganda Information Research Department of British intelligence.

George Young had reappeared on the scene of right-wing Tory politics in the early 1970s. He joined the Monday Club and, assisted by Harvey Proctor, tried to take it over. He formed a group called Unison which comprised right-wing elements from business circles and the legal profession who were convinced that Britain was heading for a 'collapse of law and order'. Their most prominent member was Ross McWhirter. Young also developed links with recently retired General Walter Walker whose task was to enrol 'volunteers' prepared to save Britain from the red menace. David Stirling who had founded the SAS and loathed Young set up GB75 as a rival to Unison.

It has been easy for some politicians and journalists to dismiss these activities as the work of a lunatic fringe but the views of MI5 chief Sir Michael Hanley are well known. When asked at a seminar for junior officers what would happen if Michael Foot became Prime Minister, he replied, 'I and every other officer in the service will have to consider our position.'

Other officers in MI5 did not share Hanley's sense of resignation and they found a natural leader in Peter Wright. By Wright's own admission in the years that followed thirty MI5 officers engaged in twenty-three criminal conspiracies and committed twelve acts of treason against the elected government of the day.

The group that formed around Wright had three main objectives. First was to force Wilson to resign. Their preferred replacement was Callaghan whom they considered sound on security issues.

The second objective was to replace Heath with someone they found sufficiently right wing. Initially, they tried to discredit Heath and rumours of his alleged homosexuality were given a new lease of life. An expensive, illustrated, glossy booklet detailing the 'evidence' was printed in Sweden and began to circulate widely, although the restrictive British libel laws meant that no paper would touch it. An attempt was made to get round this problem by having Tony Benn raise the issue. During 1974 an American woman appeared in Bristol who worked hard on Tony's election campaign. After establishing herself she gave Tony a copy of the Swedish booklet and suggested that he raise the issue publicly. This Benn declined to do and the woman disappeared. It is, of course, impossible to prove MI5 involvement in the production of the booklet but it is the same tactic used by the MI5 agent, and Tory MP, Captain Henry Kerby who had passed similar allegations of Heath's 'alleged' homosexuality to George Wigg.

The initial choice of the MI5 plotters to replace Heath was Sir Keith Joseph who had started a public campaign to move the Tory party to the right, just a few weeks after the February 1974 election defeat. He announced that he would be a candidate against Heath following the Tories loss of the October 1974 general election, but before much could be done to advance his cause Joseph self-destructed with a remarkable speech in which he warned that the poor were breeding more rapidly than the middle classes and the government should 'deal' with the problem. The resulting furore forced him to drop out of the race against Heath and there was only one other member of Heath's cabinet who had supported Joseph's shift to the right – Margaret Thatcher. In collaboration with Joseph, she announced that she would be a candidate on the day he withdrew and after some hesitation Wright and his associates soon swung behind her. The third objective of Wright's associates was, of course, to replace the Labour government with one led by Thatcher as soon as possible.

One factor that was to be helpful to the MI5 group around Wright was their informal contacts with several dubious private security firms. These had been formed by retired SAS, MI5 and MI6 officers and were often contracted to undertake work for the government that it was thought advisable should not be handled directly by the government's own security services. Thus if anything went wrong it was possible for the government to deny responsibility. The government was also able to use these companies secretly to support foreign governments whom they did not wish to be seen backing openly. In recent years, the use of these firms to spy on domestic critics of government policy has increased dramatically and there have been suggestions that in some cases acts of violence, including the murder of Hilda Murrell, have taken place.

The dissident MI5 group also maintained links with like-minded people in the world of business and politics. This was particularly easy in the case of the Tory Party as there is a long tradition of serving and former MI5 and MI6 agents seeking election as Tory MPs. In *The Wilson Plot* (1989), an excellent account of the security services by David Leigh, the author identifies ten Tory MPs with an intelligence background.

By far and away the most important of these was Airey Neave, the MP for Abingdon. Neave was an unusual mixture of the courageous and the conspiratorial. During the Second World War he had become famous as an escaper from the notorious German prison, Colditz, and then headed MI9, which operated the escape route for others.

Neave himself kept his own close friendships and contacts with the intelligence community throughout the post-war period.

Over the years Neave had given Wright 'a lot of valuable information about ... traitors or potential ones' and Wright now approached him again, ostensibly to discuss the issue of private armies. Wright concluded that 'Neave came out of the interview very well, showing himself to be loyal to the Crown and to British democracy'. We can only speculate about other items they might have discussed but it would be surprising if they had not touched on the need for a new Tory leader.

Neave was determined to remove Heath but although he had known Thatcher from his days as a barrister they were not close. He had already approached both Whitelaw and du Cann to volunteer his services but as both had declined to stand he now approached Thatcher, offering to organise her campaign. She willingly accepted and Neave got to work assembling a team of PR and media people to handle the campaign whilst he organised discreet lobbying amongst Tory MPs.

Following Thatcher's victory, Neave was rewarded not only with the post of Shadow spokesperson on Ireland but he also became the head of her private office and adviser on intelligence matters. Unlike her predecessors of both parties, she developed a close interest in the work of MI5 and MI6 and the relationship between Thatcher and Neave developed to the point where he soon became her closest friend and adviser – the only one with the confidence to tell her when she was wrong.

Although the MI5 dissidents had no trouble finding fellow conspirators in the Tory Party, the senior military officers whom they approached where understandably reluctant to become involved. However, this was not the case amongst more junior army officers on active service in Northern Ireland who were in frequent contact with MI5 agents in the field.

Once 'the troubles' had flared up in 1969, the British government discovered that there was no reliable intelligence gathering operation in place and both MI5 and MI6 were dispatched to Northern Ireland to remedy this defect. After a long period of infighting between the two organisations MI5 took overall control of operations there. Wright himself was given a roving brief on Irish matters and spent much time in the province advocating more interventions south of the border and tougher measures to eliminate the IRA.

Many of the thirty MI5 officers conspiring to bring down the Wilson government spent periods of time in Ireland. Constraints on illegal activities there were much less than in Britain and this gave scope for MI5's plotters to get down to work, spreading disinformation and smears. Operating under the codename Clockwork Orange, documents were forged and an illegal Swiss bank account was established in the name of Edward Short, the deputy leader of the Labour Party. The rumours about Wilson's alleged KGB links, sex life and finances were spread far and wide and similar suggestions were disseminated about his friends and associates. Forged documents were circulated 'proving' that David Owen was a dangerous leftist. The rumours about Heath were given further emphasis and Jeremy Thorpe was also the object of attention because of his opposition to the South African government.

These activities, whilst they are acts of treason, definitely have the air of rather nasty public schoolboy pranks, as befits the social background of most of the plotters. Yet in their determination to get the sort of government they really wanted, they were prepared to take actions which were despicable, literally murderous and aimed at wholly innocent members of the public.

When Blunt had been granted immunity from prosecution, he had insisted that the immunity cover all crimes he had committed in addition to his treason. Desperate to ensure the success of the cover-up MI5 granted his demand. In his 'interrogations' by Wright, Blunt is almost certain to have admitted that one of his crimes was involvement in a child sex ring based on the Kincora boys home in Northern Ireland.

The origins of this child abuse ring dated back to his days at Cambridge where he had become involved sexually with a group of upper class paedophiles from Northern Ireland. In the years after Cambridge, Blunt maintained his contacts and occasionally travelled to Ireland for long weekends spent abusing young boys at parties attended by some well-known names from British and Irish ruling circles.

The Kincora boys home was run by men who were members of Tara, an extreme loyalist organisation, and paedophiles themselves. They must have assumed that provided they maintained a regular supply of young boys for the pleasure of these upper-class loyalists (including a member of the judiciary), they would be immune from prosecution themselves. As they succeeded in getting away with it for over twenty years, this was a reasonable assumption to make.

MI5 decided to take no action against the Kincora ring for fear that any prosecutions would inevitably lead to the exposure in court of the immunity granted to Blunt. For the same reason, MI5 did not even warn the local social services department so that they could bring this child abuse to an end.

When, in 1969 (five years after Blunt's confession), Ireland erupted and large numbers of MI5 officers arrived in the North to begin the painstaking work of establishing a proper information gathering system, Kincora was still festering away. It would be ten years before the truth emerged about Blunt and MI5 therefore was still interested in keeping the lid on Kincora. Now, however, Wright's fellow officers realised that good old-fashioned blackmail could give them control over leading figures in Northern Irish politics. MI5 was soon aware of the identities of the public personalities who visited Kincora to avail themselves of the paedophile service run by the loyalist Tara organisation, and actually went so far as to photograph surreptitiously these respected members of the establishment about their pleasure. Far from complying with the law and stopping this dreadful abuse of young boys, MI5 effectively adopted the role of brothel-keeper. One disgusting aspect of the whole affair was the way in which MI6 visitors to MI5 headquarters in Ireland were sometimes treated to a salacious glimpse of photographs, taken from the Kincora file, showing public figures in the act of sodomising young boys.

Things did not go all MI5's way, however, and the Kincora scandal threatened to erupt into public view when a former lover of Guy Burgess and Blunt became disaffected. Mr ABC began writing to newspapers and politicians recounting what had gone on and listing the names of the great and the good who had been members of the paedophile ring. His local police force (West Sussex) conducted the initial investigation into the allegations and decided to take no action. Mr ABC stepped up his letter writing campaign and the establishment began to panic. In the end the Lord Chancellor's office (under Lord Hailsham), brought a government prosecution against Mr ABC who was forbidden by the courts from continuing his campaign. MI5 was thus left to get on with its work and Blunt continued to operate as a respected member of the British establishment.

Once the Blunt story was blown in 1979, it was only a matter of months before the Irish press printed an exposé of the Kincora scandal, in 1980, and in 1981 the three local Tara members who ran the home went to prison. No one else was ever prosecuted. The government set up three enquiries. The first was carried out by the RUC which had known what was going on but whose files on Kincora inexplicably went missing. The report was never made public. The second inquiry was conducted by the chief constable of another police force which the government claimed had no involvement in the case. This was a lie. The enquiry was by Sir George Terry, the Chief Constable of West Sussex police, whose force had been responsible for investigating the claims of Mr ABC. The report was never published. The third enquiry report, conducted by Judge William Hughes, was published but it only dealt with the lessons for social services arising out of the Kincora case. Its terms of reference spelt out that it would not investigate any of the allegations involving the security services or politicians.

Another disturbing fact is the number of violent deaths amongst those interviewed by the RUC in connection with Kincora. This was unusually high even by the standards of Northern Ireland. John McKeague, the leader of the Red Hand Commandos, was interviewed informally by the RUC but shot dead before they could return to take his statement. Thomas Edgar was found shot dead in 1982. The RUC said it had all the 'hallmarks of a professional assassination'. Michael Wright's death was alleged by the paramilitary Ulster Defence Association to be part of a dirty tricks campaign by the Dublin government. Pastor Billy Mullan was found in circumstances which suggested he had shot himself. Finally, Senator Joshua Cardwell, a former Stormont MP, was found gassed. Rubber tubes connected to the gas mains had been thrust up his nose. The RUC stated it was suicide. Cardwell had been Minister of State for Health and Social Security in Northern Ireland.

In 1988, I gave the Prime Minister the name of a senior civil servant now employed in the Ministry of Defence who had been a member of the Kincora paedophile ring. Mrs Thatcher refused to take any action. Finally, in 1989, more than two decades late, the British government started paying substantial damages to some of the ex-residents who had been abused in Kincora. All were out of court settlements and they were all told not to talk to the press. The MI5 officers who first covered up the Kincora scandal and then presided over it as an entrapment ploy have either retired with the usual honours or been promoted.

Amazing though it may seem, Kincora is not the worst crime in MI5's long history of the abuse of human rights in Ireland.

The security forces were very dubious about Wilson's commitment to defeating the IRA. Wilson had toured the area whilst Leader of the Opposition and had returned to Britain convinced that the only solution was eventual British withdrawal. Although he kept his views confined to close colleagues, it was not long before MI5 heard of his new position.

The first chance for MI5 officers to block Wilson came when the new government had to face the loyalist workers' strike against the power-sharing executive which the Heath government had established. MI5 and the local army officers (who were often the same people) resisted Wilson's instruction to take over and run the electricity stations simply insisting that it was not possible to use the army to break the strike. They thus forced the government to agree to the strikers' demands. After the strike the loyalist leader, James Miller, claimed that MI5 had told him to encourage the idea of the strike.

Wilson continued to search for a way out of the Northern Ireland conflict, and it began to look as though a solution might be possible when the new Northern Ireland Secretary, Merlyn Rees, was able to negotiate a cease-fire with the IRA in February 1975. MI5 was horrified. Not only was it politically opposed to the creation of a united Ireland, it was also realised that a Labour government which could negotiate a peaceful withdrawal from Ireland would win great popularity and the possibility of an election at which it might win a working majority.

MI5 officers and their agents in both the army and the RUC began to undermine the cease-fire by supplying weapons and information to loyalist paramilitary organisations. This enabled the loyalists to assassinate members of the IRA and other republicans on both sides of the border. As the cease-fire held MI5 increased its involvement with the loyalist paramilitaries and in some cases even led the assassination and bombing teams. Most of MI5's agents in the field had no idea about the political motive behind the operations they were being asked to run. They were simply loyal soldiers who believed that the politicians in Whitehall were asking them to defeat the IRA whilst fighting with one hand tied behind their backs. It was a dirty, vicious little war and like soldiers in similar situations the world over they believed in fighting as hard (or as dirty – depending on your point of view) as the enemy.

Still the cease-fire continued to hold and MI5 had to consider more extreme measures. As the killing of republican activists had not been able to shake the cease-fire, one of the sicker minds inside MI5 decided that an act of particular savagery, directed against innocent civilians, might unleash a wave of sectarian killing which would leave the IRA with no choice but to break the cease-fire or be discredited within the nationalist community.

The officer chosen for this task was Captain Robert Nirac, Oxford educated and part of the SAS 22 regiment (formally attached to the Grenadier Guards). Nirac had been trained in counter-insurgency techniques at Sandhurst by Brigadier Kitson himself and was posthumously awarded the George Cross for 'acts of the greatest heroism in circumstances of extreme peril that showed personal courage second to none'.

Nirac gave guns and bombs to seven members of the paramilitary Ulster Volunteer Force and then led them, on the night of 21 July, to a main road where they planned to intercept the Miami Showband, who were the number one pop group in Ireland at the time. Disguised as members of the army's Ulster Defence Regiment (one of them was actually a sergeant in the UDR), they waved down the van carrying the band back to Dublin after a concert in the North. In setting off the bomb that killed three members of the band they also blew up two members of the gang but this may not have been an accident. One suggestion is that part of Nirac's orders was to ensure that enough went wrong to identify the loyalist group behind the killing.

The IRA reacted by killing five people in the Bayardo Bar on 13 August and the cease-fire began to fall apart in a wave of sectarian tit-for-tat killings. As these escalated throughout the autumn pressure built up on Merlyn Rees and on 12 November he terminated the cease-fire.

The group of MI5 officers which had set out to end the truce had achieved its objective and the Wilson government had been deprived of what would have been its greatest achievement. But the people of Britain and Ireland were to pay a terrible price as the years rolled by and the death toll of the war in Ireland climbed to over 3,000 fatalities during 1989. Perhaps the truce was doomed anyway but it offered a chance to achieve a negotiated settlement and its destruction locked Britain into a further fourteen years of killing with still no end in sight.

Back in London, at about the same time that the Miami Showband were being waved down on the Dublin road, Maurice Oldfield, head of MI6, took Wright to dinner at Locketts restaurant and questioned him about the extent of the Wilson plot. Having heard him out Oldfield told Wright to put MI5 chief Hanley in the picture. This Wright did the next day. In Wright's words: 'Hanley ... went white as a sheet ... he was learning that half of his staff were up to their necks in a plot to get rid of the Prime Minister.'

Whilst Hanley pondered on how to defuse the time bomb on which MI5 was sitting, George Weidenfeld, the publisher, asked to see Wilson and warned him about the gossip at fashionable London dinner parties that MI5 considered Wilson to be a security risk.

Finally, on 7 August 1975, just eighteen days after the Miami Showband killings, Wilson called in Maurice Oldfield who confirmed that there was a problem in MI5. Wilson then confronted Hanley. How much Hanley told Wilson is not known. Indeed it is highly unlikely that Wright had told Hanley or Oldfield just how out of control the situation had become in Northern Ireland. Indeed, so great had been the growth of MI5 in Ireland that perhaps by that time even Wright himself only knew a part of what had been happening.

Wilson was planning to retire in eight months and accepted the incomplete and sanitised account of events Hanley relayed to him. In the end, there was only an internal enquiry by Sir John Hunt, the Cabinet Secretary. By the time it reported No 10 was occupied by James Callaghan – MI5's preferred choice for Labour leader and a good friend of the security services. Hunt proposed that a number of new people be recruited to MI5 to try to dilute the anti-Labour climate within the organisation and that Hanley's successor should be an outsider. The act was temporarily cleaned up but the play went on. The illegal bugging and letter intercepts of citizens whose only crime was to be active in a trade union or the peace movement continued. The growth of private security firms and their use by the government continued. The lack of accountability of MI5 and MI6 to Parliament continued. For five more years the abuse of boys in Kincora continued.

The unusual story of Captain Robert Nirac also continued. Two years later, in May 1977, following his capture in south Armagh (an area which was effectively under the control of the IRA) and his interrogation and execution by the IRA, the *Daily Mail*, who had been briefed by the army, revealed that he was 'a secret agent ... known only to top Special Branch men, to Army Intelligence and to the men of the SAS with whom he worked'. There was even a suggestion (which I have not been able to confirm) reported in *Magill*, in June 1979, that at the time of his death Nirac was working for a small, top secret unit answerable only to Sir Maurice Oldfield. Whether or not this is the case does not invalidate the question as to why Nirac was sent into such a dangerous no-go area without back-up. It seems almost as though he were being sent to his death.

There is a contradictory rumour (which it is not possible to confirm without access to army records) that there was an army unit in hiding around the Three Steps public house outside which Nirac was overpowered by the IRA. If this is true then the events are even less explicable.

The unusual story of Airey Neave also continued. For four more years he was the Shadow Cabinet spokesperson on Ireland, Mrs Thatcher's adviser on the intelligence services and head of her private office – the filter between her and the rest of the world. In reality he was the second most important person in the Tory Party.

But there was another side to Airey Neave that neither the public nor even most of his parliamentary colleagues knew about. He kept in close touch with the MI5 dissidents who were, albeit with greater discretion, continuing their treasonable activities.

After Colin Wallace (who had been one of the Army Intelligence officers working for MI5 involved with the Clockwork Orange project) left his job as an information officer in army headquarters in Northern Ireland, he was approached by Neave. Although they had never met before, Neave obviously knew that he had been working for MI5 and involved in the disinformation and propaganda campaigns against both the IRA and the Labour government.

Neave's proposal to Wallace was simple. Continue the same work but do it directly for Neave. Wallace agreed and over the following months prepared background papers and speeches for Neave which dealt with the growing strength of the British left and its 'links' with the IRA and the USSR. Another favourite propaganda line of Wallace's was the wholly unsubstantiated assertion that a united Ireland would become the Cuba of the North Sea. These themes were taken up by Neave in a series of speeches which were widely reported. Further proof of Neave's involvement with Wallace comes from the fact that Wallace retained the correspondence which is in Neave's own handwriting.

When questioned about this on the floor of the House of Commons, John Wakeham, the Leader of the House, was unable to explain how Neave would have known that Wallace was working for MI5 or have been so well informed about the nature of Wallace's work. Mrs Thatcher simply refuses to answer the questions.

Confirmation that Neave was more than just an observer on the fringes of the plotters' group comes from former MI6 officer Lee Tracey who was and remains firmly anti-communist and very right wing. Tracey had been one of MI6's electronics experts but had left the service by the time he was phoned by Neave in March 1979 and asked to come to the Cumberland Hotel in London. As Tracey explained to journalist Duncan Campbell in early 1981: 'I'd never met him before. But I had a very high regard for his reputation.'

At the hotel Neave told Tracey that if the Tories were elected at the forthcoming general election he expected to become the security overlord. He intended to carry out a purge of unreliable officers in MI5 and the Metropolitan Police. But although he expected the Tories to win he was worried that if Labour got back Callaghan would soon retire and that would leave the way clear for Benn to become Premier. Both men believed that there was a real danger of Britain being taken over by communism.

Neave said that he was setting up a team of intelligence and security men, an undercover 'army of resistance' who would 'make sure that Benn was stopped'. Tracey insists that Neave was prepared to use violence to achieve this end. They agreed to meet again but one week later Neave was assassinated by the Irish National Liberation Army.

Duncan Campbell, who was working for the *New Statesman*, had picked up enough information to be aware that these meetings were taking place, but in the aftermath of Neave's murder decided that 'there was nothing we could or would have done to investigate further'.

Campbell believes Tracey to be a reliable witness. Information from Tracey used in other stories has always been confirmed by other sources and by the facts where this was possible. In this case, Campbell sought and got corroboration from another former intelligence officer.

When all the evidence and the witnesses are assembled the full scale of the conspiracy aimed at the heart of our democracy is truly shocking. Any one item examined on its own, even the killings, can be dismissed as the work of right-wing eccentrics or just part of the violence that has become a way of life in Northern Ireland. But taken together they prove beyond a shadow of a doubt that during the 1970s a substantial, and powerful, minority of the British establishment was involved in activities which in any other country would be called treason.

I happen to believe that, irrespective of these treasonable activities, Callaghan would have succeeded Wilson and the Tories would have won the 1979 election. I suspect that Mrs Thatcher would have defeated Heath but I am not as certain as I am about the other two propositions. On this there are genuine grounds for suspecting that the treason may have changed the whole course of British politics and it is the involvement of Airey Neave that makes it so.

Neave knew of the treason but how much he knew is a secret he took to the grave. From his contacts with Peter Wright and Colin Wallace we can deduce that he most probably knew quite a lot of the detail of what was happening. From his activities we can see that not only did Neave know of the treason but that he played a key part in it.

What made Neave such a vital part of the plotters' campaign was the fact that whereas the others could create mayhem and mischief, Neave alone was in a position to change the course of events positively. Neave alone was in a position to choose, promote and organise the election of Margaret Thatcher.

This is the real reason that the Prime Minister now blocks every attempt to enquire into or expose what happened in those years. This is why such a vast effort was expended to try to prevent the publication of *Spycatcher*. This is why all questions in Parliament are met with evasive and stonewalling answers.

There is no reason why this government should try to cover up scandals which took place during a Labour government's time unless it is to protect the reputation of old and faithful supporters. Mrs Thatcher knows better than anyone else that a full independent enquiry into these events would almost certainly lead to the question of how much did Airey Neave know and what was his role in these events? Once that question is asked it inevitably leads to another.

Neave became Mrs Thatcher's closest friend and adviser; as head of her private office he decided who saw her and as her unofficial security adviser he introduced her to the world of MI5 and MI6. Are we to believe that in all that time he never once indicated to her, even in the barest or most general outline, the treason he was involved in? And if the answer to that question is no then did she not once ever suspect that some very unparliamentary work was being organised by the man who ran her private office and stood like a praetorian guard at her door?

Instead of investigating these acts of treason Mrs Thatcher decided to push two bills through Parliament which will make it very difficult even to write about such events. When they become law it will no longer be possible to publish a *Spycatcher*.

The contrast between Britain and other Western democracies could not be more stark. Here in Britain systematic acts of treason and murder are committed by our own security agents and we are told that in the interests of national security even MPs cannot be allowed to investigate them. Yet in the USA former President Nixon was forced to resign after Congressional and judicial inquiries established that his campaign managers had authorised the bugging of the Democrats headquarters and that Nixon had used his position to cover up the crime and impede the investigations.

The separation of powers between the executive, legislative and judicial branches of the US government, coupled with the freedom of speech and press which is enshrined in the US constitution, guaranteed the eventual emergence of the truth. Had Nixon been a British premier the Watergate scandal would never have been exposed and Nixon would have retired with honour. He would have been able to use his powers of patronage over MPs to control the House of Commons and prevent the issue being raised there in any meaningful way. The media would have been told that this was a matter of national security involving officers of MI5 and MI6 and therefore subject to a 'D' notice banning any reporting of the incident. The judges, who are simply appointed by the Prime Minister of the day without any scrutiny by an independent body, would have been sympathetic to discreet lobbying that it was not in the national interest that any court proceedings should lead to the exposure of the background of the burglars. In fact given that the Metropolitan Police, who would have made the arrest, are directly answerable to the government it is possible that the burglars would not even have been charged.

When I meet politicians from other countries they are always amazed at Britain's lack of a written constitution and are either appalled at or envious of the concentration of power around the Prime Minister, which is the inevitable consequence. There is only one other country in the world that lacks a written constitution and that is Israel. But if they ever tried to write one the whole country would be torn apart over the proposals the religious parties would make and they might not even be able to agree on the definition of who is a Jew.

Britain has no such excuse yet we have not even adopted a set of basic civil rights. Therefore, whilst everywhere else people are citizens of their country here in the UK we are SUBJECTS of the monarch. When elected MPs make their oath of allegiance it is not to the people, the Parliament or even to the defence of democracy but to the monarch and his or her heirs. Although this may seem a trivial point it underlies the whole basis of law and governmental practice in the UK because the powers of the monarch are devolved on the Prime Minister of the day.

Whilst this system has always been wrong in principle, in the past it has been tolerated in practice because former premiers have operated self-imposed constraints on the use of the power concentrated in the office of Prime Minister. They have also usually sought to achieve a consensus behind the government that is wider than just their own party supporters and have been prepared to moderate their policies accordingly.

Instead of operating within this long-established consensus, Mrs Thatcher has deliberately set out to behave as though she is running the 'elective dictatorship' which Lord Hailsham once warned that Britain was in danger of becoming. It is Mrs Thatcher's contempt for the self-imposed constraints implicit in the British system that has created the demand for constitutional reform among such a wide range of people and institutions. As she has proceeded with each measure – the abolition of the GLC, the imposition of total government controls on local councils, detention without trial for up to seven days, increased surveillance of the domestic population, the use of internal exile, the increasing censorship of the media, the removal of dissidents inside her own Cabinet, the abolition of the right to silence in court, the use of the civil service to lie to Parliament and the people – she has made the issue of a written constitution and a Bill of Rights come to life as key issues in British politics.

The creation of Charter 88 is the first sign that the way Britain is governed has become a cause for concern to a wide range of public opinion. Socialists have nothing to fear from such concern because unaccountable bureaucracy is inherently inimical to socialism and democracy. Socialism is about the redistribution of power as well as wealth and any idea that socialism could be imposed from above on a reluctant population is a betrayal of socialism. The old idea that all we have to do to bring about socialism is to elect a few hundred good socialists to Parliament was a chimera fifty years ago, let alone in the vastly more complex society of today. A constitution which made government more accountable and shifted the balance of power away from central and local government bureaucracy towards the individual would dramatically increase the number of ways in which socialism could be built from below. As we have seen in the Thatcher decade, it is all too easy for a reactionary government to capitalise on public antipathy to unaccountable bureaucracies and use that anger as a cover to hide the real intention of cutting into social provision for the poor.

Instead of Neil Kinnock dismissing (at an off the record press briefing) those who are campaigning for Charter 88 as 'whiners, winge-ers and wankers', Labour should have devised a full package of constitutional reforms which would create a governmental structure which was more sympathetic to socialist principles. But this would have to go far beyond the demands of Charter 88 to include economic and social rights.

The first step in a new constitutional settlement is to implement a Bill of Rights. There are many things which could be included but we should ensure that it enshrines the rights of the individual rather than the rights of property and wealth.

It should recognise freedom of speech and publication except for the incitement to racial hatred.

It should recognise that the right of access to information is essential for the exercise of democratic rights and therefore ban any censorship or restrictive control of radio, television or the press by government, rich individuals or powerful corporations.

It should recognise the right to live free of discrimination on the grounds of race, sex, religion, sexual orientation or disability.

It should reinstate the right to trial by jury and ban the government's right to vet or weed out jurors whose politics it does not like.

It should reinstate the right to peaceful assembly and the right to travel freely without obstruction. This would prevent a repetition of the banning of citizens from travelling from one part of the UK to another, as was the case in the miners' strike and the prevention of Sinn Fein representatives travelling to London in 1982.

It should establish a right to privacy with citizens able to see and challenge the accuracy of all files held on them by governmental and private agencies.

It should establish a freedom of information right so that the complementary Freedom of Information Act could not be eroded by a future Conservative administration.

It should establish a right to basic services such as education, health, housing and social security so that the individual citizen would have a recourse to law if the national minimum standards laid down by government were not available locally.

It should re-establish the right to free trade unionism by asserting the inalienable right of people to withdraw their labour – which means repealing Thatcher's anti-trade union laws.

As well as catching up with the rest of the Western democracies (the USA adopted its Bill of Rights in 1791), we also need to follow other countries in the more recent trend towards devolution and decentralisation and end the concentration of power around Whitehall. Most modern democracies have a separation of power between central, regional and local government, so that it would not be possible for the US President or the West German Chancellor to abolish the elected city administrations of New York or West Berlin.

For far too long governments in Britain have thought that they know best, Labour governments being no better than Tory ones in this respect. Everyone in the Labour Party bemoans the fact that Mrs Thatcher's controls are so extensive that local councils have become little more than instruments for the execution of central government decisions, but it was the last Labour government which started to increase central government controls. Within a year of their being elected, in March 1974, the first step on the road of total government control was announced by the Housing Minister, Reg Freeson. Instead of leaving councils free to administer their own housing programmes, new controls were imposed which meant that the government had to agree each individual modernisation of each council flat. Within weeks these controls had been used by DoE bureaucrats to involve the government in nit-picking decisions about the exact size of rooms or the quality of fixtures and fittings to be used. The result was an immediate slow-down in the modernisation of homes throughout the country. At great cost, highly paid local government officers commuted backwards and forwards to London to argue with more highly paid civil servants about design details of individual council flats.

Even when the decisions taken by central government have been right in principle, it has still not been possible for central government to impose its will on councils determined to resist. When Tony Crosland issued a government circular requesting education authorities to submit plans to reform their selective schools along comprehensive lines, he soon discovered that local councils could thwart his plans in various ways. Fifteen years later when Callaghan was defeated by Mrs Thatcher 10 per cent of councils had still not created comprehensive schools and another 10 per cent had done so in ways which completely negated the comprehensive principle.

How much better it would have been if Labour had mobilised parental pressure to force councils to introduce comprehensive education, instead of being seen as remote bureaucrats imposing their will without regard for local opinion. It might also have led to greater parental involvement in schools, preventing the disillusion which eventually arose when first Labour and then Tory governments denied comprehensive schools adequate funding to make the scheme work.

The growing awareness of the importance of economic and cultural differences between the regions of the UK has come at a time when it is more obvious than ever before that governments cannot adequately administer the whole country from Whitehall.

Labour should welcome the cultural differences between regions, accept the principle that government is best conducted closest to the community, and implement a major shift of real power down to directly elected regional parliaments and local councils.

Central government's main roles should be reduced to defence, foreign affairs, macroeconomic policy, the redistribution of wealth from rich to poor areas and the setting of national minimum standards for the provision of all public services and the protection of the environment.

Scotland and Wales are clearly separate nations which require their own devolved parliaments. The most vigorous campaign possible is needed on this to counteract Labour's earlier weakness which opened the door to the SNP. As regards England, the Northern, North West, Yorkshire, East Midland and West Midland regions would all have clear boundaries. The present divisions of southern England are not so satisfactory. Many people in the South West believe that so much of southern England is wrongly included that it dilutes the cultural distinctiveness of the region. And there is an obvious case for including Essex in the East Anglian region.

However, the main problem lies with the present South East region which, with its disproportionate share of both population and economic strength, could dominate the whole nation if it was not broken up into its three quite distinct subregions – Greater London, the south coast and the corridor between Bristol and Heathrow. Each of these three areas has a different cultural history which would be submerged in a south-eastern superregion, and which in any case would be so large as to lose the benefits of devolution.

The above structure would give Britain ten regional and two national parliaments with manageable populations between just under 2 million and not more than 7 million. Within each region there should be a single tier of local councils replacing the present two tier system of districts and counties.

The split of responsibilities between regional parliaments and councils should once again reflect the principle of devolving government as close to the local community as possible. The local council should be responsible for the provision of virtually all the services that the individual requires, including housing, education, health, police, social services and social security. The regional parliaments main responsibilities would be transport, industrial regeneration and training, environmental protection, the provision of public utilities such as water, electricity and gas, to legislate on regional matters, and the provision of those elements of policing, education and health care which are only economic on a regional scale. (The distribution of functions between the three tiers of government is meant to be indicative not exhaustive.)

The poll tax should be abolished and replaced by a local income tax which would be collected by the local council. The national and regional governments would set their own taxes to be collected by the local council and passed up. Thus each individual's tax bill, whilst it would be one total sum, would have three separate elements clearly identified so that the proportion emanating from each tier of government, and its value, could be judged.

Local councillors and regional MPs should be full time with an adequate salary and secretarial and research staff. There would obviously be no need to continue having so many MPs at Westminster, and given the shift of power and responsibility away from Whitehall many MPs would choose to become full-time politicians on their local council or regional parliament in preference to staying in London.

In devolving power from Whitehall, however, we must beware of replacing unmanageable government bureaucracy with unmanageable local bureaucracies. To do this there must be a further element in the devolution package – wherever possible the control of local services should be further devolved to the consumers and providers of the service.

One of the tragic lost opportunities of the last two years was Labour's unimaginative response to Thatcher's radical social programmes. As her government pushed through the changes in the management of schools, council housing and the NHS, it talked about giving parents, tenants and patients real choice whilst in reality giving greater control over schools to Kenneth Baker, private landlords the chance to take over council estates and turning local doctors into penny-pinching accountants. But instead of simply opposing Thatcher's changes we should have advocated real democratic reforms.

As regards council housing this would mean tenants being given the right to take over and run their own estates with powers to appoint and dismiss their caretakers and maintenance teams. Local committees and coops would be directly elected by tenants with a minority of places on the committee for representatives of the workforce. The local council would retain nomination rights to empty homes and ensure that local committees did not discriminate.

Similarly, schools should be run by committees of parents, teachers and pupils. The role of the head teacher who has total power over the conduct of the school has long been an anachronism in a modern democracy. Many heads already consult widely before taking decisions and the best practice collective leadership. If we really want our children to grow into confident citizens we need to ensure that their experience of school life is one which encourages confidence in their own decision-making abilities, rather than just following the orders relayed down the hierarchy of teachers.

Whilst it is easy to see how the control of council estates and schools could be devolved there is less experience in the areas of health and social work. But although the problems are greater I have no doubt that, to take just one example, the many horrifying accounts of brutality in private and public homes for the elderly would not arise so often if pensioners occupying them elected the local management committee. Equally, if we are to tackle the problem of child abuse we must find some way to ensure that all children are aware of their rights and empower those who are taken into care with some say in how they are treated.

I have no doubt that many teachers and social workers will claim that such reforms undermine their status as 'professionals', but there is no logic in the suggestion that workers in some, mainly middle class, jobs have a right to be exempt from scrutiny by those who are the consumers of the service (and in many cases pay for it through their taxes).

The separation of powers between the three tiers of government should be enshrined in a written constitution so that subsequent governments would not be able to change the boundaries or responsibilities for party advantage.

The question then arises as to how this constitution (including the Bill of Rights) should be protected and amended as society develops. The devolution of power away from Parliament would not only justify a reduction in the number of MPs, it would make the case for the abolition of the second chamber even more unanswerable. Its defenders have justified retaining the House of Lords on the grounds that it is a check on a dictatorial House of Commons and that it would stop the government of the day from being able to postpone elections. The last ten years of Thatcherism have exposed the hollowness of this claim. No substantial Thatcherite measure, however unpopular, has been rejected by the House of Lords. The abolition of the GLC, the imposition of the Poll Tax, the extension of police powers, censorship of the media have all been passed after some obligatory hand wringing by the peerage. And if a dictatorial government did want to abandon an election then a house so totally dependent on the patronage power of a prime minister to create new peers would be no obstacle. All that is required is to create enough new peers to pass the bill abandoning the election.

Instead of trying hopelessly to achieve constitutional safeguards by preserving this relic of the *ancien régime*, there are more modern ways to defend the frequency of elections. It would be essential to include in the new constitution a fixed limit on the life of each parliament and then ensure that any amendment to the constitution cannot simply be agreed by the House of Commons. Whilst an amendment would have to be agreed, first, by a majority in the Commons, it should then need the endorsement of either a referendum of all voters or a majority of the regional parliaments. A variation on this safeguard would be a second chamber composed of representatives of the regional parliaments which would be convened whenever there was discussion of constitutional amendments. There is also the option of requiring a constitutional amendment to achieve a two-thirds majority in the House of Commons and/or amongst the regional parliaments.

With these proposals for the devolution of most of government's functions to the regions and the introduction of proper constitutional checks and balances into the system, it may seem anomalous to propose a real increase in the powers of the House of Commons but that is the next vital step in modernising British democracy.

Up until the First World War Parliament was the real centre of power in the British Empire. What happened on the floor of the House of Commons determined which section of the ruling class was predominant in Britain, most key establishment figures being present in either the Lords or Commons. Before the vote was extended to the majority of men in 1870, governments were made and brought down by shifts in the various factions comprising each party. As issues vital to one particular section of the ruling class became less or more important, whole blocks of MPs would simply cross the floor of the House. The result was that governments were more often changed between rather than at elections.

However, following the First World War (and just as the Labour Party arrived in the House of Commons as a real force), power began to shift away from Parliament to the Prime Minister and the Cabinet, the civil service and the emerging great national and international corporations. Over the years this process has accelerated so that Parliament has been reduced to little more than a circus whilst real power is exercised elsewhere and behind firmly closed doors.

This does not mean that MPs are inherently incompetent, just that their capacity to be effective is deliberately undermined by the government and civil service. The last thing that those who run Britain want is a well-resourced, independent-minded legislature able to investigate and expose what is really going on in Britain today.

There are two ways by which the legislature is kept toothless. First, there is the massive use of patronage by party leaders which means that anyone who wishes to be a minister (which is most MPs, given the lack of power of backbenchers) needs to keep in with the Prime Minister. This pressure to conform also works in opposition because it is largely front-bench spokespeople who get publicity, thus advancing their careers whilst attacking government ministers. Therefore, Leaders of the Opposition have an interest in preserving the *status quo* since they hope one day to be running the system and do not approve of those MPs who argue for a democratisation which would curtail their powers.

All too easily Labour Party leaders and their most senior colleagues are seduced into thinking that they will one day be able to sit at the desk of the Prime Minister or secretary of state and use all that centralised power to change Britain as they wish. The way Thatcher has behaved has reinforced that idea, although any socialists who have served on their local councils rapidly learn that the system that works so well for the Tories seldom responds so easily to socialist politicians trying to carry out radical policies. This is not surprising since the Tories have been in power for fifty-one of the seventy-one years since the end of the First World War and have created an administrative structure geared to their interests. On those occasions when Labour wins office it always seem to fall for the same old assurances that the civil service and judiciary are neutral instruments of government, and only discover this is not the case when it is too late.

The second way of keeping MPs toothless is by denying them the resources to carry out the job. Whereas even a new member of the US House of Representatives has an average of twenty-two staff (but represents eight times as many people) an MP has a total annual allowance of only £21,000. Out of this we need to pay for a secretary based in Parliament, any equipment such as word processors, a constituency office and staff to help with people's problems locally, and a researcher (the employers' national insurance contribution also has to be paid from the allowance). Unless you underpay your staff it is simply not possible to employ more than one full-timer and one part-timer – a local office is out of the question. Whilst many Tories have additional staff provided by the companies which retain them as lobbyists, the few Labour MPs who get assistance from a trade union find it is seldom enough to employ even one other person.

Even these limited resources have only been achieved in the last five years – before that the parliamentary allowance was £6,000 and as recently as the 1960s MPs were restricted in the length of long-distance phone calls they could make. After one speech I made attacking inadequate resources for MPs, Merlyn Rees told me how, when he was first elected in 1964, he had to use a special phone box when calling his constituents in Leeds and after five minutes an attendant with a stop watch would tap on the phone booth to remind him that he had had his time! Even today, MPs cannot phone abroad without booking the call through the switchboard and paying for it out of the allowance.

With such restricted means it is almost impossible to have much impact on government ministers who have the backing of an entire Whitehall department and large personal staff. With these odds it is remarkable that any government is ever defeated in argument or embarrassed by exposure of its wrongdoings, and yet by a vast amount of diligent work, often with a lot of help from campaigning groups and a fair bit of luck, MPs still manage to be effective. But that effectiveness could be increased tenfold if MPs had adequate resources.

To make the House of Commons really effective involves changing the rules by which it works. The existing committee system should be expanded so that every government department is shadowed by a Commons' committee and any legislation affecting a particular committee's area of policy would have to be submitted to that committee for consideration and amendment. At present, a new government bill is given to a special committee of MPs established by the government whips who ensure that there is a safe majority of government supporters on the committee. A few rebels might be included but never enough to endanger the bill if they voted with the opposition. Usually, the government packs the committee with members who have little interest in that particular legislation but just sit quietly at the back of the room and get on with their correspondence until they are called upon to vote down the various amendments moved by the opposition.

If, instead of this farce, legislation had to be submitted to standing Commons' committees of MPs who had specialised in that particular area of policy, then there would be a much greater chance of bad legislation being amended or rejected.

In addition, if civil servants were made responsible to the Commons collectively instead of the government, then the increasing corruption of the role of civil servants by the government of the day would be reduced. We would no longer have to tolerate civil servants being used for straightforward party political purposes, lying to Parliament and the public, and being banned from giving evidence to parliamentary committees.

One of the most important and abused powers Prime Ministers have is the choosing of the time of the election, for partisan purposes. Apart from engendering endless, terminally boring, press speculation about the date of the next election, it gives the incumbent government an even bigger advantage than it already has, causing increased instability and waste for those in business and administration whose decisions are affected by the electoral cycle.

There is no reason why we cannot have fixed-term elections so that we know the date of an election decades ahead. Bearing in mind the British weather, a fixed-term election every fourth June would have considerable advantages for everybody except the Prime Minister. The reduction of the term from five to four years is not much of a change as the only two governments seriously to try to survive into their fifth year in recent times were those of Home in 1964 and Callaghan in 1979. In both cases this was simply an attempt to stave off inevitable defeat.

Governments are usually tired and directionless in their fifth year and an election is a reviving and renewing process for MPs as well as the political process.

Fixed-term elections would also do away with one of the most damaging features of the British political system which occurs when a government is elected with a only a small majority and then proceeds to waste a year or two while it defers all difficult decisions, particularly those on the economy, and bribes voters with short-term give-aways and gimmicks in the hope of calling and winning another election. A fixed-term Parliament would stop all that nonsense as the government would know it had to proceed on the basis of a full four-year term.

It is not logical to consider reform in Britain without looking at the issue of the voting system. The only honest justification for the present system is that it favours the two main parties which are its beneficiaries and strongest defenders. This venal approach is nothing new – in the days when Labour was still the third party it supported PR and the Liberals, who were one of the two main parties, did not.

Unfortunately, the justification for the introduction of PR is currently overshadowed by the debate about how to get rid of the Tories. Leading members of Labour's Shadow Cabinet and NEC, who privately do not believe that Labour can win the next election, are talking about doing deals with David Owen and Paddy Ashdown so that there would only be one anti-Thatcher candidate in each Tory marginal constituency.

There is one simple reason for rejecting this sort of deal – there is no evidence that it would work. Every academic study has demonstrated that economic policy is the most important factor in determining why people vote as they do, and Mrs Thatcher has won the last two elections by bribing the voters in the run-up to the election, thus reinforcing her claim to have a coherent package of economic policies which are slowly getting Britain back on its feet. If at the next election the choice is between continuing with the Tory economic policies or voting for an unprincipled alliance of opposition parties who agree on nothing except the need to get rid of Mrs Thatcher, then people will continue to vote for the devil they know rather than risk their standard of living.

It may very well be the case that voters would like to vote for a government which would introduce PR but when finally facing the ballot box, they are not going to risk their economic prosperity simply in order to change the voting system.

The SDP and the SLD are both: (1) opposed to the government having controls on capital in order to direct investment into rebuilding the economy; (2) not prepared to reduce defence spending; and (3) opposed to changing Mrs Thatcher's anti-trade union laws. It is hard to imagine them agreeing on a common economic package with Labour that would look credible enough to have a chance of overturning the Tory majority.

Without an agreement on economic policy, in those constituencies where Labour voters were being asked to support a centre party candidate, many would either abstain or vote for the Green candidate. But in those cases where centre party supporters were being told that they had to vote Labour, many would either abstain or even vote for the Tories in preference to letting Labour 'ruin' the economy.

Whilst it is important to reject the idea that there is some simple short cut to getting rid of Thatcher which avoids the hard task of assembling a coherent alternative package of policies, we should not reject reform of the voting system. There is simply no justification for a system under which Mrs Thatcher can be rejected by 56.1 per cent, 57.6 per cent and 57.7 per cent of those who vote and yet win, respectively, 53.4 per cent, 61.1 per cent and 57.8 per cent of the seats in Parliament.

Unfortunately, the whole debate on PR over the last decade has been quite fraudulent with the centre parties claiming to support it whilst in fact trying to replace the present unfair system which discriminates against them with a different unfair system which discriminates against the Labour Party. What they have argued for is the system of the single transferable vote (STV) in multimember constituencies. This is the system in southern Ireland yet it does not produce an equality between votes cast and seats gained because the process can be fiddled depending on how the constituency boundaries are drawn. We can see how this works most clearly by looking at the vote of the Irish Labour Party in the three elections of 1965, 1969 and 1973. In the first of these Labour won 15.4 per cent of the vote and twenty-two seats but in the next election whilst Labour increased its vote to 17.0 per cent it actually lost four seats! In the 1973 election, Labour's vote slumped to 13.7 per cent but it gained a seat. As in Britain, the system benefits the winning party. In 1977 when Fianna Fail won only 50.6 per cent of the vote it gained 56.8 per cent of the seats.

The system is fiddled by varying the size of constituencies. For example, during the 1983 and 1987 elections the Alliance parties proposed an STV system with five member seats in the cities and three member seats in the rural areas. This would have meant that in the rural areas Labour, whose vote is usually under 33 per cent would have failed to gain any seats, whilst in the big cities where the Alliance just manage to get 20 per cent they would have gained one in each of the five member seats. Lo and behold, by remarkable good fortune the electoral system proposed by the Alliance would unfortunately have given that party more than it was entitled to and Labour less. The single transferable vote is not genuine PR and I think there would be considerable public anger if the voting system was changed but still failed to provide a perfect match of seats gained to votes cast.

It would be easy to dismiss the sham PR proposals of the centre parties as simply an attempt to gain partisan advantage, but there is a much more cynical reason lurking in the background. The establishment knows that at some point the Tories will lose power in Britain. To counteract this the blocking power of the centre parties in a hung Parliament could be used to prevent a real democratisation of the whole British state and economy. There would be an attempt to substitute a pseudo-democratisation based on changing the voting system, giving the centre parties a permanent veto over any really radical attempt to modernise the British economy. Thus policies to create a high-tech, high-skill, high-wage economy by directing the financial sector's investment into industry and rebuilding our welfare state by cutting defence expenditure could be blocked, forcing us to live with the continuation of the changes that the Tories have pushed through during the last ten years. Therefore, there would be an apparent democratisation of the political superstructure whilst leaving the underlying economic base untouched. In short, any agreement with the centre parties would result in an impasse, making the modernising and democratising of the British economy impossible.

In any change in the voting system it is vital to maintain local accountability. It is also important to prevent any further powers of patronage accumulating in the hands of the central bureaucracies of the political parties, as is the case with the list systems used by most European countries.

An ideal system for Britain would be a variant of the West German List method which retained accountability by having two-thirds of all MPs elected in the traditional first past the post way. This would obviously mean the size of constituencies being increased but would retain the local link. The other third of MPs would be drawn from separate party lists assembled from the candidates of that party which had lost with the most narrowly defeated candidate at the top of the list down to the most heavily defeated at the bottom. MPs would be drawn from these lists in the correct numbers so that each party ended up with the exact proportion of MPs as it received votes. Under such a system the party leaders would not have any extra patronage as it would be the voters themselves who would determine a losing candidate's position on the list. It would also be the case that every MP would have had to have been selected by a local constituency party and undergone the election campaign.

If we imagine a slightly smaller Parliament with 600 MPs, instead of the present 650, and an election result like 1987, then the list system would work as follows:

Votes cast	Seats won in first stage	Additional seats	Total
Tory 42%	230	22	252
Labour 31%	140	46	186
SLD 23%	18	120	138
Others 4%	12	12	24
Total 100%	400	200	600

If the list system operated on a regional basis instead of just one national list, it would ensure that each region had its fair share of MPs.

The reason for introducing PR should be seen as part of a much wider package of reforms aimed at expanding democracy and reshaping the economy. If it is taken out of that context and introduced for its own sake, PR could end up as a blocking mechanism aimed at maintaining the shackles the Tories have placed on British society.

For historical reasons the absolute rights of the monarch – such as the power to declare war, sign peace treaties and call elections – have in reality shifted to the Prime Minister, although the monarch remains the figurehead for these decisions. Having created a Bill of Rights, a written constitution, a fair voting system and proper checks and balances between central government and the regional parliaments, it would be time to bring Britain into line with other Western democracies and pass these monarchical powers to the House of Commons.

Although there would be a wide consensus behind proposals to modernise Britain's democracy along the lines set out above, it would almost certainly take four years before the legislation could be passed, elections organised and the new bodies established. But the warning of *A Very British Coup* was that a Labour government would not survive that long. The Labour Party therefore needs to consider what measures it should take to ensure that the decision of the voters in the polling booths is respected and not overturned by the unaccountable centres of power which lie in the hands of the establishment.

The new government would have to move rapidly to secure itself from attack by the intelligence services. The new government would need to appoint a full Cabinet minister responsible for the intelligence services and that individual would need considerable support from external advisers knowledgeable of the recent history of MI5 and MI6. Along with the new minister, the immediate establishment of a Commons committee to investigate past crimes and abuses would put MI5 and MI6 on the defensive. The committee would need the power to imprison those officers who refused to cooperate and would be charged with drawing up proposals for the replacement of the present security services with a more limited and accountable department integrated into the existing police force. The role of the new service would be restricted to the prevention of actual crimes and would have to operate within the law at all times.

Disloyalty in the civil service is also nothing new. During the financial crisis of 1976, whilst the Labour government was trying to secure a loan from the IMF in Washington, top officials in the Treasury were secretly phoning their opposite numbers in the IMF urging them to impose tougher conditions on the loan, thus forcing the government to make bigger cuts in its social programmes. Since then things have worsened. The new government would be working with a civil service in which every senior appointment had been agreed by Mrs Thatcher, subject to the condition 'Is he one of us?'

The new government would need to pension off those top bureaucrats who were not prepared to carry out its orders impartially and loyally, as well as bringing into Whitehall a large contingent of advisers and academics who could understand and implement our policies. The new government should also recognise that having just three or four ministers at the top of a vast department like Defence is simply too few to establish firm ministerial control. Instead Labour should appoint a team of at least a dozen MPs to each ministry.

There would also be a problem with senior judges. By the time of the next election every member of the Court of Appeal and the Law Lords is likely to have been appointed by Mrs Thatcher. Unlike previous Prime Ministers, she has taken a close interest in every appointment and has ensured that each is sympathetic with and in some cases even to the right of her own politics. The bias this has produced is a major problem facing any trade union, Labour council or black or Irish person who is trying to get a fair trial from the two highest courts.

Whilst this may seem an outrageous allegation we only need to examine the record of recent judgments to confirm the charge. There are just over eighty High Court judges which is too many for a Prime Minister to be involved in each appointment, and frequently not much is known about their politics before their appointment. But once in the High Court they are faced with many controversial decisions and it soon becomes apparent as to who are progressive and who reactionary. When Mrs Thatcher then meets the Lord Chancellor, whom she also appoints – and dismisses, to decide on the filling of vacancies in the Court of Appeal and the Law Lords, she is completely aware of the politics of each High Court judge. It is obvious from the record of their judgments that she has been successful in packing both the Court of Appeal and the Law Lords with the most reactionary and biased of the High Court judges. This has now produced the situation whereby a trade union or a Labour council or a black person fighting deportation may often win their case in the High Court, but in almost every 'political' case the High Court decision is overturned in the Court of Appeal and that decision is invariably upheld by the Law Lords.

A Labour government would soon find that the judges were wilfully misinterpreting legislation to block its policies. The judges did this to a certain extent with the Trade Union and Race Relations laws of the Wilson/Callaghan administration, but the political shift that Mrs Thatcher has engineered amongst the senior judiciary ensures that it would occur on a much greater scale in future.

To show that it did not intend this to happen Labour should take immediate steps to change the composition of the Court of Appeal and Law Lords. The easiest way would be to reduce the age of retirement to 65 and then appoint less partisan judges to fill the vacancies that would automatically be created. Labour would have to create enough new peers to carry the legislation in the House of Lords if it looked as though the Judges (Retirement at Age 65) Bill was not going to pass.

Such an early demonstration that Labour was not prepared to tolerate judicial sabotage would most probably be enough to remind the judges that they are there to interpret the law – not to make it and give Labour time for a more wide-ranging reform of the law along European lines. Certainly the narrow social base from which the judges are drawn (from private schools to Oxford and Cambridge and then the Bar) must be widened and there is also no reason why the bulk of the administration of justice should not be carried out at the new regional level.

Many of the attacks on a radical Labour government would, of course, be led by the Tory press and there would be no chance of Labour's policies gaining a fair hearing whilst 80 per cent of all national newspapers are under the control of just three men – Murdoch, Maxwell and Stevens. Not only is this a completely unacceptable concentration of power in a few hands, but the unbridled pursuit of profit by Murdoch in particular has led to a massive decline in the standards of reporting and good taste.

In his book *1984*, George Orwell described a Britain where Big Brother sought to maintain power by constantly falsifying the news and reducing the number of words in use so that ordinary people could not even begin to articulate anger at their oppression. In a much more subtle way that is precisely what Murdoch has done with papers such as *The Sun*, in which the English language is in danger of being reduced to bum, boobs, bingo, Argie, Frog and poofta. And although many people claim that this does little harm, I have a gnawing suspicion that the increased rate of rape, and in particular the growth of violent rape, may be influenced by the constant depiction of page three women as sexually available for man as and when required, together with the almost pornographically detailed way in which accounts of rape are reported in these papers.

Although Murdoch is by far and away the most degrading influence on life in Britain, the simple fact is that anyone who is rich enough to own a paper will be tempted to use it as a vehicle for personal politics and beliefs. When dealing with these people, the assurances they give about editorial independence are not worth the paper they are written on. A good example is my own relationship with Robert Maxwell. He started a new London daily paper during the year between the abolition of the GLC and the 1987 general election and employed me to write a regular weekly column. The paper turned out to be a real improvement on the *Evening Standard* and everything was fine for six months until I made a speech in Parliament in which I raised the allegations about the involvement of MI5 and Captain Robert Nirac in the Miami Showband assassinations. The following day I received a hand-delivered letter, signed by Maxwell himself, saying that he thought my speech was a disgrace, that he was not prepared to have someone like me working on a paper of his and that my contract was terminated. The next day came a letter by post from the editor of the paper asking to speak to me about my column. It was quite obvious that Maxwell had sacked me without even bothering to tell the editor of the paper.

The abuses of the press have become so blatant that we are now getting bills in Parliament which are trying to deal with the problem and this has led to increasing efforts on the part of the worst papers to divert the pressure by 'balancing' their coverage with the inclusion of a token left-winger. In the last two years, I alone have been offered £40,000 from Murdoch to serialise my GLC memoirs in the *Sunday Times*, a regular weekly column in *The Sun* at about the same rate and a weekly column in *The Star* (whilst it was under the editorship of the pornographer Gabbett) for a similar sum. All these I rejected not just because Murdoch sacked thousands of his own staff, but because they want to use a left-wing name to try to legitimise the way they abuse the power that press ownership gives them.

Of course, if you refuse to cooperate then these media millionaires, with their rapid expansion into book publishing and satellite broadcasting, can make your life difficult in many ways. One small example occurred when Murdoch was able to get back at me for my refusal to be interviewed by or write for his papers.

When I decided to write this book Collins (who published my previous book on the GLC and had been delighted that it became the best-selling political book of that year) were keen to publish it, and the details were agreed over a very friendly lunch. I knew that Murdoch had made a take-over bid for the firm in the early 1980s and although he had been fought off he had acquired 42 per cent of the voting shares in the company. Therefore, it was only fair to warn the executives negotiating on behalf of Collins that the book would include a strong attack on Murdoch and propose that his entire media holdings should be removed from his control. They said they did not think this would be a problem as Murdoch only had a minority shareholding and when we parted I had no doubt that we would soon sign a contract.

A few days later, however, I received an apologetic message that the board of Collins had rejected the proposal on the grounds that 'It is too soon for another book by Livingstone'! Fortunately, Unwin Hyman came to my rescue but if the concentration of newspaper, television, radio and book publishing in such a few hands continues, it may not be long before it becomes almost impossible for dissenting voices to break into any of the mainstream channels of communication.

Whilst there is no doubt the public is alarmed by this concentration of power there is rightly no support for any form of state ownership or censorship. Labour should ensure that we free the media from the clutches of the rather unsavoury press barons so that it can represent the full diversity of opinion and cultures in Britain today. We should change the system to allow journalism to become a profession of integrity in which the best guarantee of objectivity and balance is the self-respect of the journalists themselves, rather than heavy-handed government regulation.

On taking office Labour should bring the recent squalid history of the press to an end and legislate immediately to ban any individual or corporation from owning a national paper or television network. The present law which imposes on television and radio a duty to provide politically balanced coverage should be extended to all national and local papers. There should be rights of access to the media by all strands of opinion in society and a stronger regional element with the existing broadcasting bureaucracies being broken up and devolved downwards to the regions.

By turning them all into independent cooperatives, owned by the staff, subject to a legally binding duty to report news objectively and without political bias, we would usher in an era of improving standards in which the press fulfilled its vital democratic function of giving people the information they require in order to make up their own minds.

The other main source of domestic destabilisation would come from those financial institutions which opposed the redirection of investment into Britain from abroad. But it needs to be said that the sums of money invested abroad are, at £160 billion, so vast that if too much was returned too quickly to Britain it would cause economic chaos. A Labour government that wanted to reach West German levels of investment in domestic manufacturing would only need to return £5 billion to the UK to achieve that aim. If the City refused to cooperate then the public anger that such economic sabotage would arouse would allow Labour to take further powers to ensure that the mandate of the voters prevailed. If the City sees that Labour has the political will and determination to carry out its policies then it would reluctantly cooperate, but any sign of weakness or doubt would lose Labour the initiative and the City would add another Labour government scalp to its belt.

Destabilisation would, of course, be on the agenda of our enemies abroad. The USA has used Britain as its first line of defence for forty years and would do everything in its power to retain that advantage. Acting through the CIA, it would work with anti-government factions inside Britain whilst using its control of the IMF and the World Bank to undermine us internationally.

Labour's best chance of resisting US destabilisation would be through a policy of openness. By publishing the secret treaties in which previous British governments have signed away so many of our rights over the US bases here in the UK, Labour would be opening up a major debate about the erosion of our right to act as a free nation. By publishing the details of the collaboration of Britain's security services in the various US campaigns to destabilise and overthrow the governments of other nations around the world, we would make it more difficult for the US to do the same to us. By campaigning to change the control of institutions such as the IMF and the World Bank so that they were no longer simply under the control of the USA, we would gain the support of nations around the world.

It would be madness for a Labour government to sit back and wait for the destabilisation to begin. It should go on to the attack against the abuses of US power and campaign for a new world order based on openness and respect for the independence of nations. This would return us to the original ideals of the founders of the United Nations.

An equally vital key to surviving US destabilisation would be a Labour government's ability to retain the support of its own people. That is what makes the commitment to the democratisation and modernisation of Britain's institutions so vital. If a Labour government was seen to be breaking with the bureaucratic and paternalistic traditions of old-fashioned Labourism, it would excite and liberate the British people in a way that we glimpsed was possible, in a small way, in the heyday of the GLC.

Such a government could survive any attacks from outside because it would be a 'popular' government in the genuine democratic sense. We only have to look at the massive support for Gorbachev's reforms in the USSR to see how strongly a people will rally behind a movement that is really passing power to the people. And if we are honest we will admit that no other Western democracy has so many unsavoury characteristics in common with the old regime that Gorbachev is reforming than the elective dictatorship of these islands.

4

Sons of the Footbinder

Nothing characterises the succession of Labour leaders from Callaghan to Kinnock so revealingly as the total resistance each has shown in turn to the demands for reforming the Labour Party made by its feminist members. Nor are our leaders alone as they wallow in their chauvinism. Unlike most other issues where the leadership's reactionary views are rejected by the rank and file membership of the movement, it is uniquely the case that the majority of male activists will, on this one issue, find much common ground with their leaders.

I well remember a meeting in Sheffield, in the spring of 1982, where Valerie Wise announced that the GLC intended to establish a Women's Committee to fight to improve the lot of women in London. Only the women in the audience applauded whilst the men looked either bemused or contemptuous, and up on the platform David Blunkett (then leader of Sheffield Council) leant back in his chair and whispered, 'You're not really setting up a Women's Committee are you?' and chuckled so much that he almost fell off his chair when I confirmed that this was the case.

If the opponents to the idea had done no more than chuckle we would have had an easier life. Instead, our decision unleashed a torrent of vicious ridicule and abuse that continued up until the last day of the GLC. No other policy that we implemented produced such sustained opposition both inside and outside the party. Yet by the time the Women's Committee was finally abolished along with the rest of the GLC some four years later, the needs it had identified meant that its budget had grown to £16 million a year and a staff of 150 women were administering a vast network of woman and child oriented services and campaigns across the capital. Without any warning we had discovered a vast catalogue of needs and problems which we could only begin to tackle and an unused and ignored pool of talent beyond anyone's imagination, eager to be resourced and set to work.

Whilst the Women's Committee (as shown by opinion polls) became very popular amongst both women and men, the political and media attacks against it continued, and for whatever reason virtually no other council leadership in England or Wales was prepared to establish more than a token commitment in this area of policy. At the time of the demise of the GLC, we conducted a survey in London which revealed that most other Labour councils had failed to establish a women's unit, and of those that had only Camden (with six women) had more than one and a half staff in post to deal with the problems of women in their areas.

Thus the problem of sexism is one which afflicts all parties and classes in society, including the left. This is not a new phenomenon as Lenin admitted in his book *On the Emancipation of Women*: 'Unfortunately, we may still say of many of our comrades, "Scratch the communist and a philistine appears". To be sure, you have to scratch the sensitive spots – such as their mentality regarding women.' And it was certainly the case that when the Soviet revolution came under pressure and sacrifices had to be made, it was the gains of women which were the first to go.

Before we can understand the continuing and violent opposition to the full emancipation of women in our society, we need to comprehend the depth, scale and origin of the discrimination that women have faced. Those origins run so deeply through our culture that it was possible to live through a complete replacement of feudalism by capitalism without improving the balance of power between men and women.

It is only in the last few years that a convincing hypothesis of the origins of women's oppression has been articulated. The earlier hypothesis, that male dominance was linked to the man's role in hunting and his resulting control over the distribution of the spoils, may have played some part in the emergence of male dominance but is clearly not the whole story.

Much the best and most concise guide to current feminist thinking on the subject is to be found in *The Women's History of the World* by Rosalind Miles, which was published in 1988. She demonstrates that in the 100,000 to 300,000 years since our species emerged in Africa, the vast bulk of that time was spent in hunter-gatherer and tribal societies in which women played an equal if not superior food-gathering role to that of men, as hunting seldom provided more than 20 per cent of a tribe's food. There is no evidence for or against the existence of discrimination against women in those early societies and this situation seems to have prevailed until the last few thousand years. Although largely ignored (or even denied) by professional social anthropologists, during the first 4,000 years of organised human civilisation goddess worship and matriarchies were common, though it would be wrong to assume that a matriarchy implied discrimination against men. Equally this does not mean that every society went through the same developments at the same time, that there was some lost 'Golden Age' of sexual equality or that goddess worship automatically preceded belief in male gods.

But for many early human societies the magical fact of birth (which was not at that stage believed to be related to sex), of women as the givers of life, was at the base of goddess worship, and the likely consequence was an acceptance of women in terms of access to power and wealth as codified in the laws and civil structures of the societies which comprised many early civilisations. In those societies it was inevitable that men would envy the power of women to give life and this is still reflected in the Australian Aboriginal saying, 'The baby, the blood, the yelling, the dancing, all that concerns the women, men have nothing to do but copulate.' Many Aboriginal tribes practised what early white settlers believed to be ritual mutilation, whereby the penis of every boy had a thin bone inserted into the urethra and a flint knife was then used to slash through the flesh down to the bone. The split penis was then referred to as a vagina and regularly cut again in order to simulate menstruation.

However, as many early civilisations developed enough science at the beginning of the Iron Age (1500 BC) to realise that the male was essential to the reproductive cycle, a shift in power began to take place with the advent of male-dominated religions devoted to phallus worship. This shift of religious power would have reflected a real change in economic power based around the move from simple horticulture to agriculture. From the earliest evidence of cultivation in Egypt, 18,000 years ago, grain harvesting had been a predominantly female activity and this would have reinforced the role of woman as 'earth mother' and priestess of the Great Goddess. But then somewhere between 3,000 to 6,000 years ago the population exploded. Depending on the cultural stage reached, and certainly by the time iron farming tools became available, agriculture had become more physically demanding and this factor allowed men to supplant the women's traditional role. As Rosalind Miles describes it:

Where previously women had worked with nature in a kind of sympathetic magic as her natural ally, now men had to tame and dominate nature to make it deliver what they determined ... As planned ... [agriculture] ... replaced casual cultivation, the more the role of the male strengthened and centralised ... failure of crops brought enforced migration, which also necessarily involved warfare ... Both in ... nomadic wanderings and in any fighting ... men had the advantage, as they had superior muscle power and mobility, over women encumbered with children ... All women's ... skills of cultivation became useless when the tribe was on the move ... clashes of force ... produced winners and losers, determining rank, slavery and subjection, it was not possible for women to escape from this framework.

This economic shift of power is reflected in the mythology of many religions in the thousand years before the birth of Christ. The Babylonian god-king Marduk hacks to pieces Ti'amat, the Mother of All Things, and re-forms the world from her body as it should rightfully be. For the Tiwi of Africa the goddess Puvi made the world but her son, Iriti, killed her. The Greek god Apollo seized the sacred oracle at Delphi, whilst more recently in the Americas the son of the Aztec Earth Mother, Xochiquetzel, killed her daughter and took her place as god.

With this shift of power men changed the laws of inheritance to enshrine it and devised religious and academic logic to justify it. Thus Aristotle claimed that 'the woman is merely the passive incubator of his seed ... the male semen cooks and shapes the menstrual blood into a new human being' and Aeschylus depicts the Judgement of Apollo as, 'The mother is ... only the nurse ... the parent is he who mounts.' Although Aristotle and Aeschylus are representative of the more extreme misogynists of their time their prejudices did not go unchallenged.

Inexorably, the cult of the Goddess was replaced by that of the Phallus and across the world women's role and rights, and even control over their own bodies, were subordinated to the will of men so that eventually they became the property of men, a commodity to be bought or sold as the need arose.

Female sacrifice to the newly dominant male gods was commonplace but so was resistance, whether it was the women's riots against the misogynist laws of Cato in 215 BC or the work of Theodora, wife of the emperor Justinian, who fought and won for women laws of property, divorce and inheritance, whilst banishing pimps and brothel-keepers from the sixth century Byzantine Empire.

In the same way that a colonial power will justify its imperialism by denigrating the culture of those it enslaves, so men would have sought to legitimate their new-found power over women in the same way. In particular, the adoption of Christianity by the Roman Empire combined the worst misogynist features of both to open the way for a whole new ideology of woman as inherently corrupt and dangerous.

Thus did the monk Roger de Caen proclaim, 'If a woman's bowels are cut open you would see what filth is covered by her white skin. If a fine crimson cloth covered a pile of foul dung, would anyone be foolish enough to love the dung because of it?' Martin Luther went one better with his advice to 'let them bear children till they die of it'. Equally pernicious nonsense was believed about the menstrual cycle. Judaic law defined the menstruating woman as impure, 'the ultimate in corruption, a walking, reeking suppurating presence ... her breath was poisonous ... she polluted the very air about her'.

Jacob Sprenger, the Dominican monk and ideologist of the Inquisition warned of those witches

> who ... collect male organs in great numbers, as many as twenty or thirty members together, and put them in a bird's nest, or shut them up in a box, where they move themselves like living members and eat corn and oats as has been seen by many and is a matter of common report.

It was precisely this climate of ignorance which ushered in the witch-hunts during the 1560s and then again in the 1580s and 1620s. These were acts of gynocide in which at least 100,000 women died in Europe alone – one woman in every 500. Some historians have estimated the death toll to be much higher. In reality, the victims of the witch-hunts were any women who did not conform to the norm as laid down by men – women who held on to some of the traditions of the old pre-Christian religions, disturbed or paranoid personalities, wives whose sexual appetites exceeded their husband's and even those whose only crime was to 'scold' their husband.

Yet as an act of gynocide even the Christian witch-hunt cannot compare with the inestimable toll of the Chinese footbinders. Spanning a thousand years, this practice involved treating the feet of a girl (at various ages between birth and 7) with alum to cause shrinkage. The four small toes were then bent into the soles of each foot and bound tightly for three years. Andrea Dworkin described the result in *Our Blood* (1982):

> The girl, in agony, was forced to walk on her feet. Hard calluses formed; toenails grew into the skin; the feet were pus-filled and bloody; circulation was virtually stopped; often the big toes fell off. The ideal foot was three inches of smelly, rotting flesh.

The above description applies mainly to peasant girls who still had to be able to get about in order to work. For the daughters of the ruling class, for whom marriageable beauty was the main consideration, the bones of the feet were usually broken and tightly bound under the foot. This was what men were capable of doing to their own children. We will never know how many hundreds of millions of girl children died from this practice but it dwarfs any act of genocide in human history.

Is there a link, however tenuous, between the footbinding of ancient China and the crippling fashions that men have devised for women in our own time, such as the high heeled shoes that so painfully hobble women and increase their dependency on men? Or have we forgotten the 1960's joke that in reply to the question 'What is a lesbian' answered, 'A woman wearing sensible shoes!'

At least the Chinese footbinders have been retired. Unfortunately, those who practise genital mutilation, or circumcision, of women across much of the Third World today are very much in business. Those who still defend this practice seldom explain that it is performed on young girls of various ages and in its most radical form can involve the removal of the whole of the clitoris, its sheath, the labia minora, and the inside flesh of the labia majora. The wound is then stitched up leaving only a small gap for urination. The majority of 'operations' are performed with the girl awake and in the most primitive of conditions. The girl's legs may be bound together for up to forty days to stop the wound opening. In some societies the opening is cut wider to receive the penis on the wedding night. This operation was performed in both Britain and the USA until the early twentieth century as a cure for masturbation and epilepsy. For boisterous girls doctors recommended the less drastic practice of curettage – the removal of the womb lining.

With the advent of the Industrial Revolution, the position of women worsened still further as they were forced from the land into factories, where they worked for much less than their husbands, sons and fathers. But it was this period also which ushered in the beginnings of the modern feminist struggle. The first shot was fired by Mary Wollstonecraft with her *Vindication of the Rights of Women* in 1792. In 1832, a petition to Parliament demanded equal voting rights for women and in the USA, in 1848, the Seneca Falls Convention issued the same demand. The opening of the Troy Female Seminary in the USA and Girton College, Cambridge heralded the first breakthrough in the struggle for women's education, and the first steps to breaking down the male monopoly of the professions.

Yet at every stage in this struggle the resistance from men, and some women, was ferocious. Scientists 'proved' that the male brain was greater than the female counterpart and the philosopher Herbert Spencer warned that 'brain-forcing' (education) women would lead to stunted growth and flat chests.

Some feminists always recognised that complete emancipation meant not only gaining the vote and equality of opportunity in education and employment, but also regaining control of their own bodies. Therefore, the struggle for voting rights went hand in hand with the struggle for access to contraception and abortion. As the douche syringe became available in the 1870s (shortly after the appearance of the modern condom), campaigners for contraceptive rights such as Marie Stopes and Margaret Sanger began the battle to overcome the legal and professional obstructions placed in the way of women who sought control over their own fertility and their right to enjoy sex for pleasure. Typical of the worst was Dr C. H. F. Routh of the British Medical Association, who warned that contraception in women was 'indirect infanticide' and could lead to suicide and the 'most repulsive nymphomania'.

However, the tide of history was on the side of women and in the early years of this century, in one country after another, women began to gain both voting and contraceptive rights. Strengthened by the vast social and economic changes that followed in the wake of the First World War, it began to look as though women were on the brink of a historic victory.

It was then that male supremacy struck back by reviving and modernising the weapon that had been the symbol of their original victory over women – Phallus II entered the struggle in the unlikely form of one Sigmund Freud. Using modern scientific jargon, he was able to 'prove' that all women were mentally crippled by their lack of a penis and were doomed to spend their lives in a state of 'penis envy'. With equal confidence he was able to demonstrate that the clitoris was a 'childish masculinity' and that a woman could only become sexually mature when the source of her orgasms switched from the clitoris to the vagina – thus neatly proving that mature female sexuality was only possible when a penis was inside the vagina.

No tribal witch-doctor from the earliest phallocentric religions could have done any better at legitimising his cult and Freud's false theories reinforced the practice of incarcerating in asylums those young women whose only crime was to have an independent or unorthodox spirit. It was not for nothing that feminists would sometimes paint the slogan 'My dreams have enslaved half the world' around the many statues and busts erected to honour Freud by grateful men the world over. It was not until 1966, when Masters and Johnson scientifically demonstrated that the vaginal orgasm was a myth, that the world was finally rid of this pernicious nonsense.

Finally, in the early 1980s Jeffrey Masson, the director of the Freud Archives and curator of the Freud Museum, discovered in Freud's files that he had deliberately suppressed evidence that many of his women patients had been the victims of sexual abuse in childhood. Crippled by his own sexism and refusing to believe his female patients, Freud invented the nonsense of the Oedipus complex to explain away the unpleasant reality of child abuse.

Today, in the light of this knowledge, it is possible to see the flaws in Freudian theory.

Unfortunately, in the 1920s new forces were arising in the world for whom Freud's nonsense provided a confirmation of their own perception of the role of women. Aided by Freud's racist disciple Carl Jung, who was a willing collaborator, the Nazis now had 'scientific' evidence to support their views that female emancipation was 'a symptom of depravity produced by frustration and malfunctioning sex glands'. Women were only for breeding and were excluded from holding office in the Nazi Party.

The titanic forces which had to be mobilised in order to defeat the Nazis required the full utilisation of both sexes in all the Allied powers. The changes that flowed from this mobilisation gave many women a taste of freedom which was rapidly clawed back once the war was over, and women were reminded of their role as housewives and mothers.

Nevertheless, there was no way back to the world that had existed before the war. The development of the pill and the IUD, as well as the limited abortion rights introduced in many countries, gave women new rights over their bodies. But underlying all these changes was a massive shift of economic power as the rapidly expanding post-war economy drew tens of millions of women into work. The balance of economic power which had been largely unchanged since men first seized control of agriculture from women was starting to shift back.

Such a movement has the power to transform our whole society and will, of course, make its impact first at work. As such this poses tremendous opportunities for trade unions and the Labour Party, but not all our leaders perceive it in that light.

In Britain, women are the majority of the electorate – 53 per cent – and one of the reasons why the Tories have maintained themselves in office for most of the time since the Second World War is because Labour has not addressed itself to the issue of winning women's votes. Labour defeated the Tories among men in 1951, 1955, 1959 and 1970 but lost all these elections because it did not reach out to women voters, thus handing the Conservatives sixteen years of power. But traditional Tory dominance of women's votes is crumbling; in 1955, 8 per cent more women than men voted Tory. This gap had fallen to 5 per cent by 1964, to 2 per cent in 1974 and to 0 per cent in 1979 and 1983. The 1987 election once more confirmed that the differential vote of women for the Conservative Party had disappeared. Winning women's votes is vital to the electoral success of all the major parties – opinion polls have shown repeatedly that it is among women between the ages of 25 and 45 that there is most at stake electorally for both Labour and the centre parties. To win the majority of the electorate, women, and to win them in conditions where they are deserting the Conservative Party, is Labour's single most important electoral task. But the reality is that Labour has not gained the votes of women deserting the Conservatives. Since 1955 Labour's support among women has fallen by fourteen percentage points. During the same time, Liberal and Alliance support has increased by twenty-three points.

A special report prepared for the Labour leadership in 1988 dramatically revealed what Labour has yet to achieve. The basis of this report was poll information showing that among those asked it was a common belief that there were *no* Labour women MPs, *no* women in the Shadow Cabinet, and most could not name a single Labour woman politician – although the SLD's Shirley Williams was remembered. The only Labour woman politician that even a substantial minority could name was Barbara Castle! Moreover, those polled, whatever their voting intentions, considered that the party with the most developed policy for women was the Tory Party. The party leadership has comforted itself for years with the erroneous belief that not only do they know what is best for women, but that women themselves think this too. The deeply male chauvinist idea that women will simply assume the political views of influential men – be they husbands, fathers or Labour politicians – has permeated the response of Labour to the interests of women in the electorate since its foundation. It never was true and is even less so today.

The entire relationship of women to society has changed fundamentally since the Second World War. Since 1950 the main change that can be identified as affecting women is their massive entry into the workforce. The significance and scale of this process can hardly be overemphasised and I will return to it in the penultimate chapter. But here it is worth pointing out one decisive development with enormous social significance, the impact on *married* women. Prior to the Second World War, the proportion of married women in paid work was both extremely low and static. By 1911, only 10 per cent of all married women of working age were in paid employment. By 1931, the last census date before the Second World War, still only 11 per cent of married women of working age were in work. From 1951 onwards, however, the rise in the proportion of married women in work constituted a social revolution. By 1973, the proportion of married women in paid work had doubled – from 22 per cent in 1951 to 44 per cent. By 1983, 49 per cent of married women were in the labour force. If women between 15 and 59 alone are considered (that is taking into account the lower retirement age for women), then by 1983 56 per cent of all women of working age, and 56 per cent of married women of working age, were in paid work. *The movement of married women into the paid workforce during the period from 1951 onwards constitutes the greatest single change in the structure of British society in the twentieth century*. If we take all women, married and unmarried, and add into this picture the number of women seeking work but currently unemployed, then on official figures, which understate the situation, 66 per cent of all women of working age are in or seeking paid work. This constitutes a radical change in the relationship of women to society, with profound social consequences and political implications for all parties, but particularly for Labour.

The first and most immediate consequence of the need to integrate women into the workforce after the Second World War was the opening up of access to education to women. This is most easily seen in the expansion in the percentage of young women compared to young men passing 16+ examinations in school. Indeed, young women leaving school today are *more* qualified than young men – and the gap is tending to increase. Yet despite these higher qualifications women are still not entering higher education at the same level as men. Between 1970 and 1985 the number of women in higher education rose by 87 per cent to 383,000, while the number of men rose by only 33 per cent to 553,000. In 1985, 43 per cent of all first degrees were awarded to women. This was not only necessary for creating a useful workforce but had the immediate effect of raising the educational, employment and income expectations of women. Women are participating in every level of education in increasing numbers.

Table 4.1   School leavers with 'O'- or 'A'-level Qualifications by Sex as a Percentage of All School Leavers, 1960–86

	Men %	Women %
1960–61	30.4	28.7
1966–67	38.5	38.8
1970–71	42.9	43.8
1975–76	50.6	53.8
1981–82	51.9	57.5
1985–86	52.7	59.3

Alongside rising educational and income expectations, other social expectations have also risen. In particular, the prospects of married women have clearly improved. Since the introduction of the new divorce laws in 1971, the number of divorce petitions filed by women has increased from 18,000 annually to 131,000. Since 1961, the divorce rate per 1,000 marriages has increased from 2.1 to 13.2 per year. The total number of marriages has remained constant since 1961, 397,000 in that year compared to 394,000 in 1986. However two other factors must also be taken into account. First, the total population of marriageable age has grown, and secondly, the proportion of second marriages has also increased. Yet the overall marriage rate among women has undergone a dramatic decline since around 1970, reversing a historic trend over the previous century for the marriage rate among women to increase.

To these fundamental changes in Britain must be added the major significance of the greater availability of contraception, particularly the pill, and the existence – even if limited – of legal, safe abortion. These have allowed women to exercise a much greater degree of control and choice over when and whether to bear children, and more importantly, as women still bear virtually the entire burden of childrearing, whether or not to devote the next period of their lives to bringing up children. Women are exercising this choice, as the information on family size and the age at which women bear their first child show. Around 17 per cent of all women born after 1955 will not have children at all, and among those who do family size is tending to average out at 2.0 children per woman. Moreover, the average age at which women bear their first child has risen to 25.8 years old. These factors, taken together with other social changes – the numbers of women who are heads of households, increases in 'cohabitation' outside marriage, the increase in 'illegitimate' births, changes in social attitudes (however inadequate) to domestic violence to women, among many others – mean that certain conclusions can be drawn which contradict the images of women which have formed the basis of the Labour Party leadership's thinking on its policies for women.

The traditional Labour leadership view that the vast majority of women are solely or even primarily 'housewives', and that this should form the basis of the Labour Party's primary political appeal to women, is a bad joke. Yet this attitude continues to run through the leadership's response to its failure to attract women voters. One of the key conclusions to be drawn from the 1988 report to the Shadow Cabinet on women was that the Labour Party's spokes*men* should make more effort to present themselves as 'family men'! This was followed by the spectacle of male members of the Shadow Cabinet being interviewed playing with children at day nurseries, and one could be forgiven for thinking that it might have been behind Bryan Gould's well-publicised 1989 New Year resolution to 'spend more time with his family'.

For a significant proportion of women (17 per cent overall and the majority of those aged between 18 and 25) domestic considerations play a small role. They are more concerned to gain a decent, satisfying job, with decent income, conditions and hours. Furthermore, women continue to carry the main responsibility for childrearing and housework, for caring for the sick and the elderly in the home, and for shopping and preparing meals. Cuts in social security payments, in the health service, in social care for the sick, mentally ill and elderly, cuts in under-5s' nursery provision, attacks on the family income through rent increases, food price rises, and so on, all affect women differentially as virtually the whole additional burden in extra work (and worry) is assumed by them. These facts must mould the policies that Labour adopts and promotes.

Yet 66 per cent of women are also paid workers either because they seek to alleviate their domestic burden by increasing the total household income or because they seek independence, or a combination of both. For women in the home money equals saving time and work and creating more liberty for themselves. Labour cannot win the support of women without tackling these issues head on.

The integration of women into the regular workforce was achieved by taking advantage of their oppressed position within the home and their lack of legal rights. Women were brought into the workforce on a sex segregated basis – more than 60 per cent are in clerical, catering, cleaning, retailing and teaching jobs. Women working in manufacturing are concentrated outside the mainstream electrical and metal industries. In all these areas of employment trade union organisation is more limited and wages are substantially lower than the norm. Women's average pay, expressed as a proportion of men's, has failed to improve since the mid 1970s. Figures for 1986 reveal that a full-time woman manual worker could only expect to receive 62 per cent of the wages received by her male equivalent. Of 9 ½ million women in work nearly 10 per cent, that is nearly a million women, currently earn less than £80 a week before tax. One quarter of all women earn less than £95 a week before tax.

Moreover, as in all Western European countries, a very high proportion of women workers in Britain are part-time. On 1986 figures more than 4 million women were working part-time, that is, 42.6 per cent of all women in paid work. They have even more unfavourable rates of pay than full-time women workers. The 1988 New Earnings Survey shows that the average gross hourly earnings of part-time women workers is £3.22p, compared to £4.30p for full-time women, and £5.61 for full-time men. These figures are more striking if average gross weekly earnings are compared. Part-time women average £62 gross per week, compared to full-time women averaging £157 gross, and full-time men averaging £236 per week. Of part-time women workers, 67.2 per cent work for less than twenty-one hours per week with well over half working in four areas: retail distribution, hotels and catering, education, and medical and other health services. Part-time work does not only lead to unfavourable rates of pay, many of these women are working fewer than eight hours per week or earning less than the national insurance threshold, and so excluded from the operation of employment protection legislation. They are thus not eligible to receive statutory state benefits. The chronic conditions of low pay, job insecurity, and difficult hours are the reality of life for the majority of working women, which Labour should be addressing.

The first impact of this changed social position of women was not felt directly in either the trade unions or the Labour Party – although developments that would have a powerful impact were already under way with a substantial increase in the number of women trade unionists. Before this there was the Women's Liberation Movement, organised in the colleges and among women who were recent ex-students, and in 'consciousness-raising' and action groups, demanding equal pay, equal access to education and training, abortion, contraception, childcare facilities, and many related rights. Germaine Greer, Juliet Mitchell, Shulamith Firestone and others reflected the concerns of a generation of young women who wanted to get more out of life than their mothers had done.

The influence of the women's movement became far broader than simply those who participated within its ranks. It spawned local women's refuges, rape crisis centres, and more recently, incest survivors groups. It produced women's studies courses at universities, colleges and eventually in schools, and women's bookshops and centres; it encouraged women musicians and entertainers, creating the conditions for a changing place for women in popular culture; it influenced local government, eventually resulting in the proliferation of women's committees (albeit inadequately funded) and equal rights departments in town halls up and down the country; and it began to connect with women who were working inside the trade unions, adding to their determination to take up sexual harassment at work, sexual discrimination in employment and promotion, maternity leave and so on.

These developments came together in a number of significant strikes by women workers for equal pay, notably – and only just successfully concluded – the struggle of Ford machinists to be graded similarly to men on the production line. The TUC and the Labour Party, after decades of resistance, had only adopted a position in favour of equal pay, in principle, in the mid 1970s. But all that came of this was the introduction of the completely toothless Equal Pay Act and the equally inadequate Sex Discrimination Act. Even these very limited measures came very late in the day, and on the key issue of abortion it took the young Liberal MP,

David Steel, to introduce a Private Member's Bill liberalising abortion law.

Although the impact of the Women's Liberation Movement was felt initially outside the Labour Party, its impact on the trade unions was enormous. The mass involvement of women in the workforce meant a radical transformation in the membership of the unions. Between 1948 and 1979 the proportion of women members increased from 18 to 30 per cent – from 1.7 to 3.8 million. This new female membership was naturally concentrated in those unions related to the areas where women worked. Some, like NALGO and NUPE, relied for their entire post-war growth (and influence in the TUC) on the recruitment of women members. Others, like the TGWU and GMB, are not majority female unions, but cover areas where there are now a very high proportion of women workers. The AEU, ISTC, EETPU and UCATT have scarcely been affected by the growth in women's trade union membership as the employment areas to which they relate have remained virtually no-go areas for women workers. The unions with a large and influential female membership include NUPE with 500,000 women members, the TGWU with 250,000, MSF 100,000, USDAW 300,000, COHSE 200,000, NALGO 400,000, NUT 150,000, CPSA 150,000 and GMB 300,000.

This reliance on a female membership has had a profound and deepening impact on the unions concerned. Increasingly, the main political influence in the Labour movement is concentrated around unions with a substantial female membership, while those unable to recruit women have suffered a decline in membership and influence as the industries they represent declined. The EETPU has responded to this by its own membership offensive, aimed at working with the employers to get privileged access to the workers in the new high-tech industries on the basis of aggressive competition with other unions, breaches of the Bridlington agreements, and single-union, no-strike deals that undermine the basis of trade unionism itself. The EETPU remains totally hostile to the demands of women within the Labour Party.

In contrast with the destructive and Neanderthal policies of the EETPU, unions like the TGWU, GMB, USDAW and NUPE have seen modern trade unionism as presenting new challenges. They have turned to organising and defending the interests of the unorganised part-time, low paid and mainly female workers who have come into the workforce since the Second World War, but have not been integrated into the Labour movement. The TGWU's 'Link-up' campaign, the special recruitment drives of the GMB, and NUPE's determination to give its women members a real voice at every level of the union, all represent a modern strategy for trade unions that want to bring themselves into line with the changed composition of the workforce – now nearly 50 per cent female in which the unskilled and part-time workers form a growing proportion of the whole.

John Edmonds, general secretary of the GMB, has explicitly recognised this, noting in *New Socialist* that

> industrial, demographic and technological trends point to a shrinking of ... well-organised sectors and the growth of a new class of exploited workers ... New jobs are being created only in private services, and these jobs are primarily for part-time women workers ... Tied to these changes, full-time jobs will fall by over a million between 1984 and 1990, whereas part-time jobs are set to rise by 900,000; and male employment will drop by 600,000 (by 1990) as against a rise in female employment of 400,000 ... These are fundamental changes. Millions of exploited workers – overwhelmingly women working part-time in service industries or service occupations in other industries – are being removed from trade union protection.

Subsequent surveys have revised upwards the number of full-time jobs which women have taken, although not the balance between the rise in female employment and the decline in male employment. Bill Morris, deputy general secretary of the TGWU, at the TGWU Conference launching the union's 'Link-up' campaign to organise part-time workers directly counterposed organising these sectors like the business unionism of the EETPU:

> Business unionism is a short step down the path. The single union deals, the sweetheart approach, follow as night follows day, and you end up in a ghastly parody of the old craft unionism, crossing picket lines, selling out the jobs of thousands of your fellow trade unionists to boost your own membership.

The unions adapting themselves to the changing workforce have all found that the assertion of policies relating to the specific needs of women workers is inadequate on its own. The internal structures of the unions have to be changed to make them more representative of and responsive to women members. NUPE is in the vanguard with five reserved seats for women on its national executive, an established network of women's committees, a national women's officer, and so on. The TGWU was the first union to appoint a national women's officer, run a national women's conference, and set up regional and national women's advisory committees.

The Labour leadership, however, has lagged behind the trade unions in this respect and the Labour Party is lumbered with an internal structure for its women members unchanged since 1918. Given this situation, it was not surprising that it was constituency activists and the trade unions, especially NUPE, the TGWU and COHSE, which forced the issue of 'one woman on every parliamentary shortlist' on to an unwilling party leadership at the 1988 annual party conference. As Ron Todd pointed out at the same conference, unions like the TGWU are not the backward-looking dinosaurs claimed by the right, but are at the core of a strategy for modernising the Labour Party and the party itself will have to run to catch up.

While the party leadership has dragged its feet, the same has not been true of the rank and file of the party. The Labour Women's Action Committee (LWAC) has campaigned around a series of proposals for restructuring the party, winning majority approval in the party's women's organisation, with some unions giving support. The LWAC itself is a feminist organisation whose founding members were influenced by the ideas of the women's movement of the early 1970s, and who have built it into the most influential women's campaign in the party. It has taken up a large number of issues but has made one matter decisive – the organisations of the Labour movement must be changed to make them instruments of women's struggles. To put it another way, no one except women will achieve their own liberation and for that purpose the Labour movement has to be reorganised: 'The labour movement is a men's movement ... the movement as a whole [has] achieved their political and industrial power by means of "masculinist" political and industrial strategies: the strategies of division ... [they] are based on labour's willingness to conform to capital's demand for the endless subdivision of our class on the basis of gender, skill, race, pay and time spent in work,' so Ann Pettifor wrote in 'Why Women Demand Power' (1984). Ann Pettifor, one of LWAC's founding members, went on to say in the same article that even the left remains trapped in a vision of the working class as white and male, on to which it sees the need to add other, subordinate and 'different' interests, particularly those of women and black people.

In fighting for a political strategy which 'would not keep women and blacks at arm's length, but which would include them in the mainstream of our party', LWAC has campaigned around proposals aimed at strengthening Labour's official Women's Organisation and ensuring that it has more say in the party as a whole, while promoting more women at every level of the party. LWAC proposed the creation of a women's executive to be elected nationally, with reserved seats for the trade unions, socialist societies and CLP women's organisations; that the national conference of Labour women should become more representative of the unions; for the inclusion of at least one woman on every short list for parliamentary selection; for resolutions from women's conferences to be included on the agenda of party conference; and most crucially, for the election of the five seats reserved for women on the party's national executive by the national women's conference.

The reason for these demands is that the 1918 constitution of the Labour Party set up a chauvinistic and anomalous situation. The NEC was divided into various groups which were to be elected by their respective constituencies – the trade unions electing the reserved seats for the trade unions, the CLPs electing the reserved seats for the CLPs, and so on – with one major exception, that the five seats reserved for women should be elected not by the Labour Women's Organisation but by the entire party conference, a body composed almost exclusively of men.

Proposals to reform this anomaly are fiercely resisted by the party hierarchy who fear it might change the political balance on the NEC. Currently, the five women's seats are actually elected by the block vote of the trade unions, and alongside the twelve seats officially reserved for the unions, the five 'women's' seats are included in the inter-union horse-trading for representation on the party executive. If these seats were elected at the women's conference, it would take them out of the trading at annual conference and almost certainly change the nature of the NEC, for two reasons. First, the women's conference is itself the most radical section of the Labour Party. Secondly, the unions which will have most weight in the women's conference are those with the highest female membership – NUPE, USDAW, TGWU and GMB. These unions, while sharing political differences, are not in the grip of the extreme right of the party, and their increased weight via the women's conference, if the five women's seats were elected there, would rebound most heavily on the more extreme right-wing unions with a very low female membership.

The party leadership, by preferring an alliance with the 'hard right' and those unions opposed to the demands of women, links itself to the forces most hostile to modernising the party. In short, the leadership, gives more weight to its alliance with the right wing than to the real task of modernisation, achieved by giving women real power within the party.

It is true that after the débâcle of the 1987 election more far-sighted sections of the front bench have started to give more serious consideration to these problems. Both for electoral reasons and because of the increasing pressure from women organised inside the party and the trade unions, there is now some recognition that change is inevitable and necessary. However, their prime concern is to introduce sufficient change to eliminate the pressure without taking any steps which would unsettle the internal political *status quo*.

The German Social Democrats' recent adoption of an internal quota system for women has been one possibility floated as an alternative to strengthening the Labour Women's Organisation. In this framework the SPD proposals have a clear advantage for the right as they contain no element of the self-organisation of women or any element of women electing their own representatives on to the leading bodies of the party. LWAC points out that 'quotas ... will be necessary to redress decades of discrimination in the party'. But these 'must be tied to steps to strengthen the Labour Women's Organisation itself, in particular through giving it the right to directly elect the seats presently reserved for women on Labour's NEC'.

The Labour Women's Action Committee proposals for modernising the Labour Party are vital to a strategy for remodelling the party in line with the changes in the electorate, and creating a framework for the party to appeal to and win the support of women electorally. In forging the beginnings of a political alliance with women in the trade unions, LWAC also has begun to prefigure the type of political alliance that could take the whole party forward, as an alternative to the backward-looking, stultifying, and electorally disastrous alliance between the centre of the party and the hard right.

This alliance has been deeply damaging not just in preventing the party modernising itself internally, but has been an obstacle to the

Labour movement adopting and campaigning for some of the key policies that are crucial to women.

In terms of reforms that would make a difference to the majority of women's lives, the proposal to introduce a national minimum wage is head and shoulders above the rest in significance, although its real effect would depend upon the level it was fixed at. A national minimum wage that applied to both full-time and part-time workers, even at the derisory level of £80, would make a material difference to women's lives. With a minimum wage of £123, 50 per cent of all women workers would benefit, that is, 4 ¾ million women.

The proposal for a national minimum wage was raised first in the Labour movement by NUPE, GMB and other unions representing the low paid, but it met violent opposition from right-wing unions containing skilled, highly paid, and almost totally white male workers such as the EETPU and AEU.

Following the adoption of the minimum wage, the same right-wing unions conducted a rearguard action to have it dropped from the 1987 election manifesto. It was only the fact that unions like NUPE and GMBATU – which championed the policy – were putting up a large part of the money for the Labour election campaign that saved it. However, it was ignored by the leadership and given no prominence in the 1987 election campaign, nor since, and most low-paid women workers were quite unaware that the policy even existed in Labour's manifesto.

The same problem occurred again with the important proposal in the 1987 manifesto for a free nursery place for every child aged between 3 and 5. The provision of pre-school education is obviously crucial to every woman with young children, whether working or not, but once again this popular policy disappeared without trace during the election campaign.

Labour also undermined its own proposal to create a Ministry for Women. The party's own polls showed that the idea was welcomed by over 60 per cent of women – and therefore an effective proposal in the battle to win votes from women. But the same poll revealed that over 90 per cent of women thought it was the Alliance and not Labour that proposed to bring in the ministry.

This time it was Neil Kinnock himself who led the rearguard battle to get the proposal downgraded, by insisting that the ministry should not have Cabinet status. Kinnock was defeated at Labour's annual conference on the issue but the price was that the Ministry for

Women has not been placed high on Labour's own agenda. The explanation for this attack was hard to fathom, beyond sheer male chauvinism.

This same contradiction runs through every decision the party has made on women. As with the minimum wage and the Ministry for Women, so with abortion rights and nursery provision – it has adopted progressive policies then failed to promote them adequately.

It seems that although the progressive trade union leaders have realised the importance of reforming their unions in order to reflect the changing composition of the workforce, the Labour Party's leaders still want to cling to the old male-dominated world rather than usher in a new and better one of sexual equality. Perhaps for fear of losing their own positions or having to change their aggressive style of working, they take every opportunity to block the reforms demanded by women in the party. They are then genuinely shocked to discover from their own polls that women voters remain convinced that the Labour Party is still an exclusively male domain.

Maybe we need to reassure these fragile egos that the pursuit of women's rights is not about doing men down, on the contrary, it is about liberating both sexes from the destructive stereotyping of the last 4,000 years so that together they can achieve their full potential and full happiness.

Women do not want to lose their inherent strengths in order to become as men. They do not wish, in the words of Andrea Dworkin, 'to betray our heroic commitment to the worth of human life so that we find ourselves, hands dripping with blood, equal heroes to men at last'.

As the relations between the sexes change, it offers men as a whole the chance to break free from the deadening role into which the accident of economic forces cast them. It offers men as a whole the chance to rediscover their feelings and not to be afraid to display them. It offers men as a whole the chance to discover the real ecstasy of sharing their sexuality rather than using it to dominate.

The Labour Party could propose the most pro-women policies it is possible to devise:

- a universal scheme of pre-school childcare for all parents who would wish to use it
- equal pay for work of equal value
- a properly funded national network of women's centres

- a properly funded national scheme for the remuneration of carers
- full equality before the law

and many more, but unless it is also committed to changing the nature of men then women will still live in fear of rape, battering and the abuse of themselves and their children.

We have to find and change what it is in the moulding of men by masculine culture that creates the father who can sodomise his infant child or the rapist who can take pleasure in terrorising an entire city for months on end. In that quest the first shocking discovery we will make is that every recent authoritative study of the psychology of the rapist shows that there is no measurable difference between the rapist and men in general. No distinguishing mental scar, no particularly unusual childhood trauma separates the rapist from other men. Nor would such news come as a surprise to the vast number of women who have been raped by their husbands or lovers, or violently assaulted by them.

The rapist in our culture is a typical man and in raping he practises the essence of masculinity – dominance, violence and the use of others for his own imagined needs.

Labour must come to terms with the unpleasant reality that it is riddled with the culture of masculinity from top to bottom. I hope that those in the leadership of our party will recognise themselves and their arguments in the previous examples of women's oppression that I have quoted earlier in this chapter. But it is not just a problem for the leadership of the party. Every sexist joke in a working men's club or act of sexual harassment on the election campaign reinforces that masculine culture and we do not have to wait for the election of a Labour government before we begin to change it. We can begin today to draw 4,000 years of women's oppression finally to an end. We can do it by stripping away the bravado of our masculinity to reveal the weak and vulnerable individuals that we truly are. We can do it when we recognise that strength comes not from aggression but from the realisation that men and women must stand together as human beings of equal worth before we can achieve the real potential of our species. We will do it when we change the thousand different ways we reach out to touch one another. Then at last there will be no more sons of the footbinder.

5

Labour Didn't Listen to Black People

Unlike the previous chapter on changes in the position of women, it is not necessary here to trace the history of the oppression of black people or write at the same length as to why this is a bad thing. In contrast to society's attitudes towards sexism, lip service is at least paid to the proposition that racism is an evil and no one seriously denies the scale of death and discrimination visited on black people in recent history.

Unfortunately, though, the attitude of the Labour leadership to those campaigning for the rights of black people is no better than their disposition towards those fighting for the recognition of women's rights. Over the last four years the leadership has waged an unrelenting, wasteful and thoroughly divisive war against the campaign of the Black Sections, who are demanding recognition for self-organisation by black members of the party.

The black population of Britain suffers more discrimination than any other section of the community. Racism itself is the uniquely destructive form of reaction that characterises the twentieth century – the holocaust is an indelible reminder of that – and any party which panders to it in any form, whether it be anti-semitism, anti-black, or anti-Irish is doomed. For that reason, even if not one single black person in Britain voted Labour, the fight against racism must be right at the top of the party's agenda. But because they are the most oppressed section of the population, more than 80 per cent of black people who go to the polls vote Labour. So in addition to its general fight against racism Labour also has the task of expressing the needs and demands of its black voters and members.

In fact the two issues are complementary. No white person can know the full meaning of racism – only the black community does. A leadership totally committed to the fight against colour prejudice would see the tremendous asset in the party's black members meeting together. After all, they form the community which experiences racism and can best reflect and develop policy to deal with it. This is vital because every white person, no matter how involved in fighting racism – and the vast majority of Labour Party members are totally dedicated to this – is indoctrinated by its ideology from birth and lives in a society in which every institution is racist in its structure. In this precise sense all white people are racist – but can be divided into those who consciously maintain it, those who fight to change it, and those not yet aware of the problem.

It was for stating this obvious truth that the black Labour candidate, Sharon Atkin, was stripped of her candidacy and subjected to an eighteen-month-long witch-hunt. This was eventually halted when the Labour leadership was forced to accept that its behaviour had been contrary to the rules of natural justice. Sadly, like so many of the internal rows that grip the party, the leadership was not motivated by malice, as sometimes seemed to be the case, but by a complete failure to comprehend the real issues involved.

Therefore, black self-organisation in the party is not a threat but a tremendous asset. If we couple the will of party members to fight racism with the knowledge that only black members can fully understand what racism is, we would create the most effective mechanism possible for combating this prejudice. The Labour leadership should therefore be helping to establish Black Sections by allocating money, appointing full-time organisers, and ensuring a wide distribution of their views. But instead of *promoting* black self-organisation the Labour leadership has waged a continuous and deeply damaging civil war against it. It is vital that the party changes this attitude and starts to consider the real needs of its black members and the fight against racism. The way to do this is to look first at the position in the trade unions.

Every study has found that black workers in Britain are more highly unionised than their white counterparts. In 1984, the Policy Studies Institute (PSI) reported that 56 per cent of black workers were in unions compared to 47 per cent of white workers. But despite the fact that blacks show a higher degree of support for unions than whites, coupled with the urgent need to combat racial discrimination in the whole of society, for a long time the trade unions failed to take up the fight against it – a fact the TUC later admitted and began to deal with. Indeed, it could even be said that trade unions collaborated with racism. In 1965, for example, a TUC official could still declare: 'There are no differences between an immigrant worker and an English worker. We believe that all workers should have the same rights and don't require any different or special considerations.'

In 1971, the TUC in its evidence to the Home Affairs Select Committee claimed: 'we treat all our members the same'. Not only was this no way to fight racism but it was demonstrably untrue. In both 1965 and 1971, regardless of the TUC's claim to 'treat all our members the same', there was not a single black, full-time trade union official in Britain. TUC affiliates had in the past supported explicitly racist laws, such as the National Union of Seamen's support for the Special Restrictions (Coloured Allied Seamen) Order of 1925. The TUC as a whole had campaigned in favour of the racist immigration laws and had opposed attempts to introduce anti-racist measures into the field of employment and industry. The TUC hotels committee had instigated a central campaign to exclude immigrant workers.

In 1972, the first ever full-time black trade union official in Britain was at last appointed. But by 1983 only eight unions affiliated to the TUC, out of more than a hundred, had even one full-time black official. The same situation, whether consciously, or unconsciously maintained, existed at every level. The 1984 PSI study, *Black and White Britain*, found that black and white workers attended trade union meetings in almost the same proportions – 40 per cent of black and white union members had attended some form of union meeting in the previous six months. However, only 4 per cent of black male trade unionists had held office compared with 11 per cent of white male trade union members, with comparable ratios for women of 3 and 6 per cent respectively. A detailed study in Lancashire, in 1985, entitled *Trade Union Structures and Black Workers Participation*, found that there was not a single black full-time trade union official in the whole of Lancashire despite the fact that 8 per cent of the population of Manchester and 12 per cent of the population of Blackburn is black.

A study of companies found the same pattern of racism. A survey of rubber manufacturing plants found that 27 per cent of the 250 workers were black, but not one out of the eight shop stewards was black. A survey of the foundry section of a heavy vehicle manufacturer reported that 19 per cent of the workers were black, but only one out of nine shop stewards was black – and that one was for a section which was almost exclusively black but where the one skilled job was held by a white worker. The only place of work surveyed where there was a major representation of black workers – a transport firm – was significant in that black self-organisation had developed in response to racist attacks. In this case, 30 per cent of the workers in the company were black but their nominees for election to the TGWU branch committee had been consistently voted down by white workers. Black self-organisation in the form of an Employees Welfare Association had been formed when the branch secretary refused to read out the names of Asian workers who were to be presented with safety awards at a social evening, on the pretext that he 'could not pronounce their names'. A united welfare committee was formed only after the white workers' representatives agreed to the demand that a written apology for the actions of a branch secretary should be posted on the notice board and that he should resign his post. The secretary of the black workers committee was first coopted on to the branch committee and then elected – to become the first black branch committee member – at the next election. By 1984, six out of ten branch committee members were black and three out of ten inspectors were black workers.

Given the pattern of racism, fights by black workers often involved a clash not only with the employers but frequently with the situation in the unions. This helped to produce a change of policy by the TUC after a series of disputes involving black workers.

The earliest of these, the first prominent strike specifically by black workers, was at Courtauld's in Preston, in 1965. Despite a large black workforce only one shop steward at the plant was black, and there was no formal relationship at all between the black membership and the union committee. The pattern at Courtauld's was repeated in the strikes by black workers at Mansfield Hosiery Mills and Imperial Typewriters in Leicester. In both strikes, white fascist and racist groups organised white scabbing committees. In addition, the official enquiry into the Mansfield Hosiery strike and the National Union of Hosiery and Knitwear Workers (NUHKW) which represented the workers there, stated that continued exclusion of black workers from all positions in the unions 'could result in the alienation of immigrant members to such an extent that they might feel the need to enlist the support of alternative organisations or to break away completely and form a union exclusively for immigrant workers'.

The situation revealed at Mansfield Hosiery Mills and Imperial Typewriters forced a change in emphasis by the TUC, whereby it began to take seriously the needs of black workers and the fight against racism. By the mid-1970s the TUC had established an Equal Rights Committee with a subsidiary Race Relations Committee. However, a comprehensive resolution on racism was still not taken at a TUC Congress. The first substantial new move came in June 1981 when the TUC issued its Black Workers' Charter. This was given urgency by the inner city rebellions which had taken place three months earlier. The charter declared in its opening sentences: 'Trade unions cannot just talk about equal opportunity they must be seen to be taking active steps to make it a reality. As a first step they should examine their own procedures and structures.'

Ken Gill, then general secretary of TASS, moving the adoption of the Black Workers' Charter at the 1981 Congress, declared that it

> demands the removal of direct and indirect discrimination at the workplace; more it demands that trade unions themselves look at their own structures and organisation, and break down the barriers within the unions, to advance to decision-making bodies, to executives and to officialdom. If in your industry or your occupation there are no blacks, why? If there are no black lay or full-time officers in your organisations, why? If there are no black activists, why? All those questions have to be asked within our movement.

However, the Black Workers' Charter did not even mention black self-organisation. So as it did not promote the organisation of those who had the most direct interest in fighting racism, the TUC's adoption of the Black Workers' Charter did not bring the hoped for results. A follow-up by the TUC a year later found that only twelve unions out of more than 100 had taken 'some action with regard to race relations matters', while the greater majority of affiliated unions had taken no action at all, 'even of a limited type e.g. articles in the union journals'.

A survey carried out by the Labour Research Department in 1983, two years after the Black Workers' Charter had been adopted, discovered that only nine unions out of more than a hundred had issued positive statements against racism and had set up bodies to monitor these policies. Only one union, the GMB, had held national meetings and conferences. Even by 1983 only eight unions had a single black full-time official.

In 1984, the most thorough recent study of the position of black workers in the trade unions was carried out by the GLC Anti-Racist

Trade Union Working Group. The GLC study was comprehensive – gaining official responses from unions representing 6 million workers out of 10 million trade union members in the TUC. Significantly, the two biggest unions which refused to cooperate in the study were the two right-wing ones – the EETPU and AEU. The EETPU refused outright to give any answers on its policies on racism and the AEU stated it would reply through an interview but 'despite numerous efforts the appropriate officer could not be contacted'.

If the EETPU and AEU were the worst, the situation was far from satisfactory with other unions. The UCW declared in its reply that: 'We have no anti-racist policy.' The UCW official interviewed declared that there were many 'coloureds' who were members of the union, and that the entire situation confirmed his view that there was no problem of racism in the UCW.

An NUR official declared:

> Most of the questions in the questionnaire appear to me to be irrelevant to the situation in this union as all of our members have equal opportunity and there is no discrimination against any member for any reason whatever ... No particular encouragement is given to members of black and other minority groups to participate actively in the union's activities or to play a leading role in the union.

The union said, however, it had 'issued propaganda inviting foreign nationals employed in the catering departments to join the NUR' a few years ago, but had done nothing since.

The CPSA reported that 'racism within the union has never been a problem'. The NGA stated: 'The need for special measures [to fight racism], i.e. seminars, etc., has not arisen and no request has been received ... We do not allow special treatment to any group.' UCATT declared: 'There have been no provisions by this union for the form of anti-racist activity referred to in the questionnaire.' The Bakers' Union, when asked to state what provisions it had taken to combat racism, replied 'None.' The TGWU said: 'All members are equal, therefore no problems. To have it [black representation] separate means that we are fighting the race issue rather than the class issues.' When asked what special provisions it was taking to combat racism, for example in shop stewards training, the TGWU declared that the responsibility for organising such courses should lie with the TUC and not the TGWU.

A number of unions however, had, taken measures to tackle racism. NUPE established a national Race Equality Advisory Committee and had had a Race Relations Advisory Committee in the London division for five years. On the needs of black women, NUPE stated: 'In addition to our Race Working Party we have an extremely active Equality Council dealing with issues affecting women particularly.' It said it had no special provisions for black women, 'but we do have a Women's Advisory [Committee] nationally and in the London division. Most members of the Race Relations Advisory [Committee] in London are ethnic minority women.'

The GMB had held a regional conference, issued publications, negotiators' handbooks, and had an officer designated 'to include Race Relations matters amongst his other duties'. The ACTT ran schools or seminars on racism. It had established a black subcommittee of its Committee on Equality. The four-day shop steward training courses run by the ACTT had a half day devoted to equal opportunities.

TASS stated that it 'operates a Positive Action Programme for appointing officials with ethnic backgrounds, or females, to the union. Divisions regularly give advice on positive action programmes.' ASTMS had established a Race Relations Subcommittee in 1978 which had organised several conferences. It had an active race relations subcommittee in the London division. The ASTMS NEC had also agreed the setting up of a Race Relations National Advisory Council which held its first meeting in January 1984. Its members, though, were mainly white and two years later the union still did not know the ethnic composition of its own employees.

The NUJ had established a Race Relations Working Party – although it still operated internal institutionalised racism. It claimed that 20 per cent of its employees were black but on investigation all these were found to be in low-level clerical jobs with little chance of promotion, and not a single one was a full-time official. At its 1986 conference, the union nevertheless took a significant step forward when it unanimously voted that: 'Chapels.should be encouraged to give support to black members organising caucuses in line with TUC policy.' It also elected a black president, Lionel Morrison, the following year.

NALGO is the union with the most experience of self-organisation by black members. The first meeting of black NALGO members took place in 1982. The executive attempted to head off black self-organisation by establishing a white-dominated Race Equality Working Party. A conference organised by this was picketed by black members and never got started. Two months later black NALGO members held their own conference attended by over a hundred delegates and branch observers. Meanwhile, support for the black members' motions was built up at the 1983 and 1984 NALGO conferences. At the 1985 conference, a resolution was passed instructing the union NEC to set up an equal opportunities committee and the NEC agreed to facilitate the meetings of the national black steering group. It was this pressure by black NALGO members that led the union to propose a successful resolution at the 1984 TUC Congress encouraging unions to set up appropriate structures, e.g. Race Equality Committees and Black Members Groups to coordinate unions' work on racism. This was the first time the TUC had taken a step towards black self-organisation.

Meanwhile, the overall situation in the unions remained unsatisfactory. The 1984 GLC survey found that 'we have yet to discover a union that has in its organisational structure black and minority group officers/executives, male and female, that is anywhere near their proportion as members of the union'. It also stated that 'no union had an officer designated to work entirely with ... the union's black and minority members, or to deal with issues affecting the union's position on racism more generally ... such as exists in a number of local authorities'.

The situation revealed by this GLC study was therefore very inadequate. Nine unions – ACTT, ASTMS, GMBATU, NALGO, NATFHE, NUJ, NUPE, NUT and TASS – with a membership of 3.3 million had taken some measures to fight racism internally and externally. Ten unions – the Bakers' Union, CPSA, Musicians' Union, NGA, NUR, NUTGW, TGWU, UCW, USDAW, and UCATT – stated explicitly that their policies were to fight racism but had taken no major organisational or political steps to combat it within their ranks. These unions had a membership of 2.4 million. Thirty-three unions – including such major ones as APEX, BIFU, Equity, IPCS, ISTC, NAS/UWT, SCPS, TSSA – did not state what policy they had, if any, on fighting racism. Between them these unions have a combined membership of 3.4 million. Only one-third of TUC unions had taken any steps to implement anti-racist measures, 25 per cent were prepared to state that they had taken no serious anti-racist steps, and 40 per cent couldn't even be bothered to state what their policy on racism was. This was despite the fact that three years previously the TUC had adopted the Black Workers' Charter.

Speaking to the TUC conference on 'Trade Unions and Black Workers', on 6 July 1985, Norman Willis stated:

The conference document – like the 1984 Congress resolution – raises a further key issue: that of black members' groups. Some unions already have groups of black members who meet to discuss their special problems ... It will happen in other unions soon. We need to consider very carefully our attitude to such groups ... handled wrongly, they could be the germ of breakaway black trade unions. Handled right, they can contribute to the effectiveness of the union ... at present we are not recommending unions to establish such groups. But equally we are not asking unions to see unofficial black members as an automatic threat to the union's constitution. If black members feel that unions do not care about their problems, they will turn to other organisations.

As with the Mansfield Hosiery Mills and Imperial Typewriter disputes in the early 1970s, as with the inner city rebellions of 1981 and 1985, the TUC had still not grasped the central role of black self-organisation. Fighting to support this issue in the unions – without which all experience shows no successful struggle against racism can be conducted – must be right at the top of today's list of priorities for socialists in the trade unions. Together, with the establishment of Black Sections in the Labour Party, they will shake the Labour movement to its foundations – and smash the virus of racism which gnaws at its heart.

There have been advances in the struggle. The election of Lionel Morrison as president of the NUJ, the selection of deputy general secretary Bill Morris in the TGWU, and the four black Labour MPs are all real gains for black people – and because of that for the entire working class. But the conflict is not about a few individuals, it seeks the liberation of the entire black community and the complete destruction of every aspect of racism. No possibility of success in that struggle exists without black self-organisation throughout the Labour movement. Acceptance of that right is the basis on which Labour can cooperate with black people. That is why a programmatic approach is necessary and socialists should welcome the publication by the Black Section of the 'Black Agenda'.

Unfortunately, within the Labour Party itself, matters have lagged behind the trade unions. The history of black political self-organisation in Britain has for a long time taken place outside the Labour movement because of errors made by the Labour Party.

The first large black communities to settle here this century were mainly composed of seafarers in Liverpool, London, Manchester, North

Shields and Cardiff. Economic decline and unemployment followed the First World War and ushered in a protracted period in which riots and street violence broke out notably in Liverpool (leading to the death of a black man, Charles Wooton, in 1919) and Manchester. The black population was forced to form 'self-help' communities which were not accepted within the structure of the Labour movement. The same situation followed the next wave of immigration after the Second World War – created by the labour shortage and the destruction of the colonial 'one crop' economies. There was a re-emergence of racism in the 1950s and 1960s, with riots in Nottingham and Notting Hill in 1958. In these conflicts the Labour Party failed to give the necessary support and black people fought rearguard actions in defence of their communities. As a result the direction taken by black political organisations reflected this for a long period. The founding of the Campaign Against Racial Discrimination, the Universal Coloured People's Association, the Indian Workers' Association and West Indian Standing Conference started a continuous line of development which was outside the Labour movement. The black community voted overwhelmingly for Labour and there were individual black members in the Labour Party – but, apart from the now defunct Standing Conference of Afro-Caribbean and Asian Councillors, there was no real organisation of black members within the party itself.

The first serious step to overcoming this occurred when black Labour Party members convened following the 1981 inner city rebellions. Out of this emerged the demand for Black Sections, on the same basis as the party's women's and youth sections. The Black Sections campaign first came on to the floor of the party conference in a big way in 1984 and won the support of a majority of CLP votes and the NUM – at that time embroiled in the miners' strike.

Earlier, at the 1983 party conference, a resolution calling for positive action for black members had been referred to the executive. This led to the establishment of an NEC Positive Discrimination Working Group which carried out one of the widest consultations ever to have taken place in the Labour Party, producing a consultative paper entitled *The Labour Party and the Black Electorate*. A majority of respondents, including constituency Labour parties and trade unions, favoured fully recognised Black Sections. The working party itself reported in favour of their establishment. The NEC went on, however, to reject even the dissenting minority report calling for the establishment of a 'black rights committee'. Instead Labour office staff dreamed up the idea of an unelected Black and Asian Advisory Committee (BAAC) as an alternative to Black Sections.

This overturning of a working party recommendation happened because of an unprecedented intervention by the leader of the party. Attacks on the working group reached such a pitch at one point that its chair, NEC member Jo Richardson MP, personally requested Neil Kinnock to refrain from obstructing the group's enquiry. Nevertheless, the Labour leader said, on 23 May 1985: 'I am adamantly against Black Sections ... I would not give a damn if the whole Labour Party was against me on this.' Indeed two-thirds of those consulted *were* against Neil Kinnock's position. Yet two months later the NEC rejected its working group's report. The terms of reference of the BAAC specifically excluded policy formulation; it was to have a purely advisory role on 'organisational' matters. Labour Party general secretary Larry Whitty said in the March issue of *New Socialist*: 'If I were a black member of the party I would be very upset that a party which can accommodate all sorts of specialised interests in its constitution has nothing for Blacks.'

The establishment of the BAAC was followed by a call for its boycott by the Labour Party Black Section and supported by the left. This was extremely successful. The committee had no real impact and collapsed. Yet repression against black party members continued. In 1986, Amir Khan, a Birmingham Councillor and Black Sections' supporter, was expelled from Roy Hattersley's Sparkbrook constituency – a decision which was later overturned following a major campaign in the party, supported not only by the CLPs but also by NUPE and the TGWU. Then, immediately prior to the 1987 election, former Black Section chair Sharon Atkin was removed as parliamentary candidate for Nottingham East. This action almost certainly cost Labour that seat and fuelled a racist backlash which hurt Labour in the East and West Midlands at both the 1987 local and general elections.

The Labour Party Black Section itself has gained increasing support and made itself not only an organisation of the black community in its own right, but has become an integral part of the left. Its 1984 conference in Birmingham showed a major step forward with 200 black party members attending. In contrast the BAAC has continued to be boycotted by all leading black people including Bill Morris and black MPs. Its divisive separation of 'black' and 'Asian' members has proved disastrous. The Black Section, on the other hand, has united Africans, Caribbeans and Asians in constituency Black Sections, and its continuing strength has forced the Labour leadership finally to begin negotiations to try to find a compromise following the 1988 party conference. Whether this was a serious move or just a gesture is not clear following the disgraceful decision of the leadership to ban the Vauxhall Labour Party from selecting and electing a second black woman to Parliament.

However, some of the arguments deployed against Black Sections are astonishing and very revealing. Neil Kinnock has proclaimed his adherence to 'democratic socialism' and pluralism. Yet his failure on this issue to grasp serious democratic questions is shown by his hostility to women's and blacks' self-organisation within the Labour Party. No one would dream of proposing that non-miners should vote in the NUM, or non-engineers should vote in the AEU. The party is at long last recognising that only women should vote in the women's organisation – the 1988 conference reaffirmed explicitly that only women could be delegates to the women's conference. But Neil Kinnock argues that whites should be able to participate in and decide the leadership of black organisation within the Labour Party.

He seems to feel that such sections might segregate black people from the rest of the party and undermine the unity of black and white workers, already active at grass roots level. The fact is that very few black people are active at any level in the Labour Party, despite the fact that a growing number of black people are joining. As an oppressed minority they need to coalesce to ensure that their demands are taken up in a serious way by the mainstream of the party.

The most worrying aspect of Neil Kinnock's argument is the claim that black and white unity already exists in the party. This is patently not the case. At the party conference black faces are few and far between, and black candidates are seldom put forward at any level of the party. Not a single black person sits on the NEC yet at least the TUC General Council can boast one representative. Outside the Labour Party, black people have to confront deeply ingrained racism within the working class itself, and this is reflected inside the structure of the Labour movement.

A Black Section is precisely the instrument to overcome the existing disunity but by talking as though black and white unity already exists, the leader covers up the real problems confronting black people and tries to divert attention from the fight that will have to be waged within the Labour movement to create a basis for real unity.

Finally, Neil Kinnock argues that a Black Section would take black people out of the mainstream of the party. The problem is that they are not there now. As Diane Abbott said at the 1984 Labour Party Women's Conference: 'It is hypocritical for people to go on about the black section creating separatism, when they haven't complained about the white separatism that exists in the party today.'

Given the current process of realignment in British politics the Black Section can begin to act as a bridge between the black community and the Labour Party. It can begin to pose the real issues of class unity in a more profound way than at any time since the abolition of slavery. But class unity can only be built on the basis of complete and absolute equality at all levels of the movement.

The argument that all Black Sections are only concerned with lobbying for more MPs or councillors misrepresents their stated aims, and totally misunderstands the nature of British politics today. Black Sections are the first step in the fight against the racist division of the working class. They are therefore an advance towards the kind of unity the working class, in its widest sense, needs to forge to take on Mrs Thatcher's offensive against our civil rights and standard of living. But until Labour is truly prepared to listen to what its black members are saying, we will fail to modernise our party let alone create the unity which can defeat the Tories.

6

A Nation Once Again

In the aftermath of the Enniskillen massacre the Labour leadership decided it was about time that the Parliamentary Labour Party discussed the issue of Ireland, and they called a special meeting in order to do so. The fact that the meeting was being held was welcomed by all who took part in the debate – indeed no one present could remember the last time the PLP had had a full meeting on the issue of Ireland, and given that some of the members had been MPs for thirty-six years that fact in itself was shocking.

Even more disturbing was the comment from one of the younger members to the effect that 'British troops would have to stay in Ireland until they had finished the job that they were sent in to do – destroy the IRA'! Yet, as I pointed out in my contribution to the debate, the IRA was virtually defunct when British troops were sent into Northern Ireland in 1969 and the first IRA killing of a British soldier did not take place until nearly eighteen months later, in February 1971. The truth is that the troops were sent in the aftermath of a riot by the RUC, the local police force, who went on a rampage of burning and shooting in the main Catholic areas of Derry and West Belfast. The rule of law had literally collapsed.

It is not surprising that the young MP in question could make such a mistake for he had still been at school when these events took place, and like the majority of the population had based his views on the stream of anti-nationalist propaganda that has spewed out of the Tory press for the last twenty years. For all that time, the disinformation and propaganda units in the army and the intelligence services have ensured that the government's view of events has prevailed.

Members of the IRA have been dismissed in Britain as 'godfathers of crime' or 'psychopaths who enjoy the slaughter', whilst audiences in the USA are warned that the IRA is really a dedicated Marxist guerrilla group similar to the Nicaraguans or the Cubans. Anyone who has dared to question this simplistic view has come under the most vicious and damaging attack from the full weight of the establishment.

However, there has always been another side and it was to hear yet another part of that 'other side' that in July 1988 I travelled to Frankland maximum security prison in Durham to interview Albert Baker, a prisoner, who had asked to see me. As a former assassination squad leader for the 'loyalist' paramilitary group, the Ulster Defence Association, he had been a key figure in the violence in Ireland during the early 1970s and was still the centre of widespread rumours that he knew much more than he had revealed at his trial.

The government was sufficiently concerned about what I might be told by Baker to make matters as difficult as possible for me. They refused to give permission for Neil Grant, my researcher (who had spent months investigating the whole issue of the illegal activities of the security services), to accompany me. The decision was taken personally at political level by Douglas Hogg, a junior minister at the Home Office. Hogg himself later came to public attention after his attack on the motives and loyalties of solicitors acting for the families of republicans triggered the assassination of Mr Finicone, the prominent Irish solicitor.

Although he could not accompany me to Durham, I spent most of the long train journey reading the comprehensive file that Neil Grant had assembled on the activities and history of Albert Baker. The story it told was chilling.

In June 1972, at the age of 22, Albert Baker deserted from the Royal Irish Rangers at Warminster and returned to Belfast where he rejoined the UDA, having previously been a member before serving in the Rangers. Within a year he was in prison, having confessed to the murder of four men, for each of which he received a life sentence with the recommendation that he serve at least twenty-five years. In three of the killings Baker shot his victims in the back of the head because the UDA had told him that even if they survived they would be brain damaged and unable to identify him. The murdered men were:

(a)   Philip Anthony Faye, a barman. Baker went to Faye's door, asked him if he was a Roman Catholic and on hearing that he was told him to turn round. He then shot Faye twice in the back of the head. As he lay dying on the ground, Baker fired three more rounds from his .32 Browning automatic into the area below his ear.
(b)   Paul McCartan, a 52-year-old man who was picked up by a UDA patrol in East Belfast. He was taken to a UDA club and tortured before being hooded and shot dead by Baker in Mersey Street.
(c)   James Patrick McCartan (not related to Paul), aged 22. He was dragged from a disco at the Park Avenue Hotel on 4 October 1972 and taken to the 'Romper room' (a torture chamber named after a popular children's TV programme) in the back of a UDA club in Clermont Lane. Later that evening he was beaten with a pickshaft, stabbed in the hands and thigh, threatened with castration and dropped head first from the ceiling in order to force him to reveal the names of any active republicans he knew. He was later taken to the Conns Water river where Baker shot him dead.
(d)   Eugene Heenan, who died when Baker bombed a bus taking Catholic men to work. Whilst one man in the team hobbled on crutches in front of the bus Baker lobbed a grenade through a window.

Baker implicated other members of the assassination team involved in the murders described above, and was believed to have given the police information on at least a dozen other murders, but the men he accused were all acquitted in the first Diplock (no jury) court ever to be held. The presiding judge, Lord Lowry, described Baker's evidence as 'manifestly unreliable' but added, 'It may be that he is telling almost the entire truth.' Certainly the information that Baker gave to the security forces after he gave himself up was reliable enough to produce immediate results, including the arrest of one senior UDA leader and a dramatic rise in the number of loyalists accused of serious crimes over the following months.

Whilst in prison Baker had continued to attract publicity with his claim that he had been coached by the police in how to give evidence, much of it false, against his UDA colleagues, whilst withholding anything that would implicate the RUC. He also claimed to have been visited in Crumlin Road gaol by the then junior minister for Northern Ireland, William van Straubenzee, to discuss arrangements for housing him and his family after early release and was promised that he would never be in gaol with other terrorists. When asked by the journalist Paul Foot to confirm or deny the details of the visit, Mr van Straubenzee unconvincingly suggested that it was too long ago for him to remember.

Frankland prison is not unfriendly although it is organised, disciplined and clean almost to the point of being antiseptic – not unlike Albert Baker himself. In contrast to the government's obstruction the prison staff were helpful, allowing me to speak to Baker informally in a recreation room and use a tape recorder. Two officers were present, at a discreet distance, throughout the interview, but given Baker's previous spectacular and nearly successful escape attempt from Parkhurst, when he took a prison officer hostage and almost reached a waiting helicopter, neither he nor I could complain about that.

If only a quarter of what Baker told me is true it would be enough to demolish both the government's policy and its record in Ireland. This is why Mrs Thatcher herself blocks any attempt to have an independent enquiry into the 'dirty war' and the widespread rumours of illegal 'dirty tricks'. Unfortunately, many who could corroborate what Baker has to say are either dead, in prison or have been discredited by the authorities with the use of trumped up murder charges or false accusations of mental instability.

What follows is an edited transcript of my hour long conversation with Baker in which I have removed the names of individuals concerned, both because of the libel laws and also because to name them would automatically run the risk of exposing them to reprisal killings.

A.B.   I have never mentioned it to anyone before but as far as I and other members of the UDA were concerned, we were operating for the UDA, but we had close links with the British Intelligence Services.

K.L.   Do you remember any names?

A.B.   'M' was an operator. He was working for the British Intelligence Services.

K.L.   What makes you so certain of that?

A.B.   It was Tommy Herron [the vice-chairman of the UDA, and controller in Belfast, who has since been assassinated], he told me and a couple of others to contact the British Intelligence controller who was a man named 'B'. We only knew his name as 'B', but the other one was 'M'.

K.L.   Did you ever meet them?

A.B.   I met 'M' and we used to go to the centre of Belfast, then York Street, to a telephone kiosk and he phoned 'B', the controller. Other officers in the inner circle of the UDA contacted 'B'. The arms we were getting to do the assassinations were coming from the Royal Ulster Constabulary.

K.L.   Who was involved in that?

A.B.   Well, William Whitelaw set up a group of twenty-one top detectives – called the 'Inner Circle Murder Squad' – and our contact, 'C', a CID man, was one of these twenty-one top detectives assembled to combat the Loyalist assassination squads in Belfast. But 'C' was the man who was passing all the information to the UDA. He was our deep penetration officer, the UDA officer who was also a member of the CID. One other policeman who was handing over the weapons was Inspector 'F'. He handed over Sterling submachine guns, pistols, revolvers, ammunition and magazines.

We were led to believe that those officers handing over the weapons were getting their orders from higher authority. But the public did not know that weapons were going missing from police stations. Ammunition and weapons were coming to UDA headquarters or down to Diamond Street to 'N's house and we were using them for assassinations. 'D' lived in Atholl Street and when they raided his house and got a .45 revolver it was never brought out in court that that weapon was a police weapon. He got twelve months for having an illegal weapon in his house but it was never exposed that the weapon belonged to the RUC.

K.L.   When were you first aware that there was more than just the UDA acting with elements in the security forces?

A.B.   When I met 'M'.

K.L.   Presumably there had been gossip in the UDA?

A.B.   Well, you see I was in the bodyguard for the Inner Council of the UDA. I knew Tommy Herron, Andy Tyrie, Ned McCreary, the whole lot of them. I used to go to the hotel where young Faye was assassinated. He was working in the hotel just under the Holywood Arches on the Upper Newtownards Road where the UDA held their meetings. I was told to assassinate Faye because he was a Catholic and was picking up information.

K.L.   Tell me about the incident at the Red Lion.

A.B.　Well, 'C' was involved in that. The UDA went over to do an assassination at the Red Lion, beside the Albert Clock, but a police Land Rover came round the corner so the guns were taken and put in 'C's car and he drove them through the police and army checkpoints back to East Belfast where he handed them back to us. The assassination was carried out later using police guns and Sterling submachine guns.

K.L.　Going back to the Faye killing. Was that carried out because he recognised Unionist politicians at the UDA meeting?

A.B.　There was me, 'D', 'R', and a few others doing security in the hotel. We'd move into the hotel and take the waiters' coats and things. We'd be armed and we'd be walking through the hotel and down the lobbies and the corridors underneath. So the Inner Council was in this room and Faye came in with drinks. Tommy Herron found out the geezer was a Catholic and ordered his assassination in case he'd overheard anything. I went down to Island Street and assassinated him.

K.L.　Were any politicians present?

A.B.　No, it was only Inner Council present. The politicians keep in the shadows. In other words, they don't appear in places where the Inner Council would normally appear. The Inner Council would hire a pub – the Bunch of Grapes on the Woodstock Road – and the politicians would go up there to the top room for their talks, but they wouldn't go into the UDA HQ or any other place that was under surveillance by the police. I've had instances where I've had Unionist politicians so drunk I've had to put them over my shoulder, put them into the car and drive them home.

K.L.　Were any of the people now serving in Parliament involved in any of the assassinations?

A.B.　No.

K.L.　Were they aware of specific operations before they took place?

A.B.　I think they must have been because they had been at meetings with leading members of the UDA like Tommy Herron. The Stalker–Sampson enquiry should have been extended back to the early 1970s because it was in the early 1970s that the RUC started getting involved in terrorism, and they were handing over weapons which went missing from Mount Pottinger RUC station.

K.L.　Do you think it will ever be possible to expose what went on in the RUC?

A.B.   I never thought the RUC would be exposed because the file on the Kincora boys home went missing from Brooklyn and the RUC's a very tight-knit family. All the information they receive is kept and that Kincora file was kept. Now if they were to charge RUC officers it's my belief that the Kincora file would reappear somewhere.

K.L.   Were you aware of the gossip about Kincora at the time?

A.B.   The whole Inner Council of the UDA knew about it but no Inner Council members were involved in it. There were politicians and senior Northern Ireland Office officials involved in it. I know one who's in the House of Commons. He's one of your own men.

K.L.   What was the attitude of the UDA towards Kincora?

A.B.   Well, as far as they were concerned it was being organised by British Intelligence and they kept away from that. They knew the intelligence services were running it.

K.L.   But was it any more than rumour about the intelligence services involvement in Kincora?

A.B.   I know for an actual fact that a Conservative MP was involved. The Inner Council members discussed Kincora and knew who was there because they had them under surveillance. The UDA have photographs of the people going into Kincora, of politicians, Unionist politicians. The Inner Council knew who was operating behind them. They knew they could be arrested, but given what they knew they could never be charged or face imprisonment for any length of time.

Take the case of 'P', he was captured with a load of AK 47s from Portadown. I told the authorities that 'P' was responsible for eighteen assassinations but they could only intern him for a few months. Suppose he had wanted to confess and become an RUC converted terrorist. Think what would happen then.

When I was captured I told the RUC that Tommy Herron was going to be assassinated, but when he was assassinated I wasn't called before the Coroner's Court in Belfast to repeat the evidence that I gave to the RUC.

K.L.   Have you any other evidence of collusion between the RUC and the assassination squads?

A.B.   Well, I was present in the UDA HQ when Inspector 'F' walked in and handed a Sterling submachine gun over. I was present in the house in Diamond Street when Inspector 'F' walked in whilst I was reassembling a self-loading rifle belonging to the Ulster Defence Regiment. We took a .38 pistol off a policeman in a red Mini car at the corner of Templemore Avenue and Finmore Street and it was kept in 'N's house. The next day Inspector 'F' came down and said, 'You've got to give us that pistol back because there's going to be raids,' and he gave us the names of the houses that were going to get done, so we handed the pistol back and anything that was in those houses was cleared out of them.

K.L. Was the pistol given to you voluntarily by the officer in the Mini car?

A.B. No, but he knew who took it and he knew where the pistol was. We gave it back in his own house.

There was also the time I was sitting in the bar in Templemore Avenue and 'C' was sitting there with 'Z' and 'X' who had two holdalls with about twelve guns in each. The CID man 'C' was there at the table beside us. Another example was when 'Y' was on the run from prison and he was sitting drinking at the bar. 'C' was standing drinking at the bar and he was supposed to be one of the twenty-one top detectives in the unit set up by Willie Whitelaw to combat Loyalist assassinations.

K.L. What about cross border activities?

A.B. The cross border activities were operated by 'D', a member of the Inner Council from the Waterside in Derry. He was in charge of all operations. His link was to a police sergeant (now he's a detective I think) in the Waterside. You know the attacks on the bars in Donegal in 1972, well, 'D' or his operators did them with two of our bombers from Belfast.

There was St Johnstown just across the border and shooting incidents in Donegal – you know, machine gunning bars. But the bombings in Monaghan and Dublin were operated by British Intelligence.

K.L. Why have you changed your attitude to all this?

A.B. I think it was the back-handers that the Inner Council were getting. They own bars, pubs, hotels – they all own property. That money was given by British Intelligence, plus the fact that they were involved in the protection rackets.

I'm sorry I got involved. There's kids in the paramilitaries who want to get out but if they do get out they'll be shot. That's the situation.

I keep myself fit considering they kept me in solitary for ten years in punishment cells. Anyone who's ever tried to expose the RUC has always come unstuck – look at Stalker. I've been in prison for sixteen years and I don't really care now. I believe the public should know what was going on. Some of them kids in the UDA believed they were working for the British army. Some of them believed that they were working for the British Intelligence Services and you can understand why. Take the case of Paul McCartan who was assassinated. We picked him up at the corner of Finmore Street. He was let out of the RUC police Land Rover about a hundred yards from where we picked him up. We were actually standing waiting for him and we took him away and shot him. The RUC knew we were there. McCartan was nobody, just a Catholic. It was just to keep the pot boiling, to frighten the Catholic community and the IRA.

K.L.   What about the younger McCartan?

A.B.   He was interrogated. He was supposedly in the IRA. This was information passed on by Special Branch and CID officers to a UDA commander.

We were sitting in a bar when we were told to drive off to the Park Avenue Hotel. We took him out of the hotel, interrogated him and then assassinated him.

'C' of CID and Whitelaw's special squad used to give us files. They were like a deck of cards. They were all joined together and there were photographs of every republican. I used to sit and drink with 'C'. Half the assassinations in Northern Ireland in the early 1970s wouldn't have been committed without RUC backing. Half the people who died in those assassinations would be alive today if the RUC hadn't supported the assassination teams. The RUC knew the assassination teams – every single one of them.

When I gave myself up the CID officer in charge, Chief Inspector 'Q', gave me a book of photographs and said, 'There you are, Albert, have a look at them and tell us who you know and tell us who you don't know.' And I just couldn't believe it because they had every single member of the assassination teams down there.

Then they came to take me to the police station and 'C' came down in the car. The sergeant with him said, 'We've come to take you to Chichester Street.' I ran back and said to the sergeant that 'C' was a member of the UDA. When we got to Chichester Street Chief Inspector 'Q' was flapping and said, 'What's all this about "C"?' I told him 'C' handed over the photographs of republicans and 'Q' said, 'Don't say nothing about this.' That night they visited my parents and warned them to say nothing.

The interview over, I returned to London to talk to Neil Grant about the best way of putting down questions to government ministers about Baker's allegations. As I expected, they continued with the cover-up, either refusing even to answer the questions on the grounds that I had become 'obsessive' about the 'dirty war' or simply telling me that if I had any information about any crime then I should give the details to the authorities. The fact that it was the 'authorities' that committed the crimes was ignored.

Of course, the government cannot ever allow a full, open investigation of the 'dirty war' that has been going on in Northern Ireland these last twenty years. To do so would completely discredit the RUC and the British Intelligence Services, thus further undermining Britain's legitimacy to remain in Ireland in the eyes of the world.

Whilst the government's position is understandable, if deplorable, the relative silence of the opposition is not. Neil Kinnock rightly condemns every act of violence by the IRA but he has been silent about the abuses of the security services. Not only does this leave many in the nationalist community suspecting a loyalist bias in Labour's leadership, but it also allows the press to suggest that anyone who does raise these issues is either a crank or a traitor.

Any politician who takes up the case of someone like Albert Baker can expect the full and unwelcome attentions of the Tory press, and it is largely because I was prepared to deal with such cases that I became identified in the public mind with Ireland more than any other cause. Yet at the beginning of the present phase of the troubles I knew virtually nothing about Ireland. Throughout my entire time at school I can only remember a single lesson devoted to Irish history – the obligatory thirty-five minutes devoted to the Great Famine. The richness of Irish culture, its distinctive arts and sports and all its history, except in relation to England, simply did not exist in the school curriculum. I was taught more about Singapore on the other side of the world than about our nearest neighbour which only forty years earlier had been fighting Britain in a savage war of independence.

Nor was this practice of contemptuous neglect confined to our schools. In Parliament, it was the convention never to discuss the affairs of Northern Ireland and this set the pattern of media coverage. A typical example of this occurred in the 1964 general election when the decision of the Sinn Fein candidate for West Belfast to fly the Irish tricolour was denounced by the Revd Ian Paisley who threatened to lead a Unionist mob to remove it if the police did not. The following day, the RUC attacked Sinn Fein headquarters to remove the flag thus provoking three days of rioting which left twenty-one police and fifty members of the public in hospital. The RUC only managed to retain control of the situation by the use of armoured cars and water cannon, and yet the media largely ignored the whole affair on the grounds that it was of little relevance to the struggle in Britain between Wilson and the Tories.

It was only in 1968, when the Catholic minority finally began their civil rights struggle to end years of discrimination in housing, employment and voting rights and the brutal daily repression by the almost exclusively Protestant police force, that a whole new generation of British people woke up to the problem on their doorstep. Like many others I began to read of the history of Ireland and debated with those involved in the campaigns to end British rule in the North. The more I learned, the more angry and outraged I became as I slowly began to grasp the scale of what Britain had done to Ireland over the centuries. As well as anger there was genuine surprise as I discovered a reality completely at variance with the dishonest propaganda spewed out by the British government and slavishly repeated by the media.

The first of my misconceptions to be shattered was the belief that the people of Ireland and Britain were united by a common language and culture. Although Ireland had been inhabited for 8,000 years, it was not until the century before the birth of Christ that the Gaels arrived from the Continent to absorb and replace the Firbolg. Along with their distinctive and artistic culture, they brought a partially democratic form of tribal organisation in which land was owned collectively by the whole tribe and the chieftain was elected for life. This guiding Brehon law and the loose control of the High Kings in their ringforts on the hill of Tara was in complete contrast to the strong, centralised control practised by Imperial Rome over most of the rest of Europe.

Thus as the rest of Europe collapsed into the Dark Ages following the fall of Rome Ireland, which had completely escaped Roman rule, experienced a golden age of Gaelic civilisation. The missionary heirs of St Patrick spread out across Europe to secure the Christian faith whilst others remained at home to produce great works of art like the Book of Kells. The strength of that Gaelic culture can best be judged by its survival in the face of the Norseman's long assault which began in AD 795. The final defeat of the Norwegians by the High King, Brian Boru, in 1014 signalled their eventual absorption into Ireland on

Irish terms. An even clearer example of the separateness and strength of Irish culture was demonstrated in the tenacious hold of the Irish Gaelic language which, right up until the last 150 years, remained the only language of the vast majority of the Irish people.

Therefore, far from Ireland being part of a predominant English culture, the reality is that we have less in common in terms of language and culture than we have with those other European nations that share a Latin base to their language, politics and culture.

The strength of Gaelic culture was demonstrated again when invading Normans led by the Earl of Pembroke, in 1169, were also rapidly absorbed. This was not an invasion backed by the authority of the English King. The Earl of Pembroke, also known as Strongbow, was an adventurer seeking land and his own powerbase which he soon achieved by victories on the battlefield and a strategic marriage which made him King of Leinster. Indeed, it was the growing power of Strongbow and the other Norman adventurers which brought the English King, Henry II, to Ireland with a force of 4,500 men to ensure that they reaffirmed their traditional feudal allegiance to the King of England. Henry's position was strengthened by the decision of Adrian IV (the only English Pope) who in 1155 had granted Henry a commission to reform the Irish Church.

These are the origins of England's claim to authority over Ireland. Strongbow did not resist that authority, nor did he need to because the problems of communication across the Irish Sea and within Ireland itself meant it was little more than nominal. In the following 350 years the Kings of England had enough problems holding down their English subjects to find time to intervene in Ireland, although they worried at the speed with which the Norman adventurers were absorbed into Irish culture. In reality, the authority of the English Crown existed only in a small enclave around Dublin known as 'the Pale' where Irish people were banned and likely to be hunted down and killed if found, Beyond the Pale the Norman invaders rapidly adopted Irish laws, wives and ways and instead of Norman French began to speak the Irish language. In 1366, under pressure from London the Irish Parliament at Kilkenny banned all 'English born in Ireland' from the use of Irish laws, language, clothes, hairstyles, names, intermarriage or subletting their land for the Irish to graze cattle on. But it was to no effect at all and the invaders continued to become 'more Irish than the Irish'.

Whilst England's Kings were engaged in the Wars of the Roses their enclave in the Pale grew even smaller and could only survive by paying 'protection' money to the surrounding clans. Into this power vacuum stepped the House of Kildare. Between 1455 and 1534 the Earls of Kildare successively occupied the post of the English King's Lord Deputy in Ireland. Yet in practice their position was strong enough to break with England and it was only by the most skilful manoeuvring that the two Tudor Kings, Henrys VII and VIII, avoided this whilst creating a strong centralised, absolute monarchy in England. It was not until 1534 that Henry VIII felt strong enough to move against Ireland and it is from this point in history that England's bloodsoaked involvement in Ireland really began.

Having been summoned to London, the Earl of Kildare was imprisoned in the Tower and his son tricked into raising an army against Henry which was rapidly crushed. Also in 1534, Henry abolished the ancient Brehon law under which the land was collectively owned by the whole tribe. Henceforth, all land would be the property of the Crown and only regranted to those subjects who gave their allegiance to the Crown. Those who had been granted the land but failed to administer it according to the laws of England were declared traitors and had their lands confiscated.

This act ushered in seven decades of rebellion as one revolt after another was crushed with maximum butchery, during which Henry and then Elizabeth developed the tactic of divide and rule to a fine art, buying off one Gaelic chieftain after another until they in their turn could be dispensed with. These tactics allowed Henry to buy enough support so that by 1541 he proclaimed himself 'King of this land of Ireland as united, annexed and knit for ever to the Imperial Crown of the Realm of England'.

In annexing Catholic, Gaelic-speaking Ireland to newly Protestant England, the Crown had taken its first major step in creating the greatest empire in human history but it had to wade knee deep through the blood of Ireland to do it, and four and a half centuries later innocent Irish and English blood still flows from that decision.

As with all colonial acquisitions, the imperial power justified its annexation on the basis that the native population were savages in need of a civilising influence. Who were the real savages, however, can be seen from a contemporary account of the military campaigns of Sir Humphrey Gilbert who led the English army to suppress one rebellion:

> the heads of all those which were killed in the day would be cut
> from their bodies ... and ... be laid on the ground by each side

of the way leading into his own tent ... it did bring great terror to the people when they saw the heads of their dead fathers, brothers, children, kinsfolk and friends lie on the ground before their faces.

By 1595 the poet Edmund Spenser could describe the scene thus:

> ere one year and a half the (rebels) were brought to such wretchedness as that any stony heart would have rued the same. Out of every corner of the woods and glens they came creeping forth upon their hands, for their legs would not bear them; they looked like anatomies of death; they spoke like ghosts crying out of their graves; they did eat the dead carrions ... the very carcasses they spared not to scrape out of their graves ... in short space there were none almost left, and a most populous and plentiful country suddenly left void of man or beast.

In the eyes of the Tudor imperialists a 'barbarous country' inhabited by savages 'must first be broken by a war before it will be capable of good government'. Some historians have estimated that as many as one third of Ireland's people died in the seven decades following Henry's annexation.

At the same time as he had annexed Ireland Henry had also finally broken with the Pope in Rome and begun the process of turning England into a Protestant nation. This now gave England another justification to hold Ireland as the fear grew that a French or Spanish invasion of England could be launched from there. This fear was given flesh when the Irish appealed to the Pope and Spain for help and were rewarded with two small and ineffectual expeditions in 1579 and 1580.

A new dimension had been added to the problem of England's relations with Ireland. Not only did the Irish speak a different language but due to the failure of the Reformation to take root there the two nations now practised different religions. To rectify this and ensure Ireland's loyalty to the English Crown and its new religion, Protestants were encouraged to settle on the lands seized from Irish rebels.

The first attempts at Protestant settlement failed and it was only the rebellion of Hugh O'Neill, Earl of Tyrone, that gave Elizabeth her chance. A descendant of the High Kings of Tara, O'Neill's base was in that part of Ireland most resistant to English rule – Ulster. His struggle to defend Gaelic culture and Brehon law began in 1595 and came close to victory in 1598 when he defeated the English at the battle of Yellow Ford. Spain intervened on the side of O'Neill by sending a fleet to Kinsale but it was there on Christmas Eve 1601 that England's decisive victory occurred, although fighting continued until O'Neill's surrender in 1603.

Although pardoned and allowed to keep his lands, he resented the imposition of English law and constant harassment of Catholics. Four years later, O'Neill and others went into voluntary exile on a French ship. With this 'flight of the earls' the last Gaelic chieftains were gone and the new English King, James I, seized the chance to confiscate the half a million acres of farmed land that had been under the control of the rebel earls in Ulster.

The Plantation of Ulster started in 1609 when thousands of Scottish and English Protestants, described by one contemporary as 'generally the scum of both countries ... abhorred at home' were 'planted' on the land. The original Catholic tenants were either dispossessed or charged high rents for the worst land. Meanwhile, the greatest number of Protestant settlers arrived on the east coast of Ulster. Unlike the Anglicans, whose settlement was organised by the Companies of the City of London, these were Presbyterians from Scotland who were themselves persecuted as dissenters.

The resentment of the dispossessed Catholics continued to grow and many of the Protestants fortified their farms against the 5,000 armed supporters of the Gaelic earls who, never having surrendered, still lurked in the wilder parts of Ulster.

It was thirty years after the Protestant settlement began, whilst England was locked in the opening stages of the Civil War between Charles I and Parliament, that resentment finally exploded. Before O'Neill's surrender in 1603 over 90 per cent of the land of Ireland was owned by Catholics but by 1640 that figure had been reduced to 59 per cent. On 23 September 1641, the Gaelic Irish rose up to reclaim their land and in the atrocities that followed 12,000 Protestant women, men and children died, the majority from exposure.

Once Oliver Cromwell had led the parliamentary forces to victory in Britain, he turned his attention to the resubjugation of Ireland. Initially, his New Model Army was reluctant to go to war in Ireland with the more progressive elements (the egalitarian Levellers) refusing to fight. But in May 1649 after a forced march to Burford, in Oxfordshire, where the rebellious Leveller regiments were gathered, Cromwell executed the dissidents and resumed preparations for his invasion of Ireland.

Cromwell arrived there in August 1649 and order was restored by 1652 following a brutal campaign of near genocide. In the years between the rebellion of 1641 and Cromwell's victory, a third of the Catholic population died and many more were transported to slavery in the colonies. Cromwell's own words are the best account of his savagery. Describing the attack on the town of Drogheda, he said:

Being thus entered, we refused them quarter; having, the day before, summoned the town ... I believe we put to the sword the whole number of the defendants. I do not think thirty of the number escaped with their lives. The enemy were about 3,000 strong in the town ... It hath pleased God to bless our endeavours at Drogheda.

Cromwell confiscated the rebels' land and those not killed or transported to the colonies were moved to farm the barren terrain of Cannacht. Thus only 22 per cent of the land remained in Catholic hands.

Irish hopes were raised with the restoration of the monarchy in 1660 and the eventual accession of James II in 1685. James began appointing Catholic officials and the Catholic majority in the Irish House of Commons passed an Act which reversed the Cromwellian land seizures. But their expectations were dashed when a Protestant led coup within the ruling class forced James II off the throne in favour of the Protestant monarchs, William and Mary of Orange. James retreated to Ireland but after losing the decisive battles at Boyne and Aughrim his armies surrendered at Limerick, in 1691, and followed him into exile.

Further repression followed this new defeat. Within fifteen years the amount of land in Catholic hands had declined to only 15 per cent. Between 1695 and 1705 legislation was passed which banned Catholics from public office, the armed forces, voting, and purchasing or leasing land for more than thirty-one years. A proposal for the castration of priests was passed but never put into practice although a bounty of £5 was paid for the head of any priest.

The Catholic majority could only continue to support its culture and religion in secret. Although Catholic education had been made illegal, illicit 'hedgerow schools' kept Gaelic traditions alive and priests conducted illegal services in the forests using any convenient large flat stone as an altar.

In response to this oppression, the Catholic peasantry eventually formed illegal secret societies of vigilantes to defend themselves from the abuses of the landlords' agents. First, the 'Whiteboys' and then the 'Thrashers', 'Oakboys' and 'Moonlighters' roamed the countryside beating up rent collectors and attacking the landlords' property. Most of the landlords were so rapacious that the idea eventually caught on and the poor Protestant peasants set up similar organisations called the 'Peep O'Day Boys' and 'Steelboys'.

The activities of the vigilantes could not stop the continuing erosion of the Catholic position, however, and by 1714 Catholics only owned 7 per cent of the land in contrast to the 90 per cent that they had held 100 years earlier. Britain also imposed restrictions on the development of Irish trade and industry so that it would not compete with Britain. In effect, Ireland was turned into a colony for the production of cheap food for workers in Britain's rapidly expanding industrial towns.

The record of first England and then Britain in the years following Henry VIII's abolition of the Brehon Law, in 1534, is a classic study of colonialism at its very worst. The slaughter and death from starvation of a third of the Irish population by the year 1600 was followed by the similar decimation of a further third of the population between 1641 and 1652; the confiscation of 93 per cent of the land and the prevention of any economic and industrial development which was not subordinate to the interests of the imperial power; and the systematic attempt to destroy all traces of Irish culture and religion and the plantation of settlers into a hostile environment. Britain's first colony was the testing ground for the brutal methods which it would eventually use, in many cases with more finesse, around the rest of the world.

Protestants as well as Catholics suffered from the economic consequences of British imperialism and so, inspired by the example of the US War of Independence, the Protestant community itself began to talk of independence. In 1782, with 80,000 armed volunteers mobilised behind the cause, the Protestant Henry Grattan persuaded the Irish Parliament to pass a unanimous Declaration of Independence. The British government responded with some cosmetic reforms but power remained firmly based in Westminster.

In 1778 and 1782, the laws banning Catholics from owning, leasing and inheriting land were repealed. But the bitter legacy of the preceding 250 years of imperial brutality could not be forgotten, and when the French Revolution ignited the hopes of oppressed peoples across the world it spurred both Catholic and Protestant Irish to rebellion.

The leader of the rebels was, like Grattan, a Protestant. Theobald Wolfe Tone declared that reform could only come from Catholic and Protestant uniting against the 'one common enemy'. A convinced republican, he had helped form the Society of United Irishmen (which welcomed Mary Wollstonecraft's book *The Vindication of the Rights of Women*). Once war broke out between Britain and France, Tone went to France to persuade the government there to provide an army capable of liberating Ireland. Finally, on 16 December 1796, at the age of 33, Tone set sail at the head of an army of 14,000 troops which, given Britain's problems on other fronts, seemed certain to succeed in freeing Ireland. Unfortunately, a strong gale aborted the invasion. Three further attempts were made in the following three years but all failed and in 1798 Tone was captured by the British and sentenced to death.

British methods in suppressing the rebellion were shockingly brutal. Flogging to death, pouring burning pitch on the head, half hanging, roasting the feet and crucifixion (using pegs on the ground) were used to identify and root out the United Irishmen. By the time the French eventually arrived it was too late and at the Battle of Vinegar Hill, in 1798, the rebellion was finally crushed. The decision to take no prisoners added dramatically to the death toll of 50,000.

Britain responded to the rebellion in two ways. In 1800, it abolished the Irish Parliament and forced a complete integration of Britain and Ireland with a hundred MPs representing Ireland at Westminster. It also set out to ensure that there would never again be a joint Catholic and Protestant movement by encouraging the violently anti-Catholic Orange Society. This was a secret society modelled on the Freemasons which had been founded in September 1795. Although the leadership consisted of squires and magistrates, they recruited the 'Peep O'Day Boys' for whatever thuggery was required to keep the Catholics in their place and smash the solidarity which the United Irishmen had created between Protestant and Catholic. Operating in much the same way as the Ku Klux Klan in the deep south of the United States, they were described by the historian T. A. Jackson 'as a "union-smashing" force . . . [that] constituted the first Fascist body known in history'.

Throughout the next hundred years Ireland continued to be a constant source of problems for successive British governments. On the one hand, the hundred Irish MPs often produced a block of reformist nationalist leaders who disrupted the workings of Parliament in order to bring about legislative changes. At the same time, there were frequent periods of violence as Fenian groups continued the fight for independence.

The economic stagnation caused by Britain's control of Ireland meant that between 1800 and 1845 unemployment was often running at 25 per cent and 1 million emigrated to the USA, whilst another 500,000 sought work in England. But this population loss was completely overshadowed by the arrival of potato blight in 1845 which triggered the Great Famine and lasted until 1849. In Ireland it was called the Great Starvation because whilst 1 million Irish starved to death and countless others were forced to emigrate, the British government exported enough corn and cattle from Ireland to feed the starving twice over.

The British Cabinet appointed the head of the Treasury, Charles Trevelyan, to take command of the situation. He concluded that as 'the numbers are beyond the power of the depots to cope with ... they must therefore be closed down as soon as possible'. He advised that 'The only way to prevent people from becoming habitually dependent on government is to bring operations to a close ... or you run the risk of paralysing all private enterprise ... for an indefinite number of years.' As typhus ravaged the Irish countryside Trevelyan finally started public works programmes and imported cheap Indian corn, but his officials warned that the object of the Relief Act was being 'perverted ... as a means of adding to the comforts of the lower classes'. To prevent this the whole cost of the scheme was thrown on to the local rates as Trevelyan warned that 'too much has been done for the people ... we must now see what independent exertion can do'. Complaining that he had never worked so hard in his life, Trevelyan departed to France for a fortnight's holiday. He returned to a knighthood.

The population of Ireland in the 1841 census was just over 8 million and was expected to reach 9 million by 1851. The combination of nearly 1 million dead and 1,500,000 emigrants meant that by 1851 the census showed only 6 ½ million. Landlords were quick to seize the opportunities presented by the vacated land and, as Marx pointed out, they increased the number of cattle grazed by 996,877!

Britain continued to obstruct the development of Irish industry outside Protestant areas in the North and therefore Catholic emigration continued. Between 1851 and 1900 another 3 million people were forced to emigrate with the result that the population continued to decline until it reached a low point of just over 4 million in the early part of this century. Even today the population of Ireland has not recovered to 5 million. Thus it is the only nation on the face of the planet which has a lower population than it had at the time of Napoleon. Had Ireland been free to develop as did independent European nations of similar size, it would today have a population of somewhere between 15 and 25 million.

The result of these genocidal policies was an upsurge of nationalist feeling and in 1858 the Irish Republican Brotherhood was formed in New York and Dublin. Also known as the Fenians, they launched an abortive rebellion in Ireland in 1867 and unsuccessfully invaded Canada from New York. Public support was alienated when a Fenian bomb killed seven workers by mistake in a bungled attempt to assist the escape of Fenian prisoners from Clerkenwell gaol.

The Liberal Party leader, William Gladstone, realised that a measure of Home Rule was necessary in order to end the continuing Fenian violence. Introducing the first Home Rule Bill in 1886, he cannot have imagined that it would take twenty-eight years before a severely truncated measure would eventually become law in 1914 (only to be suspended at the onset of the First World War).

The attitude of the British left towards Ireland at this time can best be judged by the comments of the early Fabians, Sidney and Beatrice Webb, following a visit to Ireland in 1892. 'The people are charming but we detest them, as we should the Hottentots, for their very virtues. Home Rule is an absolute necessity in order to depopulate the country of this detestable race.'

The struggle to pass a Home Rule Bill coincided with a rebirth of pride in Gaelic culture and sport typified by the founding of the Gaelic League in 1892, which established 600 branches within ten years. Also formed at this time was a new party called Sinn Fein (Ourselves Alone) which argued that Irish MPs should form their own Irish Parliament.

However, as Gaelic confidence and the demand for Home Rule grew, the loyalist backlash was stoked up by the Orange Lodges. The pattern of anti-Catholic discrimination in better paid employment was already obvious as early as 1866, when studies showed that only 7.5 per cent of the workers in the Harland and Woolf shipyard were Catholics. Between the end of the Great Famine and 1900 there were Unionist riots and pogroms against the Catholics in Belfast in six separate years.

As it became clear that the Home Rule Bill would become law the Unionist leaders began to plan an armed uprising against the Liberal government of Herbert Asquith. In 1912, 100,000 Unionists marched past the Leader of the British Tory Party, Bonar Law, who proclaimed that they would not want for help 'when the hour of battle comes'. Later he warned: 'There are things stronger than parliamentary majorities ... I can imagine no length of resistance to which Ulster will go, in which I shall not support them.'

Taking their cue from the Leader of His Majesty's Opposition, 80,000 Unionists joined the Ulster Volunteer Force and began drilling as their leaders arranged for a major gun-running operation to bring in 24,000 rifles and 3 million rounds of ammunition. In the face of this intransigence Asquith could not rely on the loyalty of the British army. Sixty officers at the Curragh camp stated that they would refuse to act against the UVF even if this meant dismissal.

Faced with civil war, Asquith and the leader of the Irish Nationalists in Parliament agreed that most of Ulster would be allowed to opt out of the new Home Rule proposals, but before anything could be done the Act was suspended following the outbreak of the First World War.

The 1916 Easter Rising came as a complete surprise to the people of Ireland. When, after five days, the weight of the British army eventually prevailed over the 150 members of the Citizens Army and they were led away to prison, the crowds on the streets of Dublin jeered and in some cases tried to assault the republicans. James Connolly and Padraig Pearse, the leaders of the rising, had known that there was no chance of a military victory over Britain but believed that their actions would ignite a greater struggle. Pearse had talked of the need for a blood sacrifice and Connolly had warned, 'We are going to be slaughtered.'

They had not underestimated British imperialism's brutal stupidity. Asquith told the House of Commons that the instigators could expect no mercy. There was to be no question of a fair and open trial. Courts martial were held in secret and the fifteen ringleaders had all been shot by 12 May. Irish opinion was outraged and forced the Irish Nationalist MPs to condemn the executions, although their first response to the rising had been to condemn it with 'horror and detestation'. The Labour Party's Arthur Henderson, a member of the wartime coalition cabinet, cheered when the executions were announced to Parliament.

Slowly, as the anger of Ireland rose to the surface, the ground began to shift from under the constitutional nationalist MPs in Westminster. At three Irish by-elections in 1917 the Sinn Fein candidates easily beat the constitutional nationalists. Sinn Fein skilfully exploited Irish fears that Britain was about to introduce conscription and was given another martyr when the Volunteer, Thomas Ashe, died on hunger strike following his arrest for a 'seditious' speech.

In the post-war general election of December 1918, Sinn Fein stood on a platform of 'independence now', winning 73 of the 105 Irish seats. The constitutional nationalists were reduced from 83 to 6 with the Unionists taking 26. In 25 seats Sinn Fein had been elected unopposed and in the contested seats had taken 47 per cent of the vote. The Unionists had a majority in only four of the six counties in what is now Northern Ireland. In what was to be the last all Ireland election ever held Sinn Fein had won a decisive majority for independence at the ballot box.

When the new MPs convened at the Dublin Mansion House to take over the administration of Ireland, Britain refused to accept the result of the election. Over the next year the situation descended into a vicious guerrilla war with acts of appalling brutality on both sides. The British government set up the Black and Tans to terrorise Ireland into submission with such brutal acts as the burning of half of the city of Cork.

By July 1921, the two sides had reached a stalemate and began negotiations but the superior strength of Britain meant that Lloyd George was able to demand and get the exclusion of the six counties of Ulster from the new state of Eire. Thus by the threat of further violence the Unionists were able to force the partition of Ireland and trap an unwilling 420,000 Catholics inside their sectarian state with its 836,000 Protestants firmly in control.

After a bloody civil war in southern Ireland in which those who accepted the treaty defeated those who rejected it, the new state set about the task of trying to develop its economy in the face of continuing British economic domination. The Protestant minority in the South accepted the situation and unlike the Catholic minority in the North faced no discrimination.

In contrast, a vast proportion of the time of the new devolved government at Stormont was taken up with perfecting the pattern of discrimination against the Catholic minority. First, the local government boundaries were changed so that it was impossible for there to be a nationalist majority elected even in those areas where there was an overwhelming Catholic majority. Then the 'B' Specials, a wholly Protestant paramilitary police force, was established to 'contain' the nationalist 'threat' and was given powers of coercion which made Northern Ireland effectively a police state. The police powers were so draconian that even the white racist government in South Africa considered them to be excessive.

The Unionists were obsessed by the fear that the higher birth rate of the Catholics would one day lead to a Catholic majority which would vote for unification with the South. To combat this the Stormont regime implemented a pattern of systematic discrimination at all levels of Northern Ireland society. Throughout its entire fifty years of its existence no Catholic ever served as a minister in any Stormont government.

The rigid discrimination against Catholics in the allocation of jobs and housing was deliberately designed to force them to emigrate in order to find a decent way of life. Although the poor conditions in the North also led many Protestants to emigrate, the policy of driving out the Catholics was more than successful. In *Northern Ireland: The Political Economy of Conflict* (1988), Rowthorn and Wayne calculate that 'in the absence of emigration the Catholic population would have more than doubled over the period 1926–81, while the Protestant population would have risen by around a third'. There would have been a Catholic majority in the North by the end of the century. This is why the longest serving Prime Minister of Northern Ireland, Lord Brookeborough, always assured his Unionist voters, 'I have never employed a Catholic on my estates.'

If the behaviour of the Unionists was deplorable, then the policy of successive British governments not to interfere was equally despicable. MPs of all parties knew what was going on but preferred to ignore the plight of the Catholics rather than offend the Unionists who had considerable support in many of Britain's main cities. We even had the hypocrisy of Labour leaders praising and supporting the black civil rights struggle in the USA whilst ignoring an identical pattern of discrimination in Northern Ireland.

What is surprising is not the bloodshed of the last twenty years but the fact that fifty years passed before there was a real campaign to demand full civil and economic rights for the minority in the North. Even when British troops were finally sent into the North in 1969, it was not to crush an armed rebellion by the republicans but to stop an orgy of burning and killing by the 'B' Specials in the nationalist areas of Belfast and Derry.

The reader will have noticed that in this brief history of Ireland I have given more weight to events in the past than to those of the last fifty years. This is deliberately done in order to place recent events in their proper perspective. However horrifying the events of the last twenty years may seem to us today, they come merely at the end of a much more violent record of British involvement in the history of what was our first and will undoubtedly be our last major colony.

Seen in the light of history, it is clear that for the last century Britain has been unwillingly engaged in the task of recognising the historical inevitability of our withdrawal from Ireland. It is just that this has been made more difficult because of the demands of the heirs of those who were 'planted' in Ulster, in order to ensure its loyalty.

The people of these islands have recently had to pay the price for the cynical way in which British governments of the past stirred up sectarian fears and religious hatreds in Ireland. It was not the only colony in which our imperial administrators developed the techniques of divide and rule to a fine art, but it is the only one close enough in physical terms to have allowed the bloodshed to spill over into our own streets and pubs.

There can be no 'comfortable' conclusion to our rule in Ireland. There will inevitably be pain. The best that we can hope for is to minimise this over the shortest possible period of time.

The leaders of the IRA know that they cannot achieve a military victory over the British army, and those commanding the British army will privately admit that they cannot ever hope to eliminate the IRA. In such a situation it is an act of criminal irresponsibility not to negotiate a political solution.

It is inevitable that Britain will one day leave Ireland. The cost of the 'security' operation at £700 million a year means that we no longer make a profit out of our last colony, and the military reasons for remaining which still weighed so importantly just fifty years ago have long been rendered obsolete by the nuclear arms race. The consistent pattern of the opinion polls shows that a majority of the British people have been in favour of withdrawal for over fifteen years, and at some point in the future a cynical party leader facing a difficult election will realise the popularity of the slogan 'Bring Our Boys Home'.

The only argument for remaining that is still used with any conviction is that of the 'bloodbath if Britain goes'. This line is echoed by those MPs who privately claim that 'we have contained the violence to an acceptable level'. This is a lie. If the same proportion of deaths in Northern Ireland over these last twenty years had taken place in Britain, we would have seen 100,000 men, women and children shot to death or blown to bits. Would we really have considered that an 'acceptable level of violence'?

I believe that Britain should negotiate an immediate cease fire with the IRA based on a guarantee of withdrawal in the lifetime of one Parliament – no more than five years. We should then ask all the parties north and south of the border to meet to discuss the problems of reunification and draw up proposals acceptable to both communities about how the new Ireland should be administered. We should make continuing British financial assistance to the new state conditional on the guarantee of the political and religious freedoms of the Protestant minority.

No one in the IRA wants the Unionists to leave Ireland – that would just undermine the economy of a united Ireland. Therefore, there would be no basis for continuing armed activity by the IRA. But would there be a new campaign of violence by the Unionists? Undoubtedly there would be some acts of violence but there is no likelihood of a sustained campaign because there is no achievable objective. The IRA have fought for so long because they see historical inevitability on their side. For the Unionists there is no such inevitability. Northern Ireland is simply not a viable economic unit. It could only survive on its own with massive economic support from Britain and that would not be forthcoming to sustain the old sectarian statelet based on a revived Stormont.

Those who reject such a solution have a duty to tell us how much longer they are prepared to tolerate the present 'acceptable level of violence' and the continuing erosion of civil liberties both in Britain and Northern Ireland that is required in order to sustain the campaign against the IRA. For Mrs Thatcher the answer is simple – she will never negotiate with the men of violence. However long the killing goes on she will make no concessions. But do the British people want to continue what has now largely become the 'War of Thatcher's Face'? All the opinion polls show that the British people have realised the basic truth that still escapes their political leaders. After 820 years of failure and violence they recognise that Britain cannot find a solution to the problems of Ireland because Britain is the problem.

7

The Vision of Omnipotence

For all that I have written concerning UK domestic politics and problems, the truth is that the first issue confronting the Labour Party in deciding its policy in the 1990s is to understand the international trends it will be facing. This is not a question of crystal ball gazing. Although detailed events are impossible to foresee, the key trends such as the role of the USA and USSR in Europe, the change in that relationship and the rise of the Pacific economy are clear. The shifts between Reagan and Gorbachev do not represent a short-term process which will be reversed. On the contrary, the present policies of the USA and USSR represent the continuation of long-term trends which are dictated by economic and political realities in both states. They will dominate the political framework of Europe in the 1990s in the same way that the United States and Russia have dominated European politics since the First World War. As Max Silberschmidt put it in *The United States and Europe: Rivals and Partners* (1972) 'During the previous four centuries world history had been dominated by Europe; from 1917 onwards the impulses which have given the contemporary world its distinctive appearance emanated from Russia and the United States, Europe's flanking powers.' The issue is no longer *whether* European politics in the 1990s will be dominated by events in the United States and the USSR but only *what type* of relation will exist between the United States, Western Europe, and the Soviet Union. The *New Statesman* noted: 'The challenge ... is now to define the kind of place that we want within a Europe in relation to ... [the] United States and Soviet Union.'

Sadly, Labour's Policy Review has barely considered these issues and has not even grasped the significance of the rise of the Pacific economy and its implications for Europe. The leadership seems to be in an even worse state. The first draft of the statement of 'Labour's

Aims and Values' (which was largely written by Roy Hattersley) contained no mention of anything beyond Britain's shores. Indeed, if an intelligent being from another planet was asked to analyse 'Aims and Values' in order to determine what it could about life on Earth, its only evidence that anything existed outside the UK would have been the statement that Britain needed a strong defence against it!

If we wish to examine these broad trends we must start with the United States – the dominant power of the modern world and the one which has shaped Western Europe. Before doing so it is necessary to separate the realities and the mythologies of politics. For over seventy years three generations have been raised on the myth of a benign USA reluctantly dragged from its preferred isolation into the affairs of Europe. We have heard at great length that in order to defend European democracy first from the Nazis and then from Stalin, the USA expended the lives of its young men and much of its wealth. A large proportion of the last three generations of politicians have found it in their own best interests to continue to propagate that view through willing newspapers and television and radio channels. It has become a perceived 'truth' and entered the curricula of schools and the courses of the universities. Those who have rejected this banal simplicity have been marginalised and ignored in the easy times but witch-hunted and driven from public service in the harsh times. The mythology of the benign USA has been integrated into our way of life so powerfully that before we can fully understand the choices now before Europe, we need a more objective view of the recent past than we have had from the pro-American lobby that has dominated the recent politics of Europe.

Even without the mythological embellishments, the rise to international economic and political supremacy of the United States is one of the most extraordinary achievements in history. It created endless confusion in European society because the rise to power of the dominant international state of this century was carried out under the banner of 'anti-imperialism'. From the Monroe Doctrine of 1823 – formally directed against European intervention in the Americas – through Wilson's Fourteen Points for ending the First World War, Roosevelt's 'Four Freedoms' of 1941, to the formation of the United Nations, the USA secured its international interests under the slogans of 'liberation', 'independence', and 'anti-colonialism'. While inhabitants of Central America or the Philippines understood far earlier than Europe the reality of US power, it was not until Vietnam that the majority of the European public came to understand it.

Nevertheless, the way the USA built its international dominance was logical. The United States arrived late on the international stage and faced hardened European political empires – notably those of Britain and France. Later it faced the Japanese empire to the west. These empires confronted the United States as economic barriers and so to secure its economic, and therefore political, domination it had first to deal with these obstructions. Whether by war, economic blackmail or encouraging movements for colonial liberation, the United States concentrated on shattering the barriers constituted by these colonial empires. The terms Gabriel Kolko used to characterise the situation after the Second World War sum up the entire course of USA expansion:

> The hallmark of American foreign policy ... was ... its intense commitment to create an integrated, essentially capitalist world framework out of ... the remnants of the colonial systems. The United States was the major inheritor of the mantle of imperialism in modern history, acting not out of a desire to defend the nation against some tangible threat to its physical welfare but because it sought to create a controllable, responsive order elsewhere, one that would permit the political destinies of distant places to evolve in a manner beneficial to American goals and interests. (*The Politics of War*, 1970)

If these colonial barriers were removed then the United States calculated that the productive power of its economy, with the military power this made possible, would solve its other tasks. As James Forrestal, US Secretary of Defence, put it bluntly in 1947: 'As long as we can outproduce the world, can control the sea and can strike inland with the atomic bomb, we can assume certain risks otherwise unacceptable' (in D. Horowitz, *From Yalta to Vietnam*, 1967).

This form of expansion served both to create confusion and attract a wide range of forces to ally with the United States. Already by the late nineteenth century, 'Henry Adams, visiting the Pacific, met a Samoan chief who assured him with emotion "that his only hope was in Christ and America".' With the outcome of the First World War, as V. G. Kiernan noted in *America – The New Imperialism* (1980), this US ideological charge was greatly strengthened: 'the US was of age, a great force in the world, equal to all ... hopes, ready to be the dispenser, arbiter, prophet of the age ... "The God of Israel", a [US] clergyman exclaimed, "has anointed us to champion the cause of the poor, the weak and the downtrodden. We also shall struggle for world power".' Liberation and domination, as often seen in America's mythology, went together.

Turning from rhetoric to reality, the path of US aggrandisement was clear. Madison, the fourth President, spoke for expansion when he argued that not to do so would lead to internal economic conflicts disrupting the fabric of US society. The USA faced the European states, its strongest rivals, to the east. Its initial expansion was southward into Latin America and westward into Asia, the first confrontation being the 1846 Mexican War. The United States seized not only those areas of Texas that Mexico occupied illegally, but the whole region to the Rio Grande which was Mexican owned and populated. Simultaneously, California was conquered. In one war the United States amputated half the territory previously held by Mexico. In Asia, Perry carried out his expedition to 'open' Japan to Western trade during 1854. In 1858, the privateer William Walker seized control of Nicaragua, receiving US government backing, before being ousted.

After a temporary respite, caused by the Civil War, US expansion developed a new momentum in the latter part of the nineteenth century: in 1867, Alaska was secured from Russia; in the same year, Midway Island was acquired; in 1875, a naval base was gained in Samoa; and in 1886 a South Pacific base was set up in Tonga.

By the end of the century, however, any further expansion could only bring the USA into conflict with the old European empires. Madison had foreseen this in 1829 when he warned that a major crisis would occur in about a century when the continent 'has filled up'. By the late 1880s this debate was at the centre of US politics. James Blaine and Benjamin Harrison individually fought and won the leadership of the Republican Party during the nineteenth century and were both committed to a policy of overseas economic expansion. The depression of 1893 to 1898 convinced many of the leaders of the American labour movement that the only way out of recession was to support the expansionists. Trade union leader Samuel Gompers wailed that 'the great storehouses are glutted'. The radical farmers' leader Jerry Simpson argued that the 'surplus must seek foreign markets'. In much the same way that Peel had created a national consensus in Britain fifty years earlier based on buying off key layers of the domestic working class out of the profits of empire, the same coalition of forces now came together in the United States. As in the case of Britain, there was a belief that such a coalition of self-interest could damp down the forces of revolution.

By the time of the election in 1912, this consensus was so solid that the Democratic candidate for the presidency, Woodrow Wilson, was able to warn:

> Our industries have expanded to such a point that they will burst their jackets if they cannot find a free outlet to the markets of the world ... We have reached a critical point in the process of our prosperity. It has now become a question with us whether it shall continue or shall not continue ... We need foreign markets because our domestic market is too small.

He also warned that the main enemy facing the USA was the growing economic might of Germany. He was well received by his audience of labour leaders.

By the time of Wilson's speech, however, the issue had already been decided. In 1898, a still more systematic United States expansion under the banner of 'freedom' started with the Spanish-American War. The official US goal in this conflict was the liberating of the Spanish colonies, although the petition from thirty-five New York business-men urging President McKinley to intervene in Cuba to put an end to the 'tremendous losses' they were suffering due to the guerrilla war being conducted against Spanish rule is a better clue to US motives. The reality was revealed as the war ended and the United States acquired the key Spanish colonies of Cuba, Guam, Wake, Puerto Rico and the Philippines as legal or *de facto* protectorates.

The war against Spain for possession of her colonies opened up a major debate within US society in which three positions were put. Broadly, the Republicans wanted to continue the policy of traditional colonial expansion while the Democrats opposed this. As the politicians exhausted each other a third group, mainly comprising business interests, won the day. It argued against classic imperialist expansion and urged the adoption of an 'Open Door' policy in which US firms would be free to trade throughout the world without the messy problem of administering colonies. This group believed that the superior economic strength of the United States would guarantee its eventual domination of the whole world.

When John Hay became Secretary of State, in late 1898, he rejected the need for the USA to acquire 'large territorial possessions' and issued the 'Open Door Notes' of 6 September 1899 and 3 July 1900. These laid down that the United States would have complete freedom of trade throughout China and within the spheres of influence of the European powers. This principle was then extended to other areas as circumstances permitted. The third 'Note' specified that loans were an integral part of commerce and that the USA must be free to make such loans throughout the world. On the premise that trade follows loans this was much the most important of the three 'Notes'. During the first fifteen years of this policy, the United States invested $2.6 billion abroad and loaned more than $1 billion. Overseas economic expansion rose rapidly to 10–12 per cent of US GNP.

Following the 'Open Door Notes' direct US acquisition of territory was exceptional. In general, given that the supremacy of its economy could secure its goals if other barriers were eliminated, the United States did not seek explicit geographic expansion – the only exception to this being the military bases in the Pacific which the USA considered indispensable in its ambitions towards China. Economic expansion was, however, coupled with the direct growth of US naval power and the formation of the chain of naval bases in the Pacific. By the end of the nineteenth century China dominated US Asian policy, indeed designs on China had been the driving force behind the proclamation of the 'Open Door'. This in turn defined the United States' most important strategic goal in Asia, namely the territorial integrity of China against the Europeans and in particular the Japanese empire.

Given this strategy, the United States came to see Japan as its principal adversary in Asia. As James Crowley noted after the 1922 Washington Conference: 'Alone of the Washington Treaty powers ... [Japan] had continental possessions in Northeast Asia (Korea); alone of these powers, it had "semicolonial" rights in China (South Manchuria) ... Japan was singled out by the ... sea powers as a potential threat to their economic interests in China.' The US goal, therefore, was first to break the alliance between Britain and Japan – the only combination that alone could pose a significant obstacle to US power. The second was to break Japanese strength. The logical outcome was the US–Japanese clash in the Second World War. Finally, after the war, the United States stood on the eve of what it believed would be an era of total domination of the Pacific – but the coming to power of the Chinese Communist Party in 1949 sharply altered its plans.

In Latin America, US policy followed the same course as the Pacific – although imperialist ambitions became clear earlier. Once again, preaching liberty and practising domination were combined. As Woodrow Wilson put it, 'I am going to teach the South American republics to elect good men.' In order to do this the United States conducted twenty-one military interventions between 1898 and 1924 and was, in the words of Senator Borah, 'party to the suppression of every natural right of citizens of South American Republics' and 'maintaining dictators in power'. At the Hague Peace Conferences of 1899 and 1907, the USA championed an Argentinian proposal that any sanctions against debtor nations by means of armed force would be in contravention of international law – a move against Britain. At the same time, the United States was seizing control of Cuba and Puerto Rico.

In the period between the First and Second World Wars the USA intervened militarily in Nicaragua against Sandino and in Cuba against the Grau government. There were also long and bitter disputes with Bolivia and Mexico as their governments tried to assert their rights over their own economies, at the expense of those US corporations who showed little interest in investing the profits they made back into the host nations. It was only when the Nazis started to challenge the US position in South America that the Roosevelt administration started to take a more reasonable attitude to these disputes. That, however, did not lead to any modification in US policy towards British involvement in South America. In the 1940s, Peron was opposed by the United States largely because he was seen as leaning too closely towards British power. US goals in Latin America, which involved the elimination of the remaining British influence, were almost completely achieved by the end of the Second World War. British exports to Latin America declined from 40 per cent in 1938 to just 8 per cent in 1948.

Europe presented the toughest case for US policy. Here it confronted not weak or disintegrating states but its chief economic rivals – Germany, Britain and France. It took the First and Second World Wars before the United States succeeded in breaking down its rivals' resistance and gaining its economic and political objectives. It was also in Europe that the United States encountered the other state that, with itself, was to dominate the twentieth century – Russia.

The First World War ensured the fate of Europe to become dominated by relations between the USA and USSR. The United States, which sold 77 per cent of its exports to the allied powers in 1913, feared that a German victory in the First World War would establish the dominance in Europe of its most dangerous economic rival. The USA therefore made war loans to Britain and France from 1914 onwards. But it was events in Russia which determined US entry into West European politics. Whatever had been its earlier intentions – and by 1917 the USA had already embarked on a course towards war – the Russian Revolution of February 1917 made rapid US entry into the First World War inevitable. The consequences of the February revolution threatened to take Russia out of the war against Germany, thereby leading to the defeat of Britain and France. The entry of US forces into Europe was critical in guaranteeing the defeat of the German offensive in spring 1918 and ensuring German surrender. Without US economic aid, and then direct participation in the war, Germany would have been victorious over France and Britain. Instead, by 1918 the United States was the arbiter of Western Europe.

It is sometimes claimed that following the First World War the United States withdrew from Western Europe into isolationism. But this is to misunderstand the situation. As Silberschmidt notes:

> isolationism in the nineteenth century, at a time when the United States was a small or medium-sized country and effectively enjoyed the protection of the British fleet, was very different from 'isolationism' at a stage where it wielded economic power, naval supremacy and the influence peculiar to a creditor nation ... If America now spoke of isolationism, it did not, and could not, mean total withdrawal, but was simply the cloak, donned in response to opinion at home, for a global policy dedicated to extreme nationalism under the isolationist banner.

On the purely political level, the refusal of Congress to support Wilson's proposal for US membership of the League of Nations did delay for twenty years an overt US political role in Western Europe. But the US economy continued to dominate Europe – and thereby the critical developments in its politics.

From 1917 to 1923 the areas of Western and Central Europe were incapable of regaining political or economic equilibrium. Revolution in Russia, in 1917, was followed by that in Germany in 1918, Hungary in 1919, and Bavaria in the same year. Social explosions shook Austria and Italy. A strike wave hit Britain. In 1923, the French army occupied the Ruhr as a result of Germany's failure to meet reparation payments.

Disorder gripped Germany and the Communist Party grew rapidly. No lasting European solution to the question of reparations proved possible. In short, in 1917–23, Europe proved incapable on the basis of its own resources, of regaining economic and social equilibrium.

The development which reversed this was increased US economic intervention. For whilst Europe teetered on the brink of famine the US State Department estimated: 'A number of our big manufacturers ... in normal times can produce enough to supply the home market in seven months.' The manufacturer George N. Peek predicted that unless the USA exported its surpluses 'we are going to have state socialism'. Under the Dawes Plan of 1924 Germany received a $200 million stabilisation loan. More importantly, in the next five years Germany received a capital inflow of more than $4 billion – most of which came from the United States. Germany in turn paid out $1.8 billion in reparations – the majority to France. When inflows of US capital stopped, German payment of reparations ceased. The economic basis of post-First World War stabilisation in Europe was therefore clear. Germany received capital from the United States. It utilised part of this itself and paid another part to France – which thereby gained indirectly from US capital flows. Nothing in the world of politics is free, however, and it was during this period that the US finally forced Britain and France to begin to open their colonies to US companies (which usually operated by the infiltration of European companies). The impact was massive. In 1919, US overseas investments were $94 million and by 1929 they had increased to $602 million. Herbert Hoover warned his fellow Americans: 'A large part of the world has come to believe that they were in the presence of the birth of a new imperial power intent upon dominating the destinies and freedoms of other people.'

Reparations were finally buried at the Lausanne Conference of 1932 but what Kees Van der Pijl has summarised on the war itself applies also to the situation following it: 'The revolution would not have been confined to Russia had it not been for the entry of the United States into the crucial final stage of the war and the tremendous power thus thrown into battle on the side of liberal capitalism by the ... American bourgeoisie' (*The Making of an Atlantic Ruling Class*, 1984).

This dependence of the European economy on the United States was graphically revealed in 1929. US capital outflows slowed in the early part of that year precipitating declines on Western European stock markets. Starved of US capital the European economies began to slide, and in October 1929 the Wall Street crash ended the financial flows to Europe. The European economies then progressively imploded, unable to resist the shockwave produced by the crisis of the US economy. The political consequence of these events was the rise of Nazism and the Second World War.

Developments during the Second World War repeated, on a higher level, those that occurred in the First World War. Once again, US economic aid and military intervention in support of Britain was decisive in securing victory against Germany – without it Britain would have been left alone in alliance with the USSR with incalculable consequences for Europe. Between March 1941 and September 1945 the US government paid out $30 billion in Lend-Lease. After the war, US intervention was again necessary to ensure that Western Europe regained political and eonomic stability.

Europe was economically devastated by war. In Germany, industrial production was half its pre-war level. European wheat production in 1947 fell to less than 50 per cent of its 1938 level. By early 1946, more than 125 million Europeans were subsisting on no more than 2,000 calories a day; a large number on no more than 1,000 – in contrast to the 3,300 calories a day average in the USA.

Most serious of all, Western Europe's trade position was impossible. British exports in 1945 were one-third of their pre-war level. In 1946–7, Europe's exports were only one quarter of its imports. By that time the United States was financing four-fifths of Italy's trade deficit, and as late as 1948, 65 per cent of West German imports were still financed by the USA. In 1947, the United States was exporting to Europe seven times as much as it imported from there, and had also gained 25 per cent of the rest of the world's gold and currency reserves. By 1948 it controlled three-quarters of the world's monetary gold compared with one-third in 1933. There was no possibility whatever on the basis of a capitalist economy of European recovery without the United States.

This situation was openly acknowledged by every West European country. Alfred Grosser described the situation in Britain:

a dismal reality began to dawn on the men governing Britain ... To finance the war effort, it had been necessary to increase external debts by $12 billion, and foreign assets of more than $5 billion had to be converted ... What would happen now. 'Everything depends on the extent the Americans are willing to cooperate,' the British National Union of Manufacturers stated. (*The Western Alliance*, 1980)

Keynes told the Cabinet that without US aid Britain faced a 'financial Dunkirk'. In France, the situation was the same and in February 1945 Jean Monnet negotiated a loan for the French government with the US Import–Export Bank for $550 million. Reporting for the French financial commission Christian Pinneau stated:

> All we can attain in 1946 in foreign exchange advances is the order of $112.5 million, while we would have to come up with billions of dollars to make up for the deficit in our trade balance ... Our real problem is therefore to obtain credits from the United States ... the United States will be the chief supplier of capital to Europe.

By 1947 the economic situation in Western Europe was deteriorating again. American efforts to penetrate the sterling bloc of the British Empire aggravated Britain's economic problems. The insistence by the USA that the British make the pound convertible in the summer of 1947 created an immediate rush from pounds to dollars, making matters much worse. On 20 August, Britain suspended convertibility of the pound. On 28 August, France was obliged to cease all purchases of non-vital goods for dollars and liquidated its last foreign currency reserves. France was followed by Italy and other West European states. Once more, as after the First World War, Western Europe proved incapable of gaining economic equilibrium on the basis of its own resources. The turning point, as with the Dawes Plan after 1918, was US aid. Marshall's speech of 5 June 1947, proposing aid to Europe, was followed by the United States assigning $22 billion for Western Europe for 1948–51. Marshall Aid represented 5 per cent of the GNP of the receiving countries and 2 per cent of that of the United States.

Nevertheless, it is clear that, as with its policy during the Second World War itself, the United States intervened in Europe to secure *its own* goals and organise the world economy according to *its* needs. The inter-war period had posed immense problems for the USA as the European states sought to escape the effects of economic crisis by raising tariff barriers. Although the United States was at the forefront in protectionism in the inter-war period, this was seen as being in its own interests. What were unacceptable were tariff barriers raised by other countries. By the end of 1932 there were fifteen European countries operating quotas or licensing systems. Indeed, it was these which set the United States on its path to war. US Vice-President Henry

Wallace noted that with 'Hitlerite methods controlling and curtailing world trade it was impossible for the US to get an adequate flow of exports'. The Secretary of State's chief adviser, John McCloy, noted: 'With German control of the buyers of Europe ... it would be well within her power ... to shut off our trade with Europe, with South America and with the Far East ... In short, the fruits of the economic gains that we have made in the last century would be lost.' This was a view shared by the labour leaders of the United States such as John Lewis. He complained in 1939 that the USA was 'gradually being driven out of trade relationships with the various markets of the world ... Unless substantial economic offsets are provided to prevent this nation from being wholly dependent upon the war expenditures we will sooner or later come to the dilemma which requires either war or depression.' Lewis W. Douglas, the Budget Director at the start of Roosevelt's administration, took an equally apocalyptic view: 'To retreat to the cyclone cellar here means, ultimately, to establish a totalitarian state at home.' The serious disruption of America's trade plans by Nazi Germany considerably strengthened Roosevelt's determination to fight – but not before Britain had been irreversibly weakened to the point where it could no longer block the plans of the United States for a completely 'Open Door' to the British Empire.

With the Second World War the United States was in a position to secure its fundamental economic goals. In 1944, Dean Acheson, Assistant US Secretary of State, explained to the House of Representatives that 'no group who has studied this problem, and there have been many, as you know, has ever believed that our domestic markets could absorb our entire production under our present system'. Speaking of the world economy, US Secretary of State Cordell Hull declared: 'We should assume ... leadership, and the responsibility that goes with it, primarily for reasons of pure national self interest.' The US goal was to eliminate the tariff barriers, which meant in practice the empires not only of its enemies, Germany and Japan, but also of its allies, Britain and France. To secure this throughout the war, and after it, the United States ensured that its aid was made conditional on recipients accepting a structure of the world economy which suited its own interests. The USA thus insisted that its Lend-Lease Treaty with Britain include the clause that the two countries would work for 'the elimination of all forms of discriminatory treatment in international commerce'. The day the French Consultative Assembly accepted the first agreement for a US loan it ratified the Bretton Woods agreements which would eliminate protective tariffs. A further loan from the United States to France, in May 1946, was accompanied by a declaration that France and the United States favoured 'abolishing the restrictions imposed on world trade'.

World politics was officially organised through the almost powerless United Nations, but more fundamental were the economic arrangements. Above all, the USA ensured that the *international* economic levers of power were in its hands. The post-war structure of the world economy was thus determined by the United States. On behalf of Britain, Keynes had proposed the creation of a new international currency, the 'bancor', to be directly linked to gold and in which exchange rates would be expressed. A supranational clearing union would use bancor to settle accounts between the central banks. Keynes had argued for automatic credit facilities for countries with deficits on their balance of payments. This plan would clearly have favoured Britain, which was no longer strong enough to propose the pound as the fundamental currency of the world economy, and anticipated the recurrent balance of payments deficits in post-war Britain. The United States vetoed this and insisted that the fundamental currency should be the dollar and that there be no automatic facility for countries in balance of payments deficit. Instead, 'commercial' criteria would operate. Keynes had sought mechanisms to force surplus countries such as the United States to modify their economic policies, but no such devices were built into the Bretton Woods agreements. In addition, the United States insisted on free trade in manufactured goods – where it expected to defeat its competitors, but demanded an exception for agricultural products – where it wished to defend its farmers. Britain, which was in no economic position to argue, gave in to the United States on all points.

Keynes also proposed to the Bretton Woods conference $20 billion in reserves for the IMF – a relatively accurate assessment of the aid necessary for rebuilding Europe. The United States, however, insisted on keeping the international reserves of the IMF small. The USA was prepared, and able, to spend $20 billion on the reconstruction of Europe but demanded that the undertaking should be under its control and not subject to international supervision. The United States revived Western Europe for its own purposes – to further its own economic interests, and to secure its own chosen structure of the world economy. The Bretton Woods currency system, the World Bank, and the IMF, enshrined the domination of the dollar in the international monetary system. The General Agreement on Tariffs and Trade ensured the type of world economy the United States demanded. In this structure of world economy and politics created by the United States no other state could possibly resist its demands except the USSR. The capitalist world after 1946 was a world 'made in the USA', which in turn determined the framework of post-war European politics.

This came as no surprise – even by the end of the First World War the United States' allies had been aware of the state of dependence in which they stood. In October 1916, McKenna, the British Chancellor of the Exchequer, warned that 'by next June or earlier, the President of the American Republic will be in a position, if he wishes, to dictate his own terms to us'. But the Russian Revolutions of February and October 1917 made the subordination of the European ruling classes to the United States complete. By June 1917 Lloyd George's Minister without Portfolio, Milner, was writing: 'I fear the time is very near at hand when we shall have to take some strong steps to stop the "rot" in this country, unless we wish to "follow Russia" into impotence and dissolution.' In November, Lansdowne published his celebrated letter in *The Daily Telegraph* urging the negotiation of moderate peace terms before the war destroyed the traditional social order. By the end of 1917 Smuts was talking of 'the grim spectre of Bolshevik anarchy ... stalking to the front'.

The United States understood this fear of socialism perfectly as a weapon to extract concessions. Walter Lippmann, chosen to explain Wilson's Fourteen Points for ending the First World War to the British government, wrote to the President from Europe: 'Utterances from the United States ... will show the way to the liberals in Great Britain and in France ... These liberals will rapidly accept the leadership of the President if he undertakes a liberal diplomatic offensive, because they will find in that offensive an invaluable support for their internal domestic trouble.' As Van der Pijl comments on the situation after the First World War: 'Hitherto, the European liberal bourgeoisie had been able both to contain domestic working-class pressures and to maintain a degree of autonomy *vis-à-vis* the United States, but the Russian Revolution threw them into the arms of Wilson.'

A symbiotic relationship grew up between the mainstream European right and the United States. Woodrow Wilson supported US aid to Europe on the basis that it would be a 'means of stemming the tide of anarchism'. The European right in turn required the assistance of the USA and stressed the dangers of the 'Bolshevik menace' to extract aid from the United States for specific national projects they were pursuing. Walther Rathenau, future German foreign minister, argued with the United States that if vindictive treaty terms were imposed on Germany under the Versailles treaty, 'one of the formerly strongest props in the European structure will be destroyed, and the boundary of Asia will advance to the Rhine'. The French Socialists were denounced as traitors by the Centre and Right for giving support to the Russian Revolution, while the same Centre/Right organised massive demonstrations of support for Woodrow Wilson. As Paul Kennedy in *The Rise and Fall of the Great Powers* (1988) noted of Wilson: 'The President's oratory, moral fervour, and belief in national self-determination, democracy, international co-operation and arbitration delighted the radicals in Britain, who had despaired of finding a democratic statesman willing to campaign for such ideals.' Or as Silberschmidt put it: 'Having fended off the threat of communism in central Europe, the Europeans needed American help in order to survive the post-war period.'

By the 1930s right-wing and liberal opinions in Europe, outside Hitler's Germany, were even stronger in their support for the United States. In 1932, Churchill toured the United States preaching its duty to stand with Britain and protect Europe against communism and returned home to write his *History of the English Speaking Peoples*. For the liberals the combination of depression, the rise of Hitler and Mussolini, and the existence of the Soviet Union seemed to pose the choice in Europe as being only between fascism, which they rejected, and socialism, which they rejected even more. Only the economic resources of the United States seemed to provide an alternative. Reformist projects in Europe, and elsewhere, were therefore all directly associated with the United States. Leon Blum's policy was hailed in Europe as 'the French New Deal'. Canadians called the policy of their Conservative prime minister 'Bennett's New Deal'. Macmillan extolled Roosevelt's bold measures and regretted that they were being ignored in England. In Belgium, Paul van Zeeland was criticised for following too closely in the footsteps of Roosevelt's New Deal. The President of Mexico congratulated Roosevelt on his large-scale programme for the relief of unemployment, and messages expressing solidarity with Roosevelt's venture came from other Latin American countries. In 1933, both Keynes and Bernard Shaw announced in the strongest possible terms that they were pinning their faith on America. In an open letter to Roosevelt, Keynes wrote, 'You have made yourself the trustee for those in every country who seek to mend the evils of our condition by reasoned experiment within the framework of the existing social system. If you fail, rational change will be gravely prejudiced throughout the world, leaving orthodoxy and revolution to fight it out.'

After the Second World War the situation was clearer still. The European right, and European liberals, understood perfectly well that only US economic and military power was a fully effective safeguard against the threat of socialism from their own labour movements on the one hand and the USSR on the other. The United States comprehended the military situation in Europe and knew that Western European capital had to choose between it and the USSR. As early as 1943, the head of War Office Information, Elmer Davis, had written: 'With Germany reduced and France in ruins, Russia becomes the only first-rate military power on the continent.' Daniel Yergin noted, 'Churchill had realised long before the war's end that the only way Britain in its weakened condition could maintain its Great Power status was as a junior partner of the United States' (*Shattered Peace*, 1980).

For its part the United States was fully confident of realising its goals as the Second World War finished. As early as 1943, Roosevelt let it be known that the system after the war would be based on 'the factor of power'. When Germany attacked the Soviet Union in June 1941 Roosevelt concluded that Germany would be defeated and that the US would be able to overcome any problems posed by the Soviet Union. Roosevelt wrote to Admiral Leahy, the US ambassador to Vichy France: 'It [the Nazi attack on the USSR] will mean the liberation of Europe from Nazi domination. And at the same time I do not think we need worry about any possibility of Russian domination.' Truman, before his first negotiations with the USSR, confided to advisers: 'We would not, of course, expect to get 100 per cent of what we wanted ... [but] on important matters ... we should be able to get 85 per cent.' Regarding the Potsdam Conference to determine post-war affairs, Truman stated he felt he had 'the cards in American hands' and proposed 'to play them as American cards ... We didn't have to go to the Russians for anything and the Russians ... had to come to us for many things.' Churchill noted that when news of the successful test of the first atomic bomb came through to Truman during the Potsdam Conference, he 'was a changed man. He told the Russians just where they got on and off and generally bossed the entire meeting.'

US confidence was increased as it believed possession of the atomic bomb would lead to others capitulating to its demands. James Byrnes, future Secretary of State to Truman, stated in April 1945 that the bomb would 'put us in a position to dictate our own terms at the end of the war'. General Groves, head of the Manhattan Project, said to the US Congress that the bomb meant 'complete victory in our hands until the time another nation has it'.

The view that the USSR would capitulate was a gross miscalculation by the United States. The technical possibility to create atomic weapons does not equal their actual possession in sufficient numbers to win a war. The USA had the capacity to produce merely three bombs per month in late 1945, and even by the end of the 1940s had only limited numbers of nuclear weapons. More than a thousand atomic bombs of the Hiroshima type would have been required to inflict on Germany the same industrial damage as was done by conventional bombs. In the late 1940s the United States possessed nothing like a thousand atomic bombs. Furthermore, the aerial bombardment of Germany had not eliminated that country's ability to wage war and was even less likely to do so in the case of the USSR with its vast area and greater population. In April 1950, US National Security Council memorandum NSC 68, the most authoritative policy document of the Cold War, still concluded that a US atomic attack by itself, with the means then available, 'would not force or induce the Kremlin to capitulate'.

If US atomic forces would not suffice for an attack on the Soviet Union neither would its conventional forces. Immediately the war ended US troops demanded demobilisation – backing this up with strikes and mass demonstrations. Whether the US wished to use its armed forces in Europe or not it was physically unable to do so.

These military realities undermined the situation of the United States *vis-à-vis* the Soviet Union. George Kennan, the leading US expert on relations with the USSR, understood the choice clearly. If the USA wished to achieve its goals in Europe it had to be prepared to go to war. Kennan spelt out the alternative – realistically outlining US goals if it could not achieve domination over the whole of Europe. He favoured 'a fully fledged and realistic showdown with the Soviet Union'. If the West was not willing, he wrote at the time of Yalta, 'to go the whole hog' to frustrate the Soviet Union, then the only thing to do was 'partition Germany, divide the continent into spheres'. The germ of the future development of Europe was contained in these phrases.

If the USA could not achieve what it wanted by military means the other weapon at its disposal, and which also failed, was economic.

Truman noted as the war ended that famine might be a useful weapon against the USSR – he suggested that the Soviet Union would face 'extensive starvation' after the war. On 8 May 1945, the United States cut off Lend-Lease assistance to all its allies. Restarting it, and declaring the earlier interruption to be a mistake, meant that it was easily understood that aid could be cut off instantly. Lend-Lease was finally ended in August 1945. When Truman sent an economic delegation to Europe he chose US oil operator Edwin Pauley to head it on the grounds that: 'This is the most important job in the United States as of this moment. It will determine the whole future of the economy of Europe, and I want somebody as head of the delegation who can throw his weight around.'

War damage to the Soviet economy was indeed devastating. Edward Crankshaw's eyewitness account of the USSR recorded:

> To travel ... was a nightmare experience. For thousands of miles there was not a standing or a living object to be seen. Every town was flat, every city. There were no barns. There was no machinery. There were no stations, no water towers. There was not a solitary telegraph pole left standing in all that vast landscape, and broad swathes of forest had been cut down all along the [train] lines as a protection against attacks by partisans ... In the fields, unkempt, nobody but women, children and very old men could be seen and these worked only with hand tools. (D. Horowitz, *From Yalta to Vietnam*, 1967)

Industrial output in the areas which had been occupied by the enemy was only 30 per cent of its pre-war level.

To maintain their economic grip the Western powers made sure that reparations from Germany would not help rebuild the Soviet economy, but went to aid their own economies instead.

In contrast to the attitude towards the USSR, any government displaying anti-Communist tendencies received immediate US help. US intervention in Western European politics was open and massive. But like Hitler the United States underestimated the Soviet ability to respond. By 1950 Soviet economic output exceeded its 1940 pre-war level. In January 1946, Stalin proclaimed the Soviet Union would produce 60 million tons of steel, 500 million tons of coal, and 60 million tons of oil within fifteen years. All these targets were easily surpassed. Stalin had stated the situation bluntly to Truman's representatives. If the termination of Lend-Lease was 'designed as pressure on the Russians in order to soften them up then it was a fundamental mistake'. If the USSR was 'approached frankly on a friendly basis, much could be done ... Reprisals in any form would have the direct opposite effect'. Soviet economic power also sustained its defence effort – producing its first atomic bomb in 1949 and its first H-bomb only months after the United States in 1953.

The possibility of crushing Soviet power in Eastern Europe did not exist. The inability of the United States to gain its objectives in Eastern Europe led it to pursue the course foreseen by George Kennan – 'to partition Germany, divide the continent into spheres'. By 1947 the United States decided it would settle for what it could get. This choice determined the post-war shape of Europe.

8

Made in the USA

The decision to divide Europe in 1945 shaped the world we live in. From that point onwards Western Europe was conditioned by the United States; as Dan Smith put it in *Prospects for a Habitable Planet* (1987), 'the USA can justly be said to have created the political entity of Western Europe'. And from the start the USA was integrally linked to the European right. The core of that, in turn, was the United States' relation to Germany.

At the end of the First World War Keynes had pointed out that any attempt to revive the European capitalist economy without a strong Germany was doomed to fail. Safeguarding capitalism in Europe after the Second World War equally required the economic and military rebuilding of Germany. The first step in this, and to the partition of Germany, was carried out in the autumn of 1946 when the American and British occupation zones were amalgamated to form 'Bizonia'. US Assistant Secretary of State John Hilldring commented explicitly: 'It will serve the purpose of getting the United States government out of the red in three years ... and it will give us a climate in which to plant our political ideas in Germany.' Chief of the US European command, General Lucius Clay put the case for the integration of the American and British zones of occupation in Germany in the following way: 'If agreement cannot be obtained along these lines ... we face a deteriorating German economy which will create a political unrest favourable to the development of communism in Germany.' US and British policy towards Germany was made easier because the key sectors of its industry were concentrated in the western zone where 80 per cent of the heavy industry had survived the war. The last crucial step in partition came in June 1948 with the introduction of a new currency into the western zones. Germany was economically sliced in two.

The policy of reviving capitalism in Germany, as well as the attitude taken towards Italy, Greece, Spain and Portugal, by the United States and Britain required the rehabilitation of fascists. This was made simpler by the fact that most Allied leaders, contrary to their claims, had not objected to fascism as such. What was unacceptable was fascism which threatened British or US interests. The US banker Morgan had financed Mussolini's Italy and Churchill had summarised his attitude towards Mussolini in his *History of the Second World War*:

> He was, as I had addressed him at the time of the fall of France, 'the Italian lawgiver'. The alternative to his rule might well have been a communist Italy, which would have brought perils and misfortunes of a different character both upon the Italian people and Europe ... Even when the issue of the war had become certain, Mussolini would have been welcomed by the Allies.

In line with this attitude, Adenauer, the United States choice to lead West Germany, was perfectly prepared to consort with Nazis. As Walter Laqueur admits in his pro-cold war *Europe Since Hitler* (1982):

> While Adenauer's anti-nazi record was above reproach, he was less than scrupulous in the choice of his closest collaborators: there could be but one opinion about the career of men like Oberlander and Globke in the nazi era, but the former was dropped only after protests from all sides and Globke, a lawyer who had provided the official interpretation to the anti-semitic Nuremberg laws of 1935, remained for years the Chancellor's close associate and confidant, despite heavy pressure.

Similar policies of rehabilitating ex-fascists were pursued in the other ex-Axis states. In Italy, out of 800,000 pre-liberation civil servants, many of whom had been members of the Fascist Party, no more than a few hundred were removed from their posts. An amnesty was granted in October 1946 after which only 3–4,000 fascists and war criminals remained in prison. The surviving fascist dictatorships of Franco and Salazar were propped up by the United States. The support later given by the United States, and Britain, to regimes such as that of South Africa, Pinochet in Chile, and Stroessner in Paraguay had its direct forerunner in the support given to rehabilitating European fascists.

The problem for the USA and Britain in this policy was that the war had been fought under an anti-fascist banner and the majority of the population of Europe was strongly anti-fascist. For that reason much work of rehabilitating fascists and war criminals had to be done under cover and its truth is coming out only today. Ed Harriman has been prominent in exposing this and it is worth quoting at length from his article in the *New Statesman and Society* of 5 August 1988:

The first to champion this dubious cause [of protecting war criminals] was Hector McNeil, the Labour government's man at the United Nations. At the UN General Assembly's second session in 1947, Soviet, Byelorussian, Ukrainian and Yugoslav delegates taxed McNeil to explain why Britain was sheltering war criminals in displaced persons camps in Germany ... 'In the town of Hoxter in the UK zone of occupation lives the butcher of the Byelorussian people, ... Rodoslav Ostroski,' charged a Russian delegate ... Ostroski ... the Nazi-groomed 'Fuhrer' who press-ganged 60 battalions of his countrymen into fighting, and killing, for the Nazi cause. The liquidation of Jews in Byelorussia ... was by then well known. Yet McNeil was unmoved. In 1961, Soviet authorities charged three Estonians with organising the mass murder of some 120,000 Jews, prisoners of war and other 'untermenschen' ... in Estonia. Two pleaded guilty and were shot. The third, Ain Mere, was then living in Leicester. The Soviets said Mere was the Estonian police boss under the Nazis who personally ordered prisoners to be exterminated in the Jagala concentration camp, and joined the local SS. The Soviet request for his extradition was refused. 'My record was checked when I came to England over 10 years ago,' Mere told *The Times*. The Foreign Office reply was to inform the Soviet government that Britain did not recognise Estonia as part of the Soviet Union.

Harriman notes:

In 1945 the Joint Intelligence Committee declared that the Soviet Union, not Nazi Germany, was Britain's prime intelligence target ... In the perverse logic of the spying world, there were few better sources for this than the Gestapo, which had devoted enormous resources and considerable vigour to liquidating communist suspects. The United States government now admits that Gestapo agents and their files were avidly sought by American intelligence.

In 1983 the US Justice Department published a hefty report spelling out exactly how the Americans recruited one such agent – Klaus Barbie [the butcher of Lyons] – and then gave him a free ride to South America. The appendix of the US report explains that before the Americans bagged him, Barbie was being recruited, in 1945, by a pair of ex-Nazis working as agents for Britain's SIS, a Dr Hoffman and his superior, a man called Markus. Markus had been aide-de-camp to SS Intelligence General Walter Schellenberg, who set up a network of spies and saboteurs among the Soviet collaborators . . . Shortly after the war Markus became the mayor of a small town in the British zone in Germany and, according to US documents, 'was given the task of forming for the British a network of agents in Germany' . . . Prosecutions of war criminals quickly became an embarrassment to [the Labour] Government. They impeded the cold war . . . Churchill was one of the first to call for an end to war crimes investigations . . . Shortly afterwards Churchill made a much publicised donation to the support fund for Nazi Field Marshal Erich von Manstein, who was being tried in Hamburg for murdering prisoners of war on the eastern front. Proceedings against Manstein's fellow officers had already been dropped by British prosecutors on grounds of the defendants' 'poor health.' In 1941, in the Crimea and short of food, von Manstein had ordered: 'The Jewish–Bolshevik system must be wiped out once and for all . . . especially in the occupied cities, a large part of the population will have to starve.' By 1952 Manstein was a free man serving in the West German army. The UN War Crimes Commission was quickly wrapped up. Prosecutors such as Gerald Draper found their efforts thwarted. The British and American authorities were not cooperative. General Lucius Clay declared that as of the end of 1947, no more suspected war criminals would be handed over for prosecution from the American zone in Germany. The British followed suit.

This policy also extended to supporting fascist dominated organisations on the grounds that they were better than communists. But while fascists were tolerated and feted, trade unions and socialists were most definitely not. At the same time as war criminals were being recruited into the secret service, the US military governor of Hesse warned on the radio that 'strikes or other activities against the policies of the military government which could in any way jeopardise the plans of the occupying powers will not be tolerated . . . Do not forget that those responsible are liable even to capital punishment.' The protection, rehabilitation, and in some case promotion of ex-fascists and war criminals gave the USA its first indelible foothold on Western Europe and the states rebuilt with US aid.

While rehabilitation of fascists was a consequence of US policy in Europe its central goal was military reinforcement. On 12 March 1947, Truman announced his new 'doctrine'. Speaking to a joint session of Congress he called for $300 million aid to Greece and $100 million to Turkey. He stated: 'It must be the policy of the United States to support free peoples who are resisting attempted subjugation by armed minorities or by outside pressure.' Exactly what was 'free' about the Greek monarchy, which had directly collaborated with fascists and continued to cooperate with them in the civil war, was not explained. However, a US dominated military alliance proceeded apace. On 17 March 1948, the Brussels Pact was signed by Britain, France, Belgium, the Netherlands, and Luxembourg, providing for a joint defence system. The only potential aggressor identified by name was Germany but the United States saw the pact as an excellent opportunity to increase Western European military readiness. Truman made three specific requests of it: passage of the Marshall Plan, enactment of universal military training, and restoration of selective service.

By 1949, the USA was engaged on a full-scale arms drive concentrated on its nuclear strike air force. By summer 1949, with funds already flowing for new bombers and jet-powered aircraft, the industry tooled up for a war boom. ' "The aircraft manufacturing industry is on its way out of the red ink for the first time since the end of the war," *Business Week* stated in June. "Reason: big military orders placed last week by the Navy and the Air Force." The change in the condition of the industry was dramatic. The Air Force's fiscal year 1949 budget ... was more than twice what it had been in 1948, while that for naval aviation had increased in almost as great a proportion. "The Federal government is spending $4,895,000,000 on aviation in the current fiscal year," said *Aviation Week* in September 1948. 'This is more than twice the $1,760,000,000 expended in the 1948 fiscal period. This is no temporary, short-term buying spree. It is the beginning of a five year plan for military air rearmament" ' (Daniel Yergin, *Shattered Peace*, 1980).

The culmination of US policy was NATO. As Yergin notes: 'For the first time since 1778, the United States was entering a formal military alliance that committed it to go to war in defence of other nations outside the

Western Hemisphere.' Despite formal equality of its members NATO was in reality an alliance totally subordinate to the United States. In the 1950s, French Marshal Juin, nominally commanding the Allied ground forces in Europe, was not even allowed to know the nature and number of atomic weapons he might eventually have at his disposal – this information was reserved for the United States. West Germany was militarily subordinate. Although formally it was granted 'the full powers of a sovereign state over its internal and external affairs,' this was accompanied by the stipulation that the three powers retained their rights to station armed forces in the Federal Republic. This became an issue in the 1970s when, as a matter of strict legality, West Germany had no right to reject the stationing of Pershing 2 or Cruise missiles on its territory. According to the October 1954 accord admitting West Germany to NATO, it was prohibited from producing nuclear, bacteriological or chemical weapons. West Germany could build guided missiles, magnetic mines and bombers only if the commander-in-chief of NATO demanded it and if a two-thirds majority of the Council of the West European Union agreed.

Economic revival ran alongside rearmament and was explicitly seen by the US as heading off any possibility of socialism. 'Europe would have been Communistic if it had not been for the Marshall Plan,' US Aid administrator Paul Hoffman declared in February 1950. Truman was warned that economic chaos in Western and Central Europe could lead to 'political revolution and Communistic infiltration'. When France was granted a $650 million credit in spring 1946 the aim, the Cabinet was told, was to combat ... Russian influence. This aid was stepped up in autumn 1947 when US leaders concluded that the Marshall Plan in 1948 would be too late unless stopgap aid was provided immediately. At the beginning of September, Truman declared to a group of congressmen at the White House: 'I do hope that we can reach some decisions on this and get things started ... We'll either have to provide a programme of interim aid relief until the Marshall programme gets going, or the governments of France and Italy will fall, Austria too, and for all practical purposes Europe will be Communist.' Truman was gripped with such forebodings throughout 1947 – writing in July of the British economic crisis of that year: 'The British have turned out to be our problem children now. They've decided to go bankrupt and if they do that, it will end our prosperity and probably all the world's too. Then Uncle Joe Stalin can have his way. Looks like he may get it anyway.' As late as 1949 *The Economist* warned, regarding France: 'Communism is in a weaker position than at any time since 1945, but it remains solidly entrenched in the working class. It can still profit by the antics of General de Gaulle. It can still exploit any resentment at the actions of the government. Above all, it waits like a tide ready to advance on any turn for the worse in the national economy.'

It was around these pillars of US economic and military power that politics in Western Europe was rebuilt. However, US influence did not stop at the borders of the European states or remain confined to their foreign or defence policy. On the contrary, the United States penetrated the entire fabric of Western European society decisively. It determined the way the post-war Western European political system was created and US interests were intertwined with it at every level. In many cases political parties had to be built almost from scratch.

As regards the parties of the right, the creation of stable political structures was more complicated than merely rebuilding the economy and creating military alliances. The right-wing parties, and in a number of countries the bulk of capital, was deeply compromised by collaboration with fascism and Nazi occupation. In the initial post-war period right-wing parties had to pretend they were on the left – or at least not of the right. The West German Christian Democrats, in their 1947 programme, stated that the 'capitalist economic system' had not served the interests of the German people, and called for 'a new order built right from the ground' based on 'an economic system of collective ownership'. Alcide de Gasperi defined the Italian Christian Democrats as 'a party of the centre moving towards the left'. The Belgian Social Christian Party proclaimed itself as 'an inter-class party, whose main objective was to achieve social and economic justice in a united, democratic Belgium'.

For their part the parties of the right, and the governments, of Western Europe had few illusions regarding their dependence on the United States. In 1947, Churchill declared: 'What is Europe now? A rubble heap, a charnel house, a breeding ground of pestilence and hate.' He went on to say in his pamphlet *Europe Unite*: 'Nothing stands between Europe today and complete subjugation to Communist tyranny but the atomic bomb in American possession.' Attlee, in March 1946, concluded: 'It may be that we shall have to consider the British Isles as an Eastern extension of a strategic area the centre of which is the American continent.' Some indeed were cynical about the situation – Pierre Mendès France declaring: 'Thank God for the Communists!

Just because we've got a "Communist danger", the Americans are going to make a tremendous effort to help us. We must keep up this indispensable Communist scare' (A. Werth, *De Gaulle*, 1965). But the United States could and did dictate the forms of the reorganisation of Europe. Supine support for US policy, both in Europe and internationally, was demanded and received; the long history of support for the United States over its military interventions in Iran, Guatamala, the Dominican Republic and a number of other countries is too well known to need repeating here.

However, while the Western European states were forced to defend the policies of the USA that country felt no such compunction in the opposite direction. On the contrary, one of the United States' objectives, as already seen, was to weaken the barriers presented by the European states to its goals. Originally, the European powers had hoped to hoodwink the United States after the Second World War and pursue the same blend of hypocrisy and duplicity as shown at Versailles. Churchill aimed to promise one thing to the Americans but in practice maintain the British Empire – thus when the Atlantic Charter was signed between Britain and the United States on 12 August 1941, it stated that the parties 'respect the right of all people to choose the form of government under which they live'. However, in September of the same year Churchill made clear that this did not apply to India, and at Yalta he insisted that 'the Atlantic Charter does not apply to the British Empire'. The French also attempted to hold on to their Indochinese and North African empires.

Nevertheless the overwhelming opposition to continued British rule in India left Britain no choice but to quit the Indian subcontinent. Secondly, the United States was not to be duped – it would leave Britain with no option of scaling down its European commitments in order to try to defend its empire. Paul Kennedy noted in *The Rise and Fall of the Great Powers* (1988): 'By 1954 ... French and American pressure compelled Eden to make a formal declaration that Britain would "continue to maintain on the mainland of Europe, including Germany", its present effective strength, which represented a hardening of its NATO commitment.' At the same time, the US Secretary of State, John Foster Dulles, declared: 'The United States cannot be expected to identify itself 100 per cent ... with ... the colonial powers.' Even where the United States was fighting on the same side as the Western European powers, for instance with the French in Indochina, it followed the same policy as during the Second World War – combining economic and military support with demands for economic and political concessions from its allies.

The example *par excellence* of US dominance was, of course, Suez. Laughably for a country which at that time held a vice-like grip on the Panama canal, the United States *de facto* aided Nasser to gain control over Suez – one need simply imagine what the US response would have been if the Panamanian government had attempted to nationalise the Central American canal! Britain and France undertook the Suez invasion to maintain what they saw as their vital interests – Britain to maintain domination over Suez and the Middle East, and France to maintain its position in Algeria.

The US crushing of Britain and France was direct and brutal. On 5 November 1956, British and French paratroops dropped on Port Said. Immediately, the pound plummeted on the New York exchange – the US government was selling sterling. As Macmillan recalled, this was at a level 'far above what was necessary to protect the value of its own holdings'. He goes on to say what occurred:

> I would not have been unduly concerned had we been able to obtain either the money to which we were entitled from the International Monetary Fund, or, better still, some aid by way of a temporary loan from the United States. The refusal of the second was understandable; the obstruction of the first is not so easy to forgive. We had a perfect right under the statutes to ask for the repayment of the British quota ... I telephoned urgently to New York, the matter was referred to Washington ... I received the reply that the American government would not agree to the technical procedure until we had agreed to the cease-fire. I regarded this then, and still do, as a breach of the spirit, and even of the letter of the system under which the Fund is supposed to operate. It was a form of pressure which seemed altogether unworthy. It contrasted strangely with the weak attitude of the Americans towards Egyptian funds and 'accounts' after the seizure of the Canal. (In A. Grosser, *The Western Alliance*, 1980)

Crushed by US economic pressure, on 3 December the British and French announced the withdrawal of their troops from Egypt.

While the USA refused to support the colonial adventures of the European powers they, however, were forced to support those of the United States. Supine support of the European powers for the United States continued up to Vietnam. Alfred Grosser comments:

> The firmest and most unconditional support [for the US over Vietnam] came from Germany, both from the government and the opposition. The communique [of December 1965] dealing with the conversations between Johnson and [Chancellor] Erhard left no doubt whatever. The President 'expressed his gratitude for the support of the Federal German Republic in the struggle to deter Communist aggression in South Vietnam.' The chancellor declared the resolve of his government to continue supporting the cause of freedom.' (ibid.)

The Italian government expressed its: 'understanding for the position and the responsibilities of the United States in Vietnam'. Equally disgusting was the grovelling of the Wilson government before the United States on Vietnam.

None of these governments had any illusions about the lack of support for US policy amongst the people of South Vietnam. They all knew that South Vietnam had been artificially created without any support from local people in order to shore up what the US perceived to be its global interests in the area. President Eisenhower had cynically admitted this in his memoirs *Mandate for Change*, published in 1963: 'I have never talked or corresponded with a person knowledgeable in Indochinese affairs who did not agree that had elections been held as of the time of the fighting [1954], possibly 80 per cent of the population would have voted for the Communist Ho Chi Minh as their leader.'

Within this overall framework of US domination, the United States had a clear project for Western Europe. The USA was aware from the beginning that a weak Balkanised Europe would be helpless – an economic burden to itself and vulnerable to socialist challenges. The United States therefore supported moves towards European unity. In 1947, the US Congress Select Committee on Foreign Aid proposed a European federation 'of which a democratic Germany will be an integral but not a dominating part'. In 1949, Senator Fulbright noted: 'For more than two years I have been urging our government to encourage, frankly and positively, the political unification of Europe.' Indeed without US support it would not have been possible for Western European states to take the steps leading to the creation of the EEC.

A fair indication of the real economic relations which existed in the post-war period was that European governments had to consult the United States over essential economic matters but not with each other. Thus when Britain devalued the pound in 1949 Washington was consulted but not Paris, Rome or Bonn. When Schuman launched his plan for the European Coal and Steel Community, in May 1950, Washington, and in this case Bonn, were informed in advance but not London. The United States was an observer at the Organisation of European Economic Cooperation (OEEC) which, in 1960, after the formation of the EEC, was extended to become the Organisation for Economic Coordination and Development (OECD). The European Payments Union was set up with American credits. No European economic integration would have been possible without the support of the United States.

Confronted with the USSR, European capital was favourable to such a project. In September 1946, six months after his 'Iron Curtain' speech at Fulton, Missouri, Churchill spoke at the University of Zurich saying: 'We must create a sort of United States of Europe.' In his memoirs Adenauer argued: 'In order to defend the tradition and the very survival of the European countries, primarily from the large Communist bloc of states which had emerged in the East, the creation of a united Europe was necessary as never before.' Adenauer further declared: 'The [West German] Christian Democratic Union has since its inception supported a European federation, guided by a profound conviction. We continue to regard its establishment as the only possibility to save the existence, the traditions and the prestige of Europe.' De Gaulle supported this project – with the proviso that France should be its leading member. Speaking in March 1948, he declared: 'Within the group of countries whose arteries will be the North Sea, the Rhine and the Mediterranean Sea, France will assume the duty and the honour of being its centre and its key.' He repeated, in February 1950, 'Europe will not be able to rebuild if it is not led by France.'

With US support the steps towards the EEC were evident. In May 1950, the French foreign minister, Robert Schuman, proposed that the coal and steel industries of France, West Germany and other Western European countries be placed under a common authority whose decisions would be binding on the participating states. A year later, France, West Germany, Italy, Belgium, the Netherlands and Luxembourg established the European Coal and Steel Community, whose practical operation commenced in January 1953. The USA gave strong support to these proposals for European economic integration. When the Schuman Plan was announced

> the idea of a united Europe enjoyed such popularity in Congress and in the American press that on a four-week trip through the United States, in 1952, Jean Monnet was received everywhere in triumph. A year later, in early June 1953, he returned to Washington as president of the High Authority of the Coal and Steel Community, accompanied by his two deputies, one of whom was the German, Franz Etzel, a circumstance which gave tangible expression both to European integration and Franco-German rapprochement. (A. Grosser, *The Western Alliance*)

The United States indicated its immediate support for the EEC and Euratom when they were formed in 1958. In November, an agreement was signed confirming US assistance, including the supply of prime materials and also equipment for atomic reactors.

Nevertheless, as always, the US promoted the economic reconstruction of Europe for *its own* purposes. John Pinder notes:

> The Americans supplied the aid and accepted the discrimination so that the Europeans should recover to the point where they could support [currency] convertibility and a general liberalisation of trade. The aim was abundantly fulfilled. By 1960 the dollar gap, as Europe's structural deficit was called, had disappeared. Between 1956 and 1962, the West Europeans gradually removed almost all their import quotas on dollar goods. By 1963, the European central banks were adapting their policies so as to provide informal assistance for the American balance of payments. Marshall Aid and temporary discrimination had indeed put the Europeans on their feet. (*Economic History of Europe*, 1976)

Within that European framework the United States understood that it was the relation between West Germany and France which was decisive. Britain was a useful ally but subordinate to this fundamental axis. US Secretary of State Dean Acheson had already written to the US ambassadors in Europe in October 1949, saying:

> The key to progress towards integration is in French hands. In my opinion France needs, in the interests of her own future, to take

the initiative promptly and decisively if the character of Western Germany is to be one permitting healthy development in Western Europe. Even with the closest possible relationships of the US and the UK to the continent, France and France alone can take the decisive leadership in integrating Western Germany into Western Europe. (A. Grosser, *The Western Alliance*)

This US understanding was parallel with the perception in Europe. The EEC was itself based on an alliance between West German industry and French agriculture. As Christopher Tugenhat put it, the EEC

gave the Federal Republic of Germany, cut off from its traditional markets in the East, continental-scale opportunities for its manufactured goods and France similar opportunities for its agriculture. Both countries were guaranteed protection against competition from the produce of the rest of the world by the introduction of the principle of 'Community Preference'. In the case of industrial goods the level of protection reflected the needs of the less efficient industries in the Community, many of which were in France, while in agriculture it was designed to safeguard the least efficient farmers so that when common prices were established their base point was the high German cereal price on which the prosperity of German agriculture had long been built. A balanced and symmetrical trade-off was thereby established which satisfied the basic economic interests of the two countries and enabled each to gain from the relative inefficiencies of the other. As the German refusal in 1985 to contemplate a significant reduction in cereal prices demonstrated, the consequences of the trade-off are still very much with us. (*Making Sense of Europe*, 1986)

While the process of integration strengthened Europe, it remained the case that the system imposed in Western Europe at the end of the Second World War left European governments subordinated in all essential aspects to the United States. It meant that no actions could be taken outside the framework acceptable to the United States – as Britain and France found out brutally at Suez. Secondly, it meant the United States in no sense acted on the basis of equality with its allies or took them into the process of decision-making on the most vital issues. As Grosser notes: 'When the United States landed troops in Lebanon in July 1958 ... units from American bases in Western Germany were used without the Chancellor's having been advised beforehand.' Adenauer's indignation explains in part his rapidly improved relations with de Gaulle. Again, the European allies were merely informed of the United States' decisions on the Cuban missile crisis, despite the fact that US actions directly threatened the Western European states with nuclear annihilation. When Nixon ordered a worldwide US military alert in 1973 over the Yom Kippur War, including US forces on European soil, he did not bother to consult his European allies.

West European subordination to the United States was based on three great pillars – the fact that since 1914 Western Europe had not been economically stable without the United States, the threatening strength of the Western European labour movement, and the fact of Western Europe's military inferiority to the USSR. Economic growth alone did not compensate for these basic realities.

Finally, it is necessary to realise that US dominance was not confined to the conservative and liberal parties – nor could it afford to be. The immediate post-war period saw a shift to the left in the political map of Europe. A crucial role in heading off the possibility of any socialist solution to the problems facing Europe was played by the right wing of the Socialist parties – and the United States Central Intelligence Agency played a decisive role in ensuring that they did so.

US influence on the labour movement had in fact already started immediately after the First World War. At that time, US economic might gave a semblance of reality to previously utopian plans put forward by Social Democratic parties. Thus Julius Braunthal said of the International Labour and Socialist Conference held in February 1919 to refound the Second International:

> The Berne conference had been called chiefly with the object of influencing the discussions of the Paris Peace Conference by putting forward a peace-programme from the International. The central item in this programme was the League of Nations. Long before President Wilson had placed it on the world agenda, the idea of a league of nations had been worked out in detail by Leonard Woolf in Fabian pamphlets published in 1915 and 1916, as well as his book *International Government*. The British Labour party propagated the idea as an essential point in its peace programme.

Kees van der Pijl notes that:

reformist socialists from 26 countries, several of them openly attacking the Bolsheviks, concurred in the opinion that the United States would be instrumental in establishing a stable world order ... The positive attitude of European socialists towards an enlightened capitalism holding out the promise of developing the productive forces would prove to be a recurrent phenomenon of the era of Atlantic integration. (*The Making of an Atlantic Ruling Class*, 1984)

The USA, for its part, was well aware of the leverage it gained in the European labour movement by its economic strength. Writing of the Berne conference, Wilson's confidant Colonel House noted that 'the entire conference showed an almost pathetic confidence in President Wilson. Speaker after speaker praised the President and insisted that the masses of Europe must stand behind him in his fight for the League of Nations.'

The declarations of the right-wing Socialist Party leaderships of this period were characterised by extreme hypocrisy. Endless theoretical declarations were made in favour of world government and the right of self-determination of nations. Yet their socialist authors approved the rapacious 'peace' treaties which served the interests of their imperialist governments. Thus the German SPD supported the Treaty of Brest Litovsk, which not only maintained German control of Poland but also seized large parts of Russia. The French and British socialist leaderships supported the Treaty of Versailles which directly added to Britain and France's colonial possessions. Indeed, the reality of the Versailles treaty revealed more clearly than anything else the hypocrisy both of Wilsonian declarations and the European Socialist parties. Whilst cynical, one cannot help but conclude that Trotsky's evaluation of the period was correct concerning the right wing of the Socialist groups:

The Social Democracy has been issued an assignment – to render political aid to American capitalism ... What are the Socialists throughout Europe doing? ... they are trying to instill in the working masses the religion of Americanism ... they are making a new political religion out of Americanism and out of the role of American capitalism in Europe. They are teaching or trying to teach the toiling masses that Europe cannot maintain herself without the pacifying role of American capitalism and its loans ... In other words, the European Social Democracy is becoming, before our very eyes, the political agency of American capitalism ... Is this development expected or unexpected? If we recall ... that the Social Democracy is the agency of the bourgeoisie, it will become clear that the Social Democracy, by the logic of its political degeneration, is bound to become the agency of the strongest and most powerful bourgeoisie, the bourgeoisie of bourgeoisies. This is the American bourgeoisie ... Yes, a great master has come to Europe, American capitalism. And it is natural that the Social Democracy should assume a position politically dependent on the master of its masters. (*Europe and America*, 1971)

The situation in Western Europe after the Second World War made the right wing of the Socialist parties lean even more directly on the United States, and at the same time it made them and the trade unions they controlled, even more vital for the United States. With the prestige of the Soviet Union increased after its overwhelming role in defeating Nazi Germany, and the local Communist parties playing a central role in the Resistance, Communist parties generally made great political gains. In the Netherlands the Communist vote reached 11 per cent, in Belgium 13 per cent, in Italy 31 per cent and in France 26 per cent. To counter this the United States, working through its CIA, intervened in the labour movement of Western Europe both directly and indirectly through dozens of foundations, charitable trusts, twenty periodicals and Forum World Features, a news service based in London which sold stories to 140 newspapers including *The Guardian* and *Sunday Times*. The United States used not only the indirect effects of its economic power but also direct instruments. By 1947, the American Federation of Labour (AFL) had endorsed German rearmament – a policy at that time vehemently opposed by the entire German labour movement.

In Britain, the USA set about organising its supporters in the Labour Party and trade union movement. In autumn 1947, *Socialist Commentary*, the organ of non-Communist German left exiles in Britain, welcomed Anthony Crosland, Alan Flanders – a former TUC official, and Rita Hinden, who had set up the Fabian Colonial Bureau, on to its editorial board. AFL organiser Jay Lovestone recruited agents from around *Socialist Commentary*. The journal became the mouthpiece of the right wing of the Labour Party and developed a close collaboration with the *New Leader* – an anti-Communist American magazine which from 1950 onwards was sponsored by the CIA. Flanders visited the United States to study the American labour movement and contributed articles to both publications. Dennis Healey became London correspondent for the *New Leader* in 1954.

When in 1960 the Labour Party Conference voted for unilateral nuclear disarmament and against two pro-NATO motions, Washington was appalled and a committee was immediately formed to reverse the decision. A large anonymous donation was received which was adequate to fund an office, full-time paid staff, travelling expenses, field workers, regular bulletins sent free throughout the labour movement and literally tons of literature. Within the year the decision was reversed. Twenty years later the politicians associated with this campaign split the Labour Party in order to form the SDP.

In continental Europe, the United States' intervention consisted not only of financing its supporters but of directly splitting the labour movement – with particular effect in France and Italy where there were strong Communist parties. In Italy, *Fortune* reported in 1949 that 'one of the brightest phenomena of the current political scene is the weekly meeting of Christian Democrat, moderate Socialist, and liberal Republican labour leaders in the office of ex-bricklayer Tom Lane, labour attaché of the US Embassy in Rome and chief of ECA's labour division'. The consequences were clear. The Italian trade union movement was split in September 1948 and June 1949. The US ambassador in Rome noted: 'We did not want the Communist Party to obtain control of the union movement ... so we did an excellent job with the support of the AFL and created both the CISL and the UIL.' This split was extended to the Socialist Party. In January 1947, Giuseppe Saragat walked out of the PSI, following a visit to Washington, to form what became the Italian Social Democratic Party (PSDI). He was immediately endorsed by the Socialist International.

In December 1947, Leon Jouhaux walked out of the united French trade union federation, the Confédération General du Travail (CGT), to found the CGT-Force Ouvrière (FO). FO received financial help from the French labour ministry, the TUC, and from the CIO and AFL. The treasurer of the AFL, David Dubinsky, came to Paris to promise a large grant. The Labour Party and TUC supported these splits fomented by the United States. They culminated in the split in the World Federation of Trade Unions (WFTU) in January 1949.

Right-wing leaders of the Socialist parties were entrusted with high office – a member of the Belgian Socialist Party, Paul-Henri Spaak, became Secretary-General of NATO in the 1950s. In turn, the relationship between the leaders of the Socialist parties and the USA became symbiotic. Jules Moch of the SFIO, and minister of the interior, declared: 'In the democracies the Socialist Party appears as the most solid rampart against communism, for it is virtually the only party that addresses itself to the same social layers.' *The Economist* considered that, 'The Socialists must defend these outposts of the Left, not only because they helped to create them but also because their ceaseless struggle to keep a footing in the working class and in the trade unions against the steady pressure of Communism will be compromised if the workers can be made to feel that the last of the gains of the Liberation have been wiped out.'

This policy was carried through internationally. Initially, the British Labour Party took the initiative in refounding the Socialist International. The provisional body emerging from this, COMISCO – the Committee of the International Socialist Conference – originally operated from Labour Party premises at Transport House in London. In particular the Socialist parties, and the revived Socialist International, strove to break any relation with the Communist parties and gave full support to the United States. While the British and Italian governments were collaborating with rehabilitating fascists, the PSI was expelled from the Socialist International in 1949 for forming an electoral bloc with the Communist Party. However, while any united activity with the Communist parties was rejected, cooperation with the right was perfectly acceptable. Thus the refounded Socialist International, re-established at Frankfurt in July 1951, declared in article 7: 'since the Bolshevik Revolution in Russia, Communism has divided the international workers' movement and thus delayed for decades the achievement of socialism in numerous countries'. But in Austria, for example, as has emerged concerning the 'Waldheim case', de-Nazification was the least of any country. This was largely due to the fact that the Socialist Party was in government with the right-wing People's Party. While fascists were rehabilitated Erwin Scharf was expelled from the Socialist Party in 1947 for advocating united action with the Communist Party.

While anti-Communism was rife, support for the United States amongst right wing 'socialists' was slavish. Bevin told members of the American Legion at a dinner at the Savoy Hotel:

My dear Americans, we may be short of dollars, but we are not short of will . . . We won't let you down . . . Standards of life may go back. We may have to say to our miners and to our steel workers:

'We can't give you all we hoped for. We can't give you the houses we want you to live in. We can't give amenities we desire to give you. But we won't fail.'

Bevin described the signing of the NATO Treaty as 'one of the greatest movements of all my life'.

During the 1950s even those Socialist parties which had initially held out were brought within the orbit of the United States' demands. Following the Bad Godesburg Congress, in 1959, the SPD affirmed its support for NATO. In 1962, Nenni, the leader of the Italian Socialists, for the first time supported NATO. Following the formation of Italian Centre-Left government, including the Socialists, the USA, in March 1964, granted Italy a credit of over $1 billion to deal with loss of foreign exchange reserves. Until 1959 the Dutch Labour Party participated in all government coalitions which included support for NATO. The Belgian Socialist Party participated frequently in coalition governments in the 1950s – although here there was significant opposition with 25 per cent of party delegates voting for withdrawal from NATO.

The policies pursued by the Socialist right wing were slavish in their subordination to the United States. The post-war Labour government was prepared to destroy its popularity, and finally its existence, through rearmament for the Korean War. It played a disgraceful role in supporting the right in the Greek Civil War. A series of ridiculous military pacts insisted on by the United States – CENTO and SEATO – were endorsed. The British Labour government at the United Nations even supported the American intervention in Santo Domingo, in April 1965. Britain undertook a level of overseas military spending far in excess of its ability to support – a major cause of its post-war economic crisis. Economic policies were pursued by the Labour government directly in contradiction to their own interests; the classic case being overvaluation of the pound which was insisted on by President Johnson as a first line of defence of the dollar. One even wonders whether Gaitskell would have been so forthright in his opposition to the invasion of Suez if it had not been opposed by the United States. Certainly his immediate response was one of total agreement with Eden.

This capitulation by the leadership of the Western European Socialist parties to the United States continued up to Vietnam. Indeed at the beginning of the Vietnam War various Social Democratic parties outdid even the right wing in their slavish attitude to US policy. For example, in March 1965, Axel Springer's *Bild Zeitung*, normally known for its virulent anti-Communism, published an editorial entitled, 'No, Sir', on the Vietnam War. It stated: 'We should tell Washington quite clearly that the Germans don't want to go to Vietnam ... As everywhere in the world, in Vietnam also the right to self-determination applies, even if free elections there should not turn out to be favourable to the Americans ... We cannot trample underfoot in other parts of the world the right that we demand for the Germans in the East, and must therefore stand aside from this "dirty war". Very far aside.' Two days later, Fritz Erler, deputy chief of the SPD, wrote to Axel Springer: 'I think it is terrible that ... the last bit of confidence in our nation by its ally is being destroyed [in this article].' In his answer Springer beat a retreat. The following month Erler and Willy Brandt flew to Washington to proclaim publicly their support for American policy. This was eight months earlier than the right-wing West German government to which they were in opposition.

In short, in the same way that Europe was divided between pro-Moscow East and pro-American West, so also its labour movement was divided between pro-Moscow Communist parties on one side and pro-American Socialist parties on the others. The domination of Western Europe by the United States, and the East by the Soviet Union, was complete at every level.

9

The Third Revolution

At the end of the Second World War the Soviet Union and its satellites were the only area of the world where the USA was unable to impose its new economic world order. Thus the predictions that political scientists had been making for nearly a century finally came to pass and the world was divided into two blocs, each based on a nation continental in size with vast natural resources and military power. These predictions that the world would one day be dominated by American and Russian spheres had first been made over fifty years before the Bolshevik revolution, but the shock to the US system when Lenin seized power ushered in the beginning of the long US obsession with the USSR. The Soviet revolution was an implicit challenge to a USA which, after a long period of internal debate, had finally decided to dominate the world with its 'Open Door' policy.

As the victorious allies gathered at Versailles in 1919 to share the spoils of victory, Herbert Hoover described the absent USSR as 'a spectre which wandered into the Peace Conference almost daily'. President Wilson was determined to overthrow Lenin's government but wanted to do so covertly, unlike Winston Churchill who argued for a 'ruthless armed assault' at a meeting on 14 February 1919. Initially, Wilson had some success and the communist government under Bela Kun in Hungary was rapidly overthrown when the USA destabilised the regime by delaying food and other vital supplies. The same tactics in Poland helped bring the right to power and Wilson then gave them finance and armaments with which to attack the USSR. But as the Bolsheviks stubbornly continued to survive Wilson eventually agreed to send US troops to join thirteen other nations, including Britain and Japan, which had already invaded the USSR.

Aided by massive domestic opposition from trade unionists in Britain and the USA, the Bolsheviks eventually defeated all foreign invaders including the United States, which had occupied Archangel. But although the Red Army defeated its opponents, much of the western lands of the old Russian Empire were lost to Poland and the newly created Baltic states.

What the USA had failed to do on the battlefield it now sought to achieve by diplomacy, as it refused to recognise the Soviet government and tried to persuade all the main powers to isolate the new republic. Not everyone in the USA agreed with the attempt to isolate the USSR. In 1925, there was a prophetic warning from Senator Borah of Idaho who said, 'So long as you have a hundred and fifty million people outlawed in a sense, it necessarily follows that you cannot have peace,' and he called for a rapprochement with the USSR as 'the key to a restored Europe, to a peaceful Europe'. Unfortunately, these views did not prevail and the fear that the Soviet revolution would be attractive to oppressed peoples around the world led the US State Department to veto any projects which might help the USSR develop its natural resources.

It was only when Roosevelt became President in 1933 that the USA finally recognised the government which had by then been ruling the USSR for over fifteen years. But the effect of Roosevelt on US–USSR relations, however, was more to do with style than substance and even in the face of the growing threat from Hitler, the USA rejected the Soviet proposal for an *entente* between the two nations. When Hitler finally invaded the USSR, future President Truman spoke for many in the USA when he said, 'If we see that Germany is winning we ought to help Russia, and if Russia is winning we ought to help Germany and that way let them kill as many as possible'.

Although some of the policy advisers around Roosevelt during the Second World War argued strongly for a political and economic deal to stabilise relations with the USSR, in the post-war world they remained in a minority. Roosevelt himself never resolved the issue and after his death Truman immediately took a hard line against the USSR. The new President first isolated and then removed anyone in the administration who did not support his hard-line anti-Soviet policy.

Roosevelt had originally expected that after the war the world would be 'policed' by Anglo-American forces for a 'transitional' period and that this would allow the USA to extend the 'Open Door' policy throughout the world. In the words of the British observer G. L.

Arnold, the USA expected a 'weakened and profoundly pacific Russia far behind the Western powers in the utilisation of atomic energy'. But as the war dragged on the massive Soviet effort ground down Nazi forces in Europe and completely dwarfed the Anglo-American contribution until the final year of the war. It was becoming obvious that the USSR could not be ignored in any post-war settlement.

Whilst the public face of the allies was one of unity, the struggle for supremacy in the post-war world was already under way. As was often to be the case, the US intelligence agencies were already pursuing a harder line and leading their political masters.

The origin of the US intelligence service is unusual. In 1929, Henry Stimson, the newly appointed Secretary of State under President Hoover, discovered that the US secret service had been breaking the codes of foreign countries including Britain and France as well as the USSR. Announcing that 'gentlemen do not read each other's mail', he closed the service down. The result of this policy was that when the USA began to prepare for the war against Germany, it had no real intelligence service other than the FBI which was restricted to activities in the western hemisphere. Once Roosevelt had decided to recreate an intelligence agency (in July 1940), he sent the strongly pro-British William J. Donovan to Britain's MI6. There Donovan arranged for advice, support and direct assistance in the form of training and officer exchanges. Thus the strongly anti-Bolshevik attitudes of MI5 and MI6 were infused into the Office of the Coordinator of Information (COI) and its successors, the Office of Strategic Services (OSS) and the Central Intelligence Agency (CIA).

Although they were fighting the Germans, the key personnel in Donovan's OSS never lost sight of the fact that they expected to be locked in a further struggle for supremacy with the USSR once Germany was defeated. In John Ranelagh's *The Agency – The Rise and Decline of the CIA* (1986), an internal OSS document prepared by the Foreign Nationalities Branch in August 1943 makes vivid reading: 'peace will not be long enduring until either our way of thought and life, or somebody else's, becomes general and controlling in the world ... we are a nation of nations peculiarly well-equipped for the undertaking'. Therefore, when it was proposed that the OSS should work with German communists to form an anti-Nazi underground the idea was vetoed by Arthur M. Schlesinger, junior, an OSS officer who was eventually to become a key adviser in the Kennedy administration.

It was the OSS who controlled the operation (code name Paperclip) which seized large numbers of German scientists in order to prevent them falling into Soviet hands. Many of these scientists were guilty of war crimes but this was ignored as long as the criminal concerned was prepared to be a good anti-communist.

By late 1944 Donovan decided that the Red Army should be penetrated by US intelligence but although this plan was vetoed by Roosevelt, Donovan went ahead on his own initiative with an extensive monitoring programme. Also in late 1944, Donovan had purchased 1,500 pages of Soviet codes from the Finnish intelligence service, but was ordered by Roosevelt to return them to the USSR without taking copies. He disobeyed orders and made a full set of copies which were brought into use as soon as death removed Roosevelt from the scene. Donovan had also decided by late 1944 to work with the former pro-Nazi intelligence service of Rumania against the local communist party in order to try to prevent Stalin establishing a ring of pro-Soviet buffer states between the USSR and the West after the war was over.

Stalin's desire to secure his borders with a ring of satellite states is more understandable in the light of the knowledge that the head of the OSS operation in Switzerland, Allen Dulles, was in constant contact with the Nazi army leadership, and even the German SS, about a possible deal which would allow the removal of Hitler and the conclusion of a peace treaty before the Red Army advanced too far into central Europe. One of Dulles' officers wrote that when Dulles heard of the failure of the July 1944 bomb plot against Hitler, he warned that 'American policy had suffered a terrible defeat' and that 'the continuation of the war would provide the Russians with a pathway to the Elbe in the heart of Europe'. Dulles' willingness to work with the Nazis to prepare the ground for a post-war conflict with the USSR proved no bar to promotion and he was appointed Director of the CIA as soon as Eisenhower assumed the presidency.

Donovan's obsession with the USSR lead him to propose, at the beginning of 1945, the creation of an all powerful central intelligence agency which would lead the post-war struggle against the USSR. The plan was sunk when Roosevelt ordered that it be leaked to the press who immediately characterised it as a 'Super Gestapo'.

Within weeks of this conflict between the President and his spymaster, however, Roosevelt was dead and any lingering ambivalence towards the USSR within the administration was immediately resolved. Had there been a chance of a post-war understanding between the USSR and a Roosevelt-led USA, the Soviets were left in no doubt that this would not be the policy followed by Truman. Truman's immediate objective was to reverse the October 1944 agreement reached between Churchill and Stalin on the respective 'spheres of influence' in the Balkans and Eastern Europe.

On 23 April 1945, the new President had his first meeting with Molotov at which the main issue was the future of Poland. The USSR was determined that the new Polish government would be pro-Soviet whilst Truman wanted Poland and the rest of Eastern Europe to be open to US influence and capital in the classic fashion of the 'Open Door' policy. Truman's attitude and the flavour of the meeting can be captured from his *Memoirs* (1955). In the pre-meeting with his advisers Truman concluded: 'It was now obvious that our agreements with the Soviet Union had so far been a one-way street and that this could not continue ... we intended to go on with the plans for [the establishment of the United Nations] and if the Russians did not wish to join us [they could go to hell].' When the main meeting finally began Truman ensured that Molotov would be under no illusions that the USA now intended to take a tougher line:

> there was little protocol and ... I went straight to the point. I was sorry to learn that no progress had been made in solving the Polish problem ... I told Molotov that the United States was determined ... to go ahead with plans for the world organisation, no matter what difficulties or differences might arise with regard to other matters.

Even though the war was still in progress, Truman crudely hinted that unless the Soviets cooperated with US plans for Poland the United States might cut off its aid to the USSR: 'I pointed out ... legislative appropriations were required for any economic measures in the foreign field, and I had no hope of getting such measures through Congress unless there was public support for them.'

Molotov explained that the Soviets felt they were carrying out the agreed policy on Poland but Truman did not agree: 'I replied sharply that an agreement had been reached on Poland and that there was only one thing to do, and that was for Marshal Stalin to carry out that agreement in accordance with his word.' Molotov replied that he did not understand why the agreement which had been reached on the composition of the Yugoslav government could not apply to Poland as well. Truman responded:

> Replying sharply again, I said that an agreement had been reached on Poland and that it only required to be carried out by the Soviet government ... I expressed once more the desire of the United States for friendship with Russia, but I wanted it clearly understood that this could be only on a basis of the mutual observation of agreements and not on the basis of a one-way street. 'I have never been talked to like that in my life,' Molotov said.
>
> I told him, 'Carry out your agreements and you won't get talked to like that.'

It takes little imagination to realise the impact that first vital meeting between the USSR and the new US President must have had on Soviet thinking and strategy. Certainly, the hawkish Senator Vandenberg had no doubts. After the meeting with Molotov he wrote in his diary, 'FDR's appeasement of Russia is over.'

The new President's attitude gave Donovan the green light to make the opening moves in the cold war. That April Donovan issued a directive to change the intelligence targets in the Balkans from German to Soviet. Within weeks he had recruited General Reinhard Gehlen, the head of German army intelligence for Eastern Europe and the Soviet Union, so that the USA could use the former Nazi spy network inside the USSR. There now began a ruthless battle for advantage inside defeated Germany with agents of both sides kidnapping and murdering in order to collect the greatest number of German scientists and technicians. There were bitter struggles within German political parties, unions and professional associations as both sides fought for positions of advantage even before the victory celebrations had finished.

The policies of the Truman adminstration left the USSR with the simple choice either to acquiesce in the policy of the 'Open Door' or to face increasing US hostility at a time when the economic and nuclear predominance of the USA was so massive that US strategists could fantasise that the USSR might disintegrate under the pressure of trying to match US military power.

The tremendous inequality between the wealth of the USSR and the USA had led Stalin to apply for a loan of $6 billion as early as 1944, so that the USSR could begin to plan the reconstruction of its economy. But the violently anti-communist Averell Harriman delayed action on the loan for so long that Truman was in the Oval Office before a decision was finally taken. Truman agreed with Harriman's proposal that the USSR should be told that 'our willingness to co-operate wholeheartedly with them in their vast reconstruction problems will depend upon their behaviour in international matters'. Harriman advised that the credit should be handed out 'piecemeal, demanding in return concessions on the political field'.

By the time that Stalin arrived at Potsdam in July 1945, he had only two ways to finance the reconstruction of the USSR. First, by a large US loan or failing that reparations for war damage from Germany. Newly appointed Secretary of State James F. Byrnes made it clear to Stalin that a loan to the USSR was out of the question, and furthermore that the USA had no intentions of giving any loan to Germany that could be used to pay for reparations to the USSR. On 23 July Byrnes told Molotov that 'each country [should take] reparations from its own [German] zone'. Stalin resisted this solution for a week before reluctantly accepting it with the pointed observation that it was 'the opposite of liberal'.

It seems that Truman and his advisers believed that US control of the atom bomb plus the vast devastation of the USSR would eventually force Stalin back to the negotiating table prepared to accept help on 'Open Door' terms. If so, it was a disastrous miscalculation that locked the world into forty years of cold war, the appalling waste of the arms race and 20 million deaths in surrogate wars as the superpowers battled for control of the Third World.

But although the victorious 'allies' were meeting at Potsdam the war in the east was not over. The USSR had promised to attack Japan within three months of the end of the war against Germany and the prospect of the USSR gaining control of part of Japan, as it had done in Germany, filled Truman with alarm. At a meeting with his advisers on 23 July, Truman decided to keep the USSR out of Japan by using the atom bomb sooner than planned in order to end the war before the Soviet attack began. It was also believed that the use of the weapon would be a sober warning to the USSR that they too could be a target. The lie that the bomb was dropped to save allied lives in the forthcoming invasion of Japan overlooked the fact that the US invasion of the island of Kyushu was not due until the autumn. By this time, the USA would have had a small stockpile of atom bombs, one of which could have been used on an uninhabited island to demonstrate to the Japanese government the futility of continued resistance.

The view that Stalin could be brought to accept the US plans for the post-war world by a continuing hard line was not shared throughout the administration. Secretary of War Stimson believed that the USA 'was on the wrong path' in its relations with the USSR and tried to persuade Byrnes, without success, to cooperate with the USSR. On 11 September, he wrote to Truman that the attempt to force the pace of change in Russian policy 'would be so resented that it would make the objective we have in view less probable'. He warned that US policy would force the USSR to develop its own atom bomb in 'a secret armament race'.

The *New York Times* joined in on 25 September with a warning: 'France, Britain, and the United States, in seeking to absorb eastern Europe into a unified continental system, are aiming to weaken the Eastern bloc, and at the same time they are being forced with varying degrees of reluctance into the formation of that very Western bloc that Russia dreads.' Unfortunately, the seeming relative weakness of the Soviet position allowed Truman to ignore these warnings. He was more impressed with the Soviet decisions, under pressure from the USA, to withdraw from Iran and drop its proposals to modify Western control of the Bosphorus Straits. The one area where the USSR was not prepared to withdraw, however, was from the Eastern European buffer zone that it saw as a vital line of defence for the western Soviet Union.

The position rapidly deteriorated and on 5 January 1946 Truman declared that the Third World War was inevitable unless Russia was 'faced with an iron fist and strong language.' On 9 February, Stalin replied with a speech which implied that wars between capitalist and communist countries were unavoidable. On 5 March, Churchill delivered his famous 'iron curtain' speech in Fulton, Missouri, whilst Truman led the applause from the platform. On 3 May General Lucius Clay announced that the USA was unilaterally ending reparations to the USSR from the Western occupied zones of Germany. Within the year the CIA and MI6 were parachuting armed guerrillas into Albania to try to overthrow the communist government and, with even greater disregard for the dangers of a 'hot' war, were sending agents into the USSR itself to run the 'Ukrainian resistance movement' which was engaged in a guerrilla war against the Red Army. In terms of international law this was an act of war against the USSR.

Thus began the public phase of the struggle for supremacy with the USSR. The struggle which some US administration officials had been preparing for since 1943 was finally under way. The creation of NATO, then the Warsaw Pact, the brutalities of Stalin in both Eastern Europe and the USSR, the development of the H-bomb, the Berlin blockade, the missile race, 'Star Wars', the string of surrogate wars from Greece, through Korea, Laos, Vietnam, Zaire, Angola, the Arab–Israeli wars and Afghanistan and Nicaragua which still continue to this day, the vicious internal 'dirty wars' in Chile and Argentina, the overthrow of democracies in Brazil and Guatemala – the history of the cold war has been too well documented elsewhere to need repeating here.

The tremendous economic imbalance between the USSR and the USA meant that instead of the popular perception of a world dominated by two superpowers, the reality was of a world dominated by a superpower and a half, or at best two-thirds. However, contrary to US expectations the USSR was eventually able to match the USA as a military equal. But as the Soviet economy never reached half the size of its US rival it had to spend twice the proportion of its GNP on its defence budget. At a terrible cost to the comforts its people had a right to expect, and with the consequence of a grossly uneven development of its economy, the USSR eventually achieved a rough military parity with the United States in the late 1960s.

All through the 1950s and 1960s the general public were fed a diet of cold war rhetoric whilst governments in the West urged themselves towards ever more destructive and expensive weapons systems. Yet the reality was that the balance of nuclear power between the USA and the USSR was so massively in favour of the USA that there was never any real prospect of an attack by the Soviets. For them to have done so would have been suicidal. In the 1950s the nuclear imbalance between the two superpowers was between a ratio of ten to one and a hundred to one in favour of the USA. Even when the USSR exploded its first atom bomb this did not substantially alter matters. After conducting a full study lasting seven months John Ranelagh says that the CIA concluded that the USSR was unlikely to start a war. 'There would appear to be no firm basis for an assumption that the USSR presently intends deliberately to use military force to attain a Communist world or further to expand Soviet territory if this involves war with a potentially stronger US.' Such assessments were, of course, withheld from the American people.

Even when the USSR had the bomb they still lacked a means to deliver it to the US mainland. Although empire-building, air force Generals like Curtis LeMay were demanding an expanded air force to 'match the Reds 1,000 bombers', the CIA knew from its U2 spy flights that even as late as 1957 the USSR possessed only ninety to 150 strategic bombers. Despite the fact that military planners knew that there was no need for a further arms build-up, the US economy became hooked on 'military Keynesianism'. The growing power of the 'military–industrial complex' that Eisenhower warned of in his last presidential message to Congress drowned out the small number of voices raised in opposition to the arms race. The scare campaigns, alleging first a wholly fictitious 'bomber gap' and then an equally fictitious 'missile gap', were successful and vast extra resources were poured into building an ever greater US military predominance which the USSR then struggled to reduce.

By the 1970s when the superpowers were finally in balance and the USA was still reeling from its defeat in Vietnam, there was a chance of building on the first stumbling steps towards disarmament which began with the *détente* of the Nixon–Brezhnev talks. Instead, this was thrown away by the brutal stupidities of first Brezhnev and then Reagan who both saw a chance for their own nation to establish an 'edge' over the other. It was only after the death of Brezhnev in 1982 and the succession of Yuri Andropov that the USSR had a leader with a real understanding of what the arms race was doing to the Soviet economy.

Because of the massive cultural and historical differences between the USSR and the multiparty systems of the West, the attempts of Western politicians and journalists to understand how struggle and change takes place inside the USSR are usually woefully inadequate and wide of the mark. Instead of the simplistic characterisation of Khrushchev and Gorbachev as progressive reformers separated by twenty years of the unimaginative conservatism of Brezhnev, Andropov and Chernenko, the reality is much more complex and subtle. The impact of *glasnost* in opening the Soviet media to many academics and intellectuals, who have felt it wiser to be silent in the past, means that for the first time it is possible for us to get a better understanding of the often contradictory forces at work inside the USSR.

Many different interest groups form alliances and compete for influence and power inside the Soviet state and its bureaucracy. Therefore, instead of seeing Soviet history as the rise and fall of individual leaders, we need to look behind the Khrushchevs and Brezhnevs to see which groups inside the bureaucracy were rising in influence and which particular individuals were associated with them. Soviet interest groups operate in much the same way as in a Western democracy except that in the past the absence of contested elections dramatically slowed down the rate of change. Bureaucracies are seldom prepared to be quite as ruthless in retiring their members at a fixed point in time as angry voters are prepared to be (except, of course, when the bureaucracy is controlled by a mass murderer such as Stalin).

In the early 1920s, the USSR was a very lively and dynamic society with organised minority factions inside the Communist Party and tolerated opposition groups outside it. Stalin often changed his policies and alliances as factions rose or fell in influence and different sets of policies and *apparatchiks* came and went. Often he slaughtered entire factions once he had broken with them, but that in itself is evidence of the strength of those groups within the factional system of the USSR.

Once Stalin died, the factions and interest groups became more obvious to the outside world as the individuals at the head of the weaker groups, first Beria and then Molotov, Kaganovich, Bulganin and Malenkov, were swept aside by the alliance led by Khrushchev. Although this was seen as a reforming alliance, in actual fact the reformists were a small minority within the governing coalition. There were many reforms such as an end to the use of terror, murder, Stalin's 'cult of personality', plus the introduction of greater artistic and individual freedoms. But the main faction in the coalition behind Khrushchev was made up of the younger, more technocratic and respectable *apparatchiks* who wished to replace the discredited old guard of Stalin's time. Unlike Khrushchev, they were more concerned with reforming the economy which was already coming to the end of its spectacular period of post-war growth, and they also disliked the unpredictable nature of Khrushchev's personality. Khrushchev's lack of priority for economic issues had undoubtedly contributed to the many disturbances when workers protested against price rises, as in 1962 at Novocherkassk. Thus Khrushchev failed to build the support he needed amongst ordinary workers and when he continued to pursue his reform programme against the wishes of the newly appointed bureaucrats, he suddenly discovered how small the genuine reform faction was and he was replaced by Brezhnev and Kosygin.

Brezhnev and Kosygin sought to modernise the economy by developing the influence and numbers of 'technocrats and managers', a position guaranteed to please most factions inside the bureaucracy. They were also able to buy peace amongst workers because rising prices on the world markets (particularly for oil and gold) allowed them to increase real wages dramatically. Thus the problems arising from the increasing stagnation of the Soviet economy could be hidden for a while, although there were alarming signs of overheating as the regime allowed excessive money growth to flood into circulation. In the meantime, attention focused on the dramatic moves towards *détente* which were possible because the weakness of the US economy in the aftermath of the Vietnam War and domestic pressure forced Nixon to the negotiating table in order to reduce US arms spending.

By the late 1970s, however, the problems were mounting for Brezhnev's USSR. Instead of building on the moves towards arms reduction Brezhnev saw the chance to steal a march on the West and continued the Soviet arms build-up, often substituting quantity for high technology quality, and worsening the debilitating impact of high arms spending on the economy. The economic reforms had been ended because of the conflicts between the managers and the party *apparatchiks* and the economy was completely stagnant. Finally, the fatal decision to invade Afghanistan and the intolerable pressure on the Polish government to crush the Solidarity movement led to the international isolation of Brezhnev.

It was against this background that Yuri Andropov, the head of the KGB, began to assemble a coalition of 'healthy forces'. This included the brighter elements in the military who realised the terrible dangers posed to the defence of the USSR as it slipped ever further behind the USA in high technology. They realised that a strong military can only be built on a strong economy. Other factions wished to reform the ossifying Soviet institutions and finally there were those who simply felt that Brezhnev's placemen had been in office too long and it was now their 'turn'. Outside the bureaucracy there was growing dissatisfaction amongst ordinary workers whose standard of living was no longer on the rise and in many instances was beginning to decline. Finally, there were the first stirrings of a left-wing opposition amongst dissidents and intellectuals who wished to democratise Soviet society. They produced and featured in *samizdat* magazines such as *Alternatives*, *Searches* and *Left Turn*. The most influential journal, however, was produced by Abel Aganbegyan and Tatiana Zaslavskaya, two economists in the research institute at Novosibirsk in Siberia.

It may seem remarkable to us in Britain that the person who pulled together the coalition of 'healthy forces' was the head of the feared KGB. But who was better placed in the whole of the USSR to know the full extent of the crisis facing Soviet society than the Soviet spymaster? Simply because Britain's spymasters have such a dreadful track record of blinkered and reactionary attitudes (and often seem none too bright) does not mean to say that this is the reality in other countries. Who else in the USSR had all the vital facts about the real state of the economy passing over his desk? Who else had enough accurate data from Soviet spies abroad to make an accurate assessment about the growing technology gap between the USSR and the US? Certainly not the sycophants and bribe-takers with whom Brezhnev had surrounded himself.

The detailed statistics and analyses which crossed Andropov's desk made devastating reading. Although the USSR still had vast resources of mineral wealth and a quarter of the total number of scientists in the world, much of the mineral wealth was being extracted in the most wasteful and environmentally damaging ways, and the deadening effect of the Soviet bureaucracy was equally wasteful of the scientific resources. The slow down of growth in the economy had reached the point by the early 1980s where there was actually a reduction in production in 40 per cent of the industrial sectors of the economy. In advanced computer related technology the USSR was at least seven years behind the USA and possibly as much as twelve years. The USSR was producing only 10 per cent as many computers as in the USA. The USSR was using 1,490 kilos of coal and 135 of steel to produce just $1,000 worth of GDP in 1979–80 compared with figures of 565 kilos of coal and 52 kilos of steel to produce the same $1,000 worth of GDP in West Germany. There was an inability to introduce new products and processes rapidly into Soviet industry. The most notorious example arose from the Soviet discovery, in 1955, of how to cast steel continuously. By the death of Brezhnev in 1982, 79 per cent of Japanese steel was continuously cast, as was 62 per cent of West Germany's, but the USSR had only reached the figure of 12 per cent! Whereas in the USA 66 per cent of new patents are in production within two years, the USSR only achieves a 23 per cent rate. The end result of these figures is that the pattern of exports from the USSR to the West is almost identical to that of an underdeveloped Third World country, mainly energy and raw materials.

In farming the position was worse. The USSR has more farmers than in all the major industrial nations combined, yet it produces only 22 per cent as much farm output as in the West. The average Soviet farmer is only one-tenth as productive as his US equivalent. Only 20 per cent of the roads in the countryside are paved and a third of vegetables rot before they reach the market. Although one-third of Soviet investment goes into farming, it is often wasted as central planners who take the decisions about what and when to sow are often unaware of local conditions and agricultural machinery needs. Yet for all the problems spelt out, above 25 per cent of farm produce comes from the private sector even though it only has 3 per cent of the available farmland.

The central planning of prices for half a million separate goods had caused appalling distortions within the economy with some prices remaining unchanged for twenty years or more. The fact that 15 per cent of the entire state budget was consumed by food subsidies produced the nonsense that it was often cheaper for farmers to feed their livestock bread than buy animal feed.

For two-thirds of the population the standard of living had begun to fall. The USSR moved from having one of the best health records in the world in the early 1960s, with a life expectancy of seventy years (equivalent to Japan), to one of the worst, with life expectancy declining by two years whilst most other developed nations saw an increase of three or four years over the same period. Spending on education had fallen from 10 per cent of GNP in the 1950s to 7 per cent, whilst over the same period the USA had increased education spending from 4 to 11 per cent of GNP.

Although these figures were a shattering indictment of the Brezhnev years there was still a bitter struggle for the succession when Brezhnev finally died. A closely fought contest between Andropov, who promised reform, and Chernenko, who offered 'Brezhnevism without Brezhnev', was narrowly won by Andropov's faction who had the backing of the armed forces. Although the reform coalition had won, the conservatives were still strong enough to block most of Andropov's policy reforms and elect Chernenko in his place when Andropov died two years later in 1984. But Andropov had made a start. Some dissidents were released from prison. New men such as Gorbachev were promoted and the drive against corruption began to remove many of the older *apparatchiks*.

Even in the brief reign of Chernenko, the economy continued to deteriorate visibly and in doing so demonstrated that the case for reform was overwhelming. When Chernenko died in 1985, Gorbachev, the 'reform' candidate, was able to defeat the conservative's choice, Grigory Romanov. But it still took Gorbachev his first year to reduce the size of the old Brezhnev faction and secure a working majority of his supporters in the Politburo, Central Committee and Council of Ministers.

The initial reform proposals of the Andropov and early Gorbachev period seem quite tame in retrospect, and it is clear that the reform coalition had no idea just how far it would have to go in order to turn Soviet society around. The radical reformer, Boris Kagarlitsky, characterised the initial package as 'an expansion of enterprise autonomy while maintaining the system of centralised planning … a small private sector, mixed international enterprises in some branches of the economy and the regulation of the administrative and legal systems'. Virtually anyone who was not an old Brezhnevite could support such a programme.

Such a limited package had no chance of correcting the deep-rooted problems of Soviet society. It was when the Chernobyl nuclear reactor disaster in the summer of 1986 brought home the need for more rapid reform that Gorbachev seized on the tragedy to increase the pace of change, and within months the terms *glasnost* and *perestroika* were in use around the world. People in all walks of life woke up to the fact that something momentous was under way in what had only recently seemed one of the most reactionary and bureaucratic of societies. From around the world academics and journalists rushed forward to poke and prod at this interesting new phenomenon.

The old classic image of the locust-like American tourists who descended every summer determined to 'do' Europe in two weeks was now under serious challenge by an equally determined horde of journalists and political scientists who arrived in the Soviet Union determined to 'do' *perestroika* in seven days. Eager to pronounce their predetermined 'definitive' verdicts on the exact extent to which Mikhail Gorbachev would be reintroducing capitalism into the USSR or to what extent the Reagan–Thatcher axis could legitimately claim to have 'won' the cold war, these worthy pundits swarmed all over the USSR. Usually, they were still in complete ignorance of the really dramatic changes taking place at the grass roots of Soviet society when they scuttled back on to their planes to zip off to give us the benefit of their opinions on the upheavals taking place elsewhere in the world.

In contrast to the media's travelling *perestroika* show, what I found striking when I visited the Soviet Union in August 1988 was not the views of the academics or the Central Committee members but the hope and confidence of ordinary citizens. Perhaps the contrast was the more stark because I was coming from Thatcher's Britain where, as the *British Medical Journal* reported, the suicide rate has doubled in the month immediately following each Thatcher election victory. But irrespective of where you are coming from, nothing can prepare you for the sense of confidence and enthusiasm for the future that you find in almost every conversation you have with an ordinary Soviet citizen.

Inevitably, the shock to the Soviet system that has been delivered by the Gorbachev reformers has caused a ferment in which many reactionary attitudes are given free rein, but they are dwarfed by the vast bulk of optimistic and progressive ideas that are being experimented with. As I travelled from factory to farm and talked to everyone from Central Committee members to the prostitutes who work the hotel bars, I was left in no doubt that the changes taking place inside the Soviet Union have absolutely nothing to do with reintroducing capitalism. Quite the reverse is the case. The Soviet reformers are trying to find their way to achieve the irreversible intertwining of socialism and democracy which is also the elusive holy grail of Western socialists.

If this sounds too wildly optimistic it is not meant to be for the reformers still face formidable obstacles. In the first place, the *perestroika* movement is split into two quite distinct camps (it is the failure to understand this which has led so many Western observers to talk so inaccurately about the reintroduction of capitalism). There are those like Nikolai Shmelev and the technocrats Lisichkin and Popov whose arguments are similar to those of Thatcher that the economy can be reformed by the creation of a pool of unemployment which will act as a spur to increase productivity. They argue that Soviet society must be led by an élite and that the welfare state is a 'survival of feudalism'.

The other faction inside the *perestroika* movement is that of the democratisers. Typified by the economists Aganbegyan and Zaslavskaya, this faction believes that the economy can only be modernised by democratising Soviet society from the grass roots upwards. Most important of all, they see the way to improve the economic performance of the USSR is by introducing democratic rights at work so that the workers elect their managers. At every stage Gorbachev has thrown his weight behind the democratisers and against the élitists. As he wrote in his book *Perestroika* (1987): 'There was an opinion ... that we ought to give up planned economy and sanction unemployment. We cannot permit this ... since we aim to strengthen socialism, not replace it with a different system ... Furthermore, a work collective must have the right to elect its manager.'

There is no doubt that at some point in the future the élitist technocrats will break with the democratisers and link up with the conservative bureaucrats and the remains of the old Brezhnev machine to try to curtail the democratic reforms which they see as undermining their rights to manage.

At that stage Gorbachev's survival will depend on two factors. First will be whether or not the conservatives can do what has so far eluded them and find an alternative package of policies which is more than just a return to the past. The second factor will be how effectively Gorbachev has been able to assemble a coalition between two vital social groups. The first of these is the workers with the highest skills plus the scientific, artistic and technical intelligentsia who have the most to gain from the modernisation of Soviet society. Equally vital is the second group, the ordinary workers and peasants who face major upheavals and dislocation from that process of modernisation.

So far the reformers around Gorbachev such as Aganbegyan have stressed that as the economy is modernised the workers must be protected from cuts in their standard of living. That is why he emphasises the strengthening of social provision such as housing, health and education. He has also spelt out the intention to keep rents low and to ensure that when price reform comes there must be compensation to protect living standards. He argues that there must be increased investment in new technology but makes the following innovative condition:

> The distinctive feature of this reform is industrial democracy moving towards self-management ... this will involve [workers] in determining the enterprise plan, the allocation of resources and the election of managers. It is a revolutionary programme. There will be much opposition, especially from management ... This can only be overcome because the ... driving force is political openness and democratization.

It is not only academic economists who talk like this. I was struck by the enthusiasm and pleasure with which Vadim Zagladin, the Head of the International Department of the Central Committee, described how a Siberian shoe factory, which had been facing closure, had been taken over by the workers. The products of the factory were notorious for falling apart within days of purchase but the Central Committee had agreed to give the workers a last chance to improve their shoes before closure. Once the workers took control their first act was to sack the incompetent managers. They then turned the business into a dramatic success within two years. Now the factory is expanding and their shoes are in demand all over the USSR. Even more innovative is the workers' proposal to begin to issue 'shares' in the factory – not to investors but to their customers who would then be in a position to exercise real consumer power.

The excitement with which progressive Central Committee members like Zagladin recount each successful experiment in workers' democracy is an indication of just how much is riding on the hopes of the reformers that democracy from below will be the key to the modernisation of the Soviet economy. If they fail the conservatives will be waiting in the wings to try the 'spur' of unemployment.

There is no doubt that such a challenge to Gorbachev and the democratisers will come. There will be many opportunities as reforms begin to take effect in the more difficult and sensitive areas. Aganbegyan expects that it will take twenty to thirty years to achieve the full modernisation of the economy, and it is in the first few years of that period that the conservatives will have many opportunities to stir up trouble. To start with over 16 million jobs will be lost as factories are modernised. Then there is the fact that the lack of high quality consumer goods for purchase means that over 160 billion roubles are sitting in ordinary savings accounts – this is the equivalent of 45 per cent of one year's GNP and there is a real danger of hyperinflation when price controls are removed or there are more goods available to buy. The reform of the six agricultural ministries into the superministry Gosagroprom does not seem to have had the desired effect, although half the bureaucrats in the old ministries saw their jobs disappear. Industrial plant is ageing fast after years of underinvestment caused by the top priority given to the needs of the arms programme. By 1985 over 20 per cent of metalworking machinery was over twenty years old – a worsening of the position since 1980 when the figure was 16 per cent. There is also a chronic shortage of people with the necessary skills to organise an increase in foreign trade such as publicity, financial advice and after sales service.

As well as these formidable problems, there is no doubt that the liberation of Soviet society that has been brought about by *glasnost* has opened the way for reactionary and in some cases even anti-Semitic views to be openly espoused. In many instances, people remain confused about the opportunities *perestroika* offers. One party official I met, who was in charge of a computer plant, told me enthusiastically that under *perestroika* surplus labour in his plant would be found work elsewhere and part of the money saved would be used to increase the wages of the workers remaining. 'With increased wages for the men, women will not need to work and they will be able to stay at home and raise their children. Then perhaps there will be less juvenile crime and drugtaking,' he optimistically assured me! Nor was this an isolated attitude. Much the weakest section of Gorbachev's book is the section devoted to women. Although the Soviet leader wrote of the need to 'promote more women to administrative posts' and of the establishment of 'women's councils throughout the country', he also drew attention to the problem of children's behaviour and morals arising from the fact that

> women no longer have enough time to perform their everyday duties at home ... This is a paradoxical result of our sincere and politically justified desire to make women equal with men in everything ... That is why we are now holding heated debates ... about the question of what we should do to make it possible for women to return to their purely womanly mission.

I should imagine the debates are very heated indeed as women point out the flaws in the reactionary ideology of biological determinism. Still, given the track record of Britain's Labour governments and the poor record of the present leadership on women's issues, we are hardly in the position to cast the first stone.

However, ignoring these occasional lapses, the USSR is still an exhilarating place to visit. The radical new ideas and questioning of past practices is forging a new moral leadership for the world, and the contrast with the stale and cautious ideology of Bush, Thatcher and Kohl is painful to behold.

I cannot avoid comparing the officials that I met who had genuinely integrated environmental concerns into their thinking about policy and administration with politicians in the West who have suddenly jumped on the ecological bandwagon. The contrast between Thatcher adding a few references to the ozone layer to her speeches, whilst continuing to defend policies that destroy it, and the way in which every Soviet official I met raised the issue of the need for cooperation across Europe, to reverse the environmental damage of the industrial age, was refreshing.

The contrast between Gorbachev's insistence that education should foster 'initiative and independence in secondary and higher school' with the dulling imposition of centralised controls by Kenneth Baker here in Britain is remarkable. That we should be adopting a Thatcherised form of Stalinist central control in our schools instead of learning from the USSR's rejection of such methods is both intellectually depressing as well as damaging for the educational prospects of our children.

The government could also learn from Gorbachev's understanding that 'Every national culture is a treasure which cannot be lost' and change the arrogant and dismissive way in which it deals with the aspirations of the Scottish nation.

But even if we cannot tempt Mrs Thatcher to introduce a spot of *glasnost* into Britain, surely it should be possible for the left to mobilise public opinion in this country to force her to drop her obstructive response to Gorbachev's disarmament proposals? Why do we not adopt the same policy as the USSR and give a commitment never to be the first to use nuclear weapons? Instead, we remain locked into the NATO strategy of 'first use' of nuclear weapons even though the presence of 200 nuclear reactors in Europe, to say nothing of the vast number of chemical works, would mean that such a strategy would turn the whole continent into a poisoned wasteland. Why do we not respond positively to Gorbachev's ideas of changing all armed forces to an 'exclusively defensive character'?

For as far back as I can remember, I have watched every British Prime Minister from Macmillan to Thatcher and every US President from Eisenhower to Reagan mouth platitudes about the West needing to have nuclear weapons because the Russians had them, and if only the sinister Russians would get rid of theirs we would get rid of ours. When, finally, a Soviet leader comes along who says, 'Why don't we get rid of all nuclear weapons by the year 2000?' it is the Western leaders who throw up their hands in horror, saying it will be impossible to get rid of nuclear weapons and that we intend to keep them for all time.

Instead of welcoming Gorbachev's proposals, Thatcher whines that they have so changed the public image of the 'Russian threat' that it is making it more difficult to get the people of Western Europe to vote for increased defence spending. In an attempt to undermine the growing ground-swell for a proper response to Gorbachev there is now a new propaganda offensive from Washington and Downing Street which warns that there is no point in disarming because Gorbachev may be overthrown and replaced by an old style Soviet cold warrior.

Yet, as I have attempted to demonstrate in this chapter, the 'Gorbachev' reforms are not happening because Gorbachev is a nice man in contrast with nasty Mr Brezhnev. The reforms are happening because the USSR has to change or face the prospect of an economic decline that could lead to the disintegration of the Soviet state with all the attendant dangers that would pose for the whole world.

The reform movement began before anyone had heard of Gorbachev and its first success was the election of Andropov. In that election, as in Gorbachev's three years later, it was the more enlightened amongst the *apparatchiks* (including key elements in the military and the KGB) who, realising the dangers of stagnation facing the USSR, swung their weight behind the reformers.

Clearly, the reformers have learnt, developed and changed their timetable as they have struggled to overcome a resistant bureaucracy.

No one would claim that progress has been smooth but we now know enough for it to be possible to make an estimate about the likely outcome of the reforms. In doing so, it is necessary to separate the democratising reforms from the economic package. I have no doubt that the experiments with democracy in the Soviet political system will survive and be extended. Having been given a taste of electoral power the Soviet people are unlikely to let it be taken back. Under the recent electoral changes 99 per cent of Soviet citizens are gainers. The only losers are the unpopular, and defeated, bureaucrats who by definition are unlikely to be able to mobilise great support for a return to past ways and abuses.

The likely outcome of the economic reforms is less clear. Aganbegyan himself predicts that it will take at least twenty years to modernise the economy. Even if the USSR could achieve a growth rate 5 per cent greater than the US, it would still take fifteen years to close the economic and technological gap between these two superpowers. So the rate of success of the economic reforms (on which the irreversibility of the political reforms must eventually rest) is uncertain.

The question for the West is do we wish Gorbachev to succeed or fail? The ambivalence of the USA is obvious. A strong and modernised USSR, which had been able to democratise its economy and improve the conditions of its people, would pose an attractive alternative system to the free market anarchy and exploitation of the US system. At the end of the day, the United States will not assist. Working with Japan it will conspire to exclude the USSR from the expanding markets of the Pacific basin, as it will also do to the countries of the EEC. The

USA will also continue to use its control over the COCOM treaty to prevent the countries of the EEC from expanding trade with the USSR.

If we are realists we should be able to see that the countries of Western Europe have a different set of interests from those of the USA. Gorbachev often uses the term 'our common European home' and there is no way that the security of our part of that common home will be enhanced by the degeneration or collapse of the USSR. We will all benefit if the Soviets and ourselves can reduce our arms spending and divert it into the reconstruction of our economies, our welfare states and our common environment. We will all be safer if we can achieve the removal of all foreign troops and nuclear weapons from the whole of Europe.

The task of modernising the Eastern bloc can be achieved a lot quicker if the economies of Western Europe would agree a major trade and development package with the USSR and Eastern Europe. The importation of the technology and management skills available in the West would allow Gorbachev to speed up the rate of change and advance the point when ordinary Soviet citizens begin to see the material improvements promised by *perestroika*. It would open a vast new market of 400 million people to the stagnant economies of the EEC and give those nations the chance to close the widening technology gap that is opening up between themselves and the USA. The scale of such a new trading bloc would rapidly change the economic and social conditions in both the West and the East and finally end the artificial division of Europe itself. Such benefits would more than compensate for the short-term increase in soft loans to the USSR and Eastern Europe that would be necessary to begin the

There is, finally, one other reason for such a deal which is particularly attractive to socialists. The scale of change that is in progress inside the Soviet Union is nothing short of revolutionary. The reformers are seeking to create an economy which is democratically managed. If they can achieve this and empirically demonstrate that efficiency and democracy are not incompatible, then they will have created a model that can and will be applied elsewhere. They will also have found a cure for what has always been the Achilles heel of Western socialists – the seeming inability to bring about social justice without creating a deadening bureaucracy that ends up alienating those it was created to serve.

In 1917, Russia passed through its first two revolutions within the space of a single year. It then had to wait seventy years for the beginning of its third revolution. If that democratic revolution, which is now daily gathering pace inside the Soviet Union, succeeds, its lessons will be studied across the whole world and its impact will change the course of human history.

10

The End of Illusions

The dependence of Western Europe on the US economy can be demonstrated very simply. From 1945 to 1973 the USA aided Western Europe whose economy then grew more rapidly than that of its benefactor. Thereafter, the USA changed the rules of the world economy in its own favour and struck vicious economic blows against Europe. After 1973 the EEC economies, far from being able to assume independence, once more fell behind the growth rate of the United States and were subject to its domination. On the military and political field Western Europe was subordinated to the United States even more than in the economic sphere.

The reasons for this change in role by the USA need further explanation. In the post-war period the USA experienced only a slow rate of growth in its productivity and this necessitated decisive counter-measures to avert profound political implications. Pressure on living standards would create internal instability and devaluation of the dollar would lead to a decline of US power and influence internationally. The history of US politics over the last two decades is largely that of attempts to prevent these consequences by increasing manipulation of the world economic system, carried out at the expense of the United States' allies in Europe. The reason the USA has had the ability to do this is because it is not simply 'another' economy. As we have seen, it structured the post-war world to meet its needs and still possesses tremendous levers of economic power to militate against all other rivals. The economic history of the last two decades illustrates how it has used these mechanisms to try to avert the consequences of its decline and in so doing has spread disorder through the world economy.

We have noted that during the first two decades after the Second World War US economic resources aided all parts of the Western world. After the Marshall Plan three further waves of United States' aid sustained Western Europe. The first was the impact of US overseas military spending. During the post-war period the USA established a chain of 400 overseas bases. In 1945–53, US military aid to Europe was $7.7 billion in addition to the $15.7 billion of assistance under the Marshall Plan. By the mid-1960s the deficit on US military spending abroad was $2.1 billion.

Secondly, there was private US investment. European investment in the USA was indirect by means of portfolio and share holdings but US investment overseas was direct, often involving the most advanced technology. European capital crossed the Atlantic to share in the profits generated by US firms and the economy generally, whereas US investment overseas served to spur production.

The third major source of aid to Western Europe was inherent in the energy policy pursued by the USA. Before 1945 the USA had been the world's largest exporter of petroleum products but after the Second World War US oil output could not meet demand. With cheap oil from the Middle East coming on stream the USA would have become an oil importer by the end of the 1950s. To prevent this, and to maintain self-sufficiency in oil, the United States imposed legal quotas – thereby cutting the world oil market in two. The American oil industry would have diminished in size to a considerable extent had it been subjected to outside competition during the 1950s and 1960s. Instead it remained the world's largest producer throughout the 1960s whilst over 250 million tons of oil was shut out of the US market.

The result of this policy was an oil glut, with low prices, in the market outside the United States. By 1970, oil prices had fallen in real terms to 40 per cent of their 1950 level which was of benefit to Western Europe and Japan. Although this 'help' on the part of the USA was quite inadvertent, its importance to the economies of Western Europe was as great as the Marshall Plan and they boomed on the basis of cheap oil.

The US current account remained in surplus until 1971 although by the mid-1950s this surplus was smaller than the deficit on military spending and capital investment abroad. The result was a flood of dollars out of the US economy and it was *this* which began to create a serious conflict between the USA and its allies because it was an economic embarrassment peculiar to *no* other country. The USA, because of the international role of the dollar, was the only country in the world that could finance capital exports without a surplus on its current account. The first problems showed up in the monetary field. The dollar, which in the late 1940s had been a scarce currency, now became common, resulting in a build-up of dollar holdings in other countries and a flow of gold out of the United States as other states exchanged dollars against gold – as they were entitled to do under the Bretton Woods system. A bench-mark was reached in 1958 when dollar claims on the United States exceeded US gold reserves – for the first time the dollar was not 'as good as gold'. After this the USA applied strong-arm tactics to prevent weaker states exchanging their dollar holdings for gold: the US Treasury made it clear that Congress could be expected to take a poor view of those countries making gold conversions when granting aid.

The decisive event which ended the era of US economic aid to Europe was the Vietnam War. The defeat of the USA in Southeast Asia was not just a tremendous *political* blow, it caused a great reduction in US *economic* power. In essence, what occurred was a classic example of what Paul Kennedy has called 'imperial overstretch'. The United States attempted a task for which it simply did not have the resources and as a result it destabilised the entire world economy.

Militarily the resources deployed by the United States in Vietnam were colossal – the greatest US military effort outside the two world wars. By 1970 it had dropped more bombs on Vietnam than in the whole of the Second World War and used chemical warfare on a scale which has still left parts of Indochina devastated. By 1969 the cost of the war was $28.8 billion annually – 3 per cent of US GDP – and Vietnam was absorbing 37 per cent of total US military spending. The US defence budget rose in real terms by one third between 1964 and 1968 while in the same period US GDP rose by only 20 per cent. Given the unpopularity of the war, the United States was unable to defray the cost by taxing its own population, so instead it was financed through greatly expanded deficit spending. It sought to transfer a large part of the burden of the war to its Western European allies.

The mechanism was simple. Throughout the war the US balance of payments deteriorated rapidly from a surplus of $6.3 billion in 1964 to a deficit of $9.5 billion by 1972. Only US income from services and overseas investments kept the current balance afloat. However, as the United States continued simultaneously to undertake a major programme of foreign investment – averaging $3.1 billion a year in 1965–71 – dollars poured out into the international economy. America was printing billions of dollars which it pumped out to pay for goods it was importing from Europe. It was in effect extracting forced loans which it used to buy up productive capacity in many of the countries which were unwillingly lending it money.

This situation hit Western Europe directly. Its central banks were forced to accept a rising flood of dollars which would eventually be devalued, making them suffer a heavy loss. Attempts to neutralise the dollar flood by selling their own currencies caused European money supplies to get out of control. The United States displayed complete indifference in its dealings with its European 'allies'. John Connally, US Treasury Secretary under Nixon, brutally declared: 'The dollar is our currency but your problem.' The USA sought to avoid its formal obligations under the Bretton Woods agreement to exchange dollars for gold. For example, in 1967 the president of the German Bundesbank, Karl Blessing, was forced to write to the chair of the Federal Reserve stating that it was the Bundesbank's policy not to convert dollars into gold, referring specifically to America's financial burden in maintaining troops in Germany in this context. The report of the Council of Economic Advisers (CEA) declared in mid-February 1971 that the USA had no intention of shaping its domestic economy to please foreign competitors. It simply called for upward revaluation of the European currencies – which would have pushed these countries into recession.

After a temporary improvement in 1969 the situation was made worse as President Nixon became desperate to reflate the economy in order to win the 1972 election. In 1971, he abruptly declared himself 'a Keynesian', lowered US interest rates and began rapidly to reflate the US economy through a 10.8 per cent expansion of the money supply in the first quarter. In consequence, dollars began to flow quickly out of the United States and new assaults on the European economies began. During the last week of February 1971 $800 million poured into the German Bundesbank. In an attempt to stem the flow of dollars through the Eurodollar market, the Europeans asked the USA to increase its short-term interest rates. US Treasury Secretary Connally replied by lowering the interest rates. The European central banks were therefore forced to begin cutting their own rates in April to deter the flow of dollars – speeding the expansion of their money supplies and the resulting inflation. By mid-April the West German money supply was expanding at an annual rate of 22 per cent. The USA, meanwhile, had exhausted most of its borrowing rights with the International Monetary Fund which now refused to accept any nation's dollars as payment of debts. At last, on 5 May, the dam burst and West Germany floated the mark after taking in $1 billion in one hour. The repercussions followed swiftly across Europe – many other nations floating their currencies or revaluing as central banks refused to support the American currency at the old parity. On 15 August, the USA suspended the convertibility of the dollar into gold, then finally, on 18 December 1971, took the decision to devalue the dollar. A new economic era had begun.

The events surrounding the Vietnam War represented a historic turning point in relations between the USA and Western Europe. For most of the period from the First World War until the early 1960s the US economy had been decisive in ensuring the economic and political stability of Western Europe. From the Vietnam War onwards the United States became a major factor in the destabilising of Western Europe. US disturbance of the post-war economy grew worse in the 1970s as it sought to avoid the consequences of its economic decline by greater and greater manipulation of the system it had created after the Second World War.

The first wave of this US offensive was signalled by the way it carried through the destruction of the Bretton Woods currency system. If the United States had succumbed to the strong pressure to devalue the dollar, this would have led to another instrument becoming the international means of payment – thus restricting the ability of the USA to run unlimited balance of payments deficits and blocking its access to funds for foreign investment. The United States therefore concentrated throughout the 1960s and early 1970s on ensuring that no other means of payment could substitute for the dollar. In particular, after the severing of the dollar's link with gold in August 1971, the USA insisted that gold should not become the basis of a new payments system. The elimination of alternatives to the dollar was a process that began in the sixties and peaked with Nixon's declaration in August 1971 that the dollar was no longer convertible for gold. The system of floating exchange rates eliminated any need for the United States to control its own balance of payments deficit, no matter what its source, because it was now possible to release unlimited quantities of non-convertible dollars into international circulation. Since 1971 the USA has increasingly exploited its ability to enforce the dollar as means of payment on its international competitors. During the period 1950–70 official US liabilities abroad rose at an annual rate of $600 million. During the 1970s the annual increase rose to $15,000 million – a twenty-fivefold increase.

To sum up so far: the decisive first step in the US offensive was therefore the destruction of the post-war system of international payments. While the dollar was the international medium of currency the fact that it was tied to gold gave other states some leverage over the USA. However, with the decision in the 1970s to break this link, all existing constraints on the US balance of payments were abolished.

The second wave of US economic aggression in the 1970s was marked by the oil price increases of 1973 and 1979. According to popular mythology pedalled by the press this was a mysterious assault on Western civilisation by 'oil sheiks'. The reality is different – the oil price increases bore the indelible imprint of US policy.

In 1973, Western Europe depended on oil to meet 65 per cent of its energy requirements of which 95 per cent was imported. Japan required oil to meet 75 per cent of its energy needs and imported 99.7 per cent of this. The USA, however, imported only 30 per cent of its oil requirements. An increase in the oil price would therefore strike harder against Western Europe and Japan. Furthermore, US domination of the world oil industry promised other benefits from the price increase. By the late 1960s investment by US oil companies amounted to $17 billion – 30 per cent of all US overseas investments. In 1973, the United States' oil industry sent home more than $2.5 billion in repatriated profits. Moreover, it was hoped that a large part of the extra profits gained by the OPEC states would be invested in the United States.

The sequence of events is now clear and initially things went according to the US plan. Preparations for an increase in the oil price began with negotiations between the international oil companies and the oil exporting countries in Teheran and Tripoli in 1971 and 1972. By this time President Nixon had commissioned a report recommending a long-term price rise for imported oil so that domestic prices might be stabilised at a higher level and investment in US energy sources promoted. The United States conveyed this message to a special meeting of the OECD called to discuss the issue. In his book *Oil and World Power* (1981), Peter O'Neill summarised the development:

The USA was fed up with a situation in which the rest of the industrialised world had access to cheap energy ... Thus, it deliberately initiated a move which was aimed at getting oil-producing nations' revenues moving strongly up. It did this by its representatives talking incessantly to the oil-producing countries about their low oil prices and by showing them the favourable impact of much higher prices. It could, of course, rely on the cooperation of the largely American oil companies for ensuring that any consequential price increases which the OPEC countries introduced ... were passed on to the European and Japanese energy consumers. In this way their energy-cost advantages over their competitors in the United States would be eliminated. In as far as the USA itself would be affected by the higher foreign-exchange costs of the increased amount of foreign crude oil that it expected to have to import, this, it was argued, would be offset entirely, or to a large degree, by the greatly enhanced abilities of the US oil companies to increase their earnings and, thus, their remittances of profits back to America. Thus, within the framework of a re-evaluation of how their best interests could be served and the consequential establishment of a somewhat 'unholy alliance' between the United States, the international oil companies and the OPEC countries, the stage was set for [the price rise].

By the beginning of 1973, as Anthony Sampson has explained in *The Seven Sisters* (1976), 'The State Department was virtually advising the Arabs to put up prices, and advertising the West's weakness.' US government oil expert Walter Levy made the situation clear: 'The United States simply cannot afford an ever-increasing over-dependence for its oil supplies on a handful of foreign, largely unstable, countries. Otherwise, its security – and that of its allies – as well as its prosperity and its freedom of action in foreign policy formulation will be in jeopardy.' While the US government officially deplored the oil price increase the *Wall Street Journal* made the situation explicit. It openly defended the price increases, arguing editorially that the big profits produced would stimulate further oil exploration and production in the United States.

The mechanism of the oil price increase, as well as dealing with the Arab oil embargo, was entirely organised through the 'Seven Sisters' – the major oil companies dominated by the United States. As the Shah of Iran noted: 'With the sisters controlling everything, once they accepted, everything went smoothly.' Similarly, Anthony Sampson said that 'if it had not been for the domination by these seven companies, the embargo would have been far more difficult, perhaps impossible, for the Arab countries to enforce'. Or as Mary Kaldor put it: 'the Arab oil embargo succeeded, not because the oil producers are exceptionally rich and exceptionally cohesive, although they are, but because the embargo was not altogether unwelcome to American oil companies and to the American government. It provided an opportunity to underpin the American oil monopoly and to strengthen the dollar.'

What was taking place was in fact well understood even before the massive price increase was finally triggered by the Arab–Israeli War of 1973. *The Economist* (7 July 1973), in a special supplement entitled 'The Phoney Oil Crisis', written *before* the Yom Kippur War, noted that it was

> a course of events to which the Americans were really not that adverse. There is probably no one outside the administration who can prove whether this suspicion is correct. It may be wholly incorrect. But even if it is, the fact that the suspicion exists in the industry is significant, as is the guess, widespread in some places, as to at least one of the reasons for the Administration's attitude. According to it, the Americans gave into OPEC so readily because they saw increased oil prices as a quick and easy way of slowing down the Japanese economy, whose exports were bothering America mightily at the time and would be more hurt by rises in oil prices than any other nation.

OECD estimates were clear, predicting that in 1974 the increased cost of crude oil would impose a burden of $40 billion on the current account balances of industrialised countries. This burden would not be spread evenly but would be concentrated in those countries heavily dependent on imported oil. Britain would see a deterioration in its balance of payments of $10.5 billion, Japan and Italy $8.5 billion each, and France $6.5 billion. The American balance of payments was expected to be in rough equilibrium.

There is no doubt that after 1973 the United States initiated a fundamental shift in the pattern of growth of the post-war world – reversing it in its own favour. The Japanese economy slowed drastically. From 1951 to 1973 its growth rate had averaged 9.2 per cent, but from 1973 to 1988 this slumped to 3.7 per cent – a reduction of 60 per cent. The US economy in contrast slowed down from only 3.4 per cent average growth to 2.5 per cent – a fall of less than half. The West German economy slowed from an average rate of growth of 5.7 per cent in 1951–73 to 1.8 per cent in 1973–87, the French fell from 5.1 to 2.3 per cent, and the Italian from 5.4 to 2.4 per cent. The United States, in 1973, gained a high proportion of its objectives and in the decade and a half that followed its growth rate exceeded that of all its European rivals.

Although spectacular in its global impact the US hoist of world oil prices was essentially short-lived. Such short-term shifts in commodity prices have never altered the long historical trend for the terms of trade to move against raw materials and in favour of industrial output – as Mrs Thatcher is now beginning to discover to her cost. After the second oil shock of 1979 the oil price began to come down rapidly. Precisely because it was based on short-term manipulation the United States, after initial gains, did not reap the long-term benefits it had hoped for. In particular Nixon's project of oil self-sufficiency by 1980 completely failed to be achieved.

With the advent of Reagan the USA abandoned even the pretence of maintaining a competitive economy. Instead the possibilities suggested by the manipulation of the international monetary system were utilised to the full. The driving force of US economic growth was a rapid build-up in military expenditure which rose in real terms by 40 per cent between 1980 and 1987. The US defence budget in 1987 reached $300 billion. As with the Vietnam War no attempt was made to fund this by taxation – on the contrary, taxes were cut. Consumer expenditure rose rapidly and Reagan, after 1981, enjoyed domestic political popularity. The budget deficit soared from $70 billion in 1980 to $200 billion in 1986. Reaganism can best be described as 'military Keynesianism'.

The *specific* feature of Reaganism is the manner in which the budget deficit was financed. During most Keynesian expansions governments cover the budget deficit by creating money thus also providing the potential for inflation. Alternatively, the USA under Reagan financed the deficit by borrowing from abroad. Between 1980 and 1986 the United States turned from a net creditor of $140 billion to a net debtor of $260 billion – the largest foreign debt of any state in the world. Given that the budget deficit was covered in this way, there was no necessity for the US government to print money and risk the potentially inflationary consequences of traditional Keynesianism. The net result was that the US economy grew rapidly under the impact of the budget deficit, while at the same time inflation was kept down.

This combination of rapid growth and low inflation was claimed by apologists for Reagan as a masterpiece of economic management. But in reality if an economy borrows more than $400 billion from abroad then, before it has to repay the loans, it will enjoy prosperity. Propelled by gigantic inflows of capital – primarily from Japan but also from Western Europe – the US economy boomed.

The consequences of 'Reaganomics' were clear. High interest rates, necessary to draw loans into the United States, drastically raised the exchange rate of the dollar so that US goods became less competitive. The high exchange rate therefore produced a balance of payments deficit running at $160 billion a year by 1987.

In this latter aspect Reaganism represented a further worsening of the competitive position of the economy – a new phase of US decline – because for the first time it transformed the US balance of trade deficit into a *balance of payments* deficit. The USA was therefore borrowing not to finance outward investment but current consumption – and this was the underlying cause of the crash. Reaganism could not last. Even the most substantial imports of capital could not compensate indefinitely for the stagnation of productivity in the United States. In order to attract capital into the country interest rates had to be raised to higher and higher levels, thus threatening a US recession. The continuous trade deficit could not be sustained forever. At some point the mechanism would grind to a halt. The way it did so was entirely logical – the October 1987 stock market crash.

In Reagan's first term the US trade deficit was financed primarily through long-term investment in the United States, including significant direct investment. This ceased after 1984 and in 1985 and 1986 portfolio investment was dominant, although even this began to decrease in 1987, putting pressure on the US stock markets. By 1987 the US balance of payments was being determined by short-term money flows. Furthermore, from 1986 onwards inflows of private capital no longer covered the deficit and large-scale purchases of dollars by foreign central banks commenced. By that time also 55 per cent of the US balance of payments deficit was being covered by bank deposit money and increases in reserves of foreign states

(Table 10.1). Funding of the payments deficit became dominated by short-term considerations – above all, interest and exchange rate fluctuations. In effect an economic bomb had been prepared.

Table 10.1 Financing the US Balance of Payments Deficit, 1984–7 (%)

	1985	1986	1987	1988
Foreign authorities' reserves	2.5	4.2	23.2	29.4
Total long-term capital	48.2	56.5	5.2	23.3
Total short-term capital	27.7	25.2	41.8	55.8

Source IMF *Balance of Payments*, May 1988

The reason the bomb exploded when it did is also clear. The necessity for central banks to step in and purchase dollars in their own currencies put upward pressure on their money supplies – as happened during the Vietnam War. By 1987 the West German and Japanese governments were attempting to push interest rates upwards to regain control of the money supply and head off inflation.

The crisis began to unfold on 1 September when the New York stock exchange fell sharply. On 4 September, the US prime rate rose from 8.25 to 8.7 per cent. On 7 October, it was raised again to 9.25 per cent. In the week leading to 19 October the developing trends came together. The Dow Jones index fell by ninety-five points on Wednesday 14 October when a record US trade deficit was announced. On 15 October, the Chemical Bank of New York pushed its prime rate up to 9.75 per cent and international bond markets began to fall rapidly on fears of higher interest rates. Wall Street fell by a further fifty-seven points.

The same day, James Baker, US Treasury Secretary, decided to launch a violent attack on West Germany for its tightening of interest rates and openly threatened, in tasteful diplomatic language but with no equivocation, devaluation of the dollar. His comments seemed to shatter the efforts made at the annual International Monetary Fund meetings to paper over deep cracks in economic policy apparent among the major industrial countries. On Monday 19 October, the stock market crashed.

The actual occasion of the crash was blamed on mismanagement – Baker's public attack on West Germany, technical matters, or absurdities such as computer trading. But these were simply the occasion for a fundamental adjustment that was waiting to happen.

The driving force was the drastic loss of competitiveness by the United States compared with its economic rivals.

What the United States could not gain by persuasion it achieved through the market. The events of 19 October directly posed the question of the US economy or threatened chaos. All the essential goals which the USA had demanded prior to October were gained afterwards: interests rates were sharply cut; the dollar was devalued.

The fear of rising interest rates sparking a recession was one of the chief problems which ignited the Wall Street crash. Another was the fact that the United States was not getting its own way over how to escape from the situation in which it found itself.

The devaluation of the dollar robbed Western Europe and Japan of a large part of their loans to the USA while simultaneously subjecting them to a trade squeeze.

The United States demanded that the crisis be resolved by Japan and West Germany, its main rivals, expanding their economies by interest rate cuts, tax reductions, and removal of tariffs in areas such as agriculture and finance. If this was done US exports would be sucked into the West German and Japanese economies and the US balance of payments crisis overcome at the expense of its rivals. The United States would thus be financed out of its crisis by its competitors and the relation of economic forces would shift in its favour. Such a development would be politically destabilising in both Western Europe and Japan, since the United States wanted those powers to ease agricultural protectionism to facilitate a major expansion of US farm exports (resulting in major farm closures in Western Europe and Japan that would undermine the main electoral base of their respective conservative parties). Instead Japan and West Germany wanted the United States to overcome the crisis by cutting its budget deficit via increased taxes – that is, through cutting the living standards of US workers. That way the US working class and not the Japanese and West German farmers, would pay for the crisis.

The events of October 1987 were in essence a fight over who was going to pick up the bill for the last seven years of Reagan's arms spending – Japan and West Germany demanding that the United States pay and the United States demanding that West Germany and Japan pay.

Until 19 October it appeared as though West Germany and Japan were winning. Far from loosening interest rates Bonn increased them – indicating that it was not going to fund the USA out of its crisis by expanding the West German market and sucking in United States imports. But West Germany's action in defending itself sparked off a drastic crisis which sharply altered matters – the entire situation getting out of hand in the most spectacular single day's events since the great crash of 1929.

It is an economic fact that, short of overt protectionism which would have plunged the world into a 1930's-style depression, there is only one way for a country to cut back imports drastically and that is to deflate its own economy – experience shows that devaluation by itself will not suffice. West Germany's interest rate increase therefore spelt potential recession in the United States in the run up to the US presidential election and the certain loss of the White House by the Republican Party.

Having deferred the difficult decisions until after the election the really gigantic test will come over the next two years. To turn round the US balance of payments deficit means reducing export markets for other countries by anything from $100 to $170 billion. And without reflation in West Germany and Japan, which would undoubtedly weaken them in relation to the United States, this means recession in these rival economies. If the US trade deficit is not reduced by means of Japan and West Germany absorbing its exports, the recession in the United States itself will deepen besides having the knock on effect of pulling West Germany and Japan into recession anyway. A huge test of strength will now take place over who is to bear the cost of the recession.

The key to the whole situation rests on the reason why West Germany and Japan tolerate these policies from the United States.

The answer lies in the fact that the USA has been the linchpin which has kept the Western post-war economies together. The United States' ultimate argument has always been 'if not us then chaos' and after 19 October its rivals know that this is no empty threat. While the United States will undoubtedly be forced to rein back on some of its policies, by cutting back the budget deficit, it will also be able to impose some of its burdens on its 'allies'. That is the privilege it gains from being the centre of the world capitalist system.

What are likely to be the political consequences of the crash? First, it means a recession in the United States now that the presidential election is out of the way. But something still more fundamental than a recession is going to happen. The crash was the most violent economic conflict since the inter-war depression and will have profound consequences for world politics.

The immediate consequence of the US currency devaluation was clear – it lowered the real value of dollar holdings of countries outside the United States. Since the beginning of 1986 $150 billion of central bank reserves had been utilised to prop up the dollar exchange rate and the devaluation after 19 October meant that a substantial loss was incurred on these dealings and on private holdings. Overall the Western European and Japanese central banks lost more than $8.5 billion through the devaluation of the dollar.

The second area affected by the dollar devaluation was the balance of payments. The dollar's decline undermines European competitiveness and results in slow growth and rising unemployment. For the United States it will have the opposite effect. A devaluing dollar tends to sustain US growth for a longer period through expansion of its export markets and a greater insulation of its domestic market from imports. As the London Business School put it, the United States is 'exporting recession to Europe'.

The most important reason why the US will not reverse its course is political. The US balance of payments deficit amounts to $2,500 dollars per year for each US household. To eliminate this by reduction of US consumption via a tax increase would provoke political consequences within the US which are unacceptable to the US establishment. The only other effective means to reduce the US budget deficit is by a reduction of arms spending.

Given this background to events we must now consider the long-term political consequences. The events of the crash drastically affected the relations between the three main international economic centres – Japan and the Eastern Asian Newly Industrialising Countries (NICs) of South Korea, Hong Kong, Taiwan and Singapore; the United States; and the EEC. Before the crash the pattern of trade between the main capitalist centres was clear. Japan and the NICs ran trade surpluses with both the United States and Western Europe. Western Europe financed this through a trade surplus with the United States – the EEC visible trade surplus with the United States in 1987 being $24.3 billion. The United States has been in balance of trade deficit both with Japan and the NICs and with Western Europe – producing the well-known US balance of trade deficit.

This situation had, in the previous seven years, allowed Western Europe to limp along. Its growth rate was less than either Japan's or the United States', but the overall economic situation of Western Europe was not particularly serious as long as it could finance its deficit with Japan and the NICs through a surplus with the United States. The devaluation of the dollar, which has taken place since 1985, however, means that the United States will rapidly close the balance of payments deficit it has been running with Western Europe. The consequences of this are already becoming clear. As regards Western Europe, David Diebold, commercial counsellor of the United States, has put forward a precise target: 'I am totally confident in saying that within two to three years we will be back in surplus.'

On the other hand, a US trade offensive against Western Europe will not lead to a lessening of Japanese pressure; on the contrary, as Japanese exports to the United States are cut by dollar devaluation Japan is going to increase its export offensive against Europe. In February 1988, Japanese exports to the USA fell by 14.3 per cent while exports to the EEC rose by 22 per cent. Western Europe is therefore going to come under a squeeze from two directions – from Japan and the NICs and also from the United States.

What is taking place is a vast redistribution of economic power which showed up very clearly on the world stock exchanges. The October crash had no lasting effect in Japan. It had an intermediate impact in the United States and it had a crushing influence in Western Europe. The result was a fundamental shift in the valuations of the world stock markets, making for the first time in history the valuation of the Japanese stock exchanges higher than those in the USA. In contrast, the UK stock exchange was worth 10.5 per cent of world valuation at the end of September 1987 and declined to 9.5 per cent at the end of March 1988. The share of world valuation of West Germany fell from 3.4 per cent to 2.8 per cent. The Japanese banking sector, accounting by itself for 10.5 per cent of the world index, is larger than the entire valuation of the British stock market. US stock exchanges, having started 1987 26 per cent larger than the Japanese exchanges finished the year 25 per cent smaller.

These figures are deeply significant as they show what capitalists are doing not with words, which is uninteresting, but with their money It is capitalism registering in a different way what the trade figures show – an enormous shift in the relation of economic power against Western Europe which will result in a tightening economic squeeze.

On current projections 'East Asia's aggregate gross national production will have grown to about 22 per cent of the world total by the year 2000, about the same proportion as both North America and Western Europe. In 1960 East Asia's economy was only half of Western Europe's and a third of North America' (*Financial Times*, 19 January 1988). This will place a special focus on the current US–Japanese relationship which some perceive as becoming increasingly adversarial. This relationship suffers a built-in contradiction: Japan has to rely on the US security commitment while its economic vitality threatens US economic supremacy. Nevertheless, a process of Japanese–US integration seems to be progressing through a massive transfer of Japanese production centres to the USA and substantial participation in its financial markets.

Arising from this global shift of power we should also be aware that there will *not* be an equal sharing of the burden within Western Europe. Within the EEC the strongest economy, West Germany, will unload the burden on to the weaker ones – including Britain. This is already occurring. With the cutback on its exports to the USA, due to the dollar devaluation, West Germany's export offensive inside the EEC is being stepped up. During the fourth quarter of 1987, German exports to the United States fell by 5 per cent, while those to Europe increased by 9 per cent. The consequences of this are clear. Sipko Huisman, director of Courtaulds, noted in *International Business Week* (16 May 1988) that West Germany is now 'much more aggressive in going after business than a year ago'. In addition to the inherent power of its economy West Germany is able to use the EEC and the EMS to reinforce its position. In 1987, for example, French inflation was 3.1 per cent compared to West Germany's of 1 per cent. This means that the West German mark has effectively devalued by 2 per cent against the franc.

The result is a mounting West German export surplus in Europe which will slow down the British, French and Italian economies – all of which are heavily dependent on exports. The Single European Act, coming into force in 1992, will of course make this situation worse and West Germany more dominant. In short, while Europe will be squeezed from two directions – from Japan and from the United States – Britain will also be squeezed inside the EEC by West Germany. This was becoming clear in 1988 as the British balance of payments deteriorated rapidly.

The British government has been attempting to get round this by tinkering – the argument between Lawson and Thatcher over the exchange rate being one symptom of this. But the truth is that the situation facing Europe, or Britain, will not be turned round by a little petty tinkering. To see why, it is only necessary to consider why the NICs of Eastern Asia are successful in crude economic terms.

The basis of the success of the NICs, and why they will survive the dollar devaluation, is their super-exploitation of their own workers. Walter Russell Mead, in his recent book *Mortal Splendour* (1987), calculates from World Bank statistics that the wage of manufacturing workers in NICs equals about 25 per cent of the value produced by their labour, while workers in Western countries typically receive 40 to 50 per cent.

In addition to this fundamental advantage, the NICs have also pursued a policy of devaluing their currencies alongside the dollar. The result is that the EEC's trade deficit with the NICs increased by 20 per cent in 1987.

Japan's superiority rests on two fundamental factors. The first is the weakness of the Japanese trade union movement. The second is its extremely low defence spending. Even though Japanese defence spending is concealed, and higher than the official 1 per cent of GDP, nevertheless it is a minute fraction of the economy compared to either the United States or Western Europe – giving Japan a decisive edge in its competition with the EEC states. It is certain that with these advantages Japan and the NICs will continue their strong economic advance and their competitive pressure against Europe.

Thus over the next decade the world economy will undergo a dramatic change. Japan and the USA may integrate their economies in order to establish a new economic bloc as powerful as the United States was on its own in the first twenty years after the Second World War. Or there may be increased rivalry between a Japanese-led Eastern Asian economic bloc and a US-led North American one. The USA has prepared for both eventualities. It has created a free trade area with Canada which, whilst it only increases the consumer population available to the US multinationals by 10 per cent, also gives the United States access to the vast mineral wealth of Canada. This was Reagan's real objective, effectively giving the USA its own version of the Soviet Union's mineral rich Siberia (though it was not, of course, sold to the Canadian people on that basis). At the same time, the Bush administration has responded positively to the initial feelers from Japan about a sharing of economic leadership, describing the US relationship with Japan as the 'world's most important bilateral relationship'.

Whether the USA eventually chooses to link with Japan or rival it with a North American economic bloc is of little consequence to the EEC which is likely to be systematically squeezed either way. In either option both the USA and Japan will conspire to exclude the EEC nations from the rapidly expanding markets of the Pacific basin, just as the UK was squeezed out of Latin America by the USA earlier this century.

The multinational corporations, which are overwhelmingly based in the USA and Japan, will continue to concentrate their research and development in their home countries, thus worsening the rapidly growing technology gap that has opened up between the EEC and its two main rivals. The trend, described by Michael Heseltine during the Westland affair, by which we are being reduced to 'tin bashers for the Americans' will continue. The United States will continue to operate the COCOM list of proscribed exports in a way which prevents the countries of the EEC from building up any advanced technological trade with the USSR and Eastern Europe.

The USA will also step up pressure on the European members of NATO to increase their military expenditure so that it can reduce its own defence spending in Europe. This has the added advantage of maintaining pressure on the USSR to keep its own defence spending at levels which will prevent it diverting resources towards the modernisation of its own economy. It will also, of course, have the same effect on the European NATO countries by diverting their resources from the productive economy into arms spending, thus reducing our economic competitiveness in comparison with that of the USA and Japan.

The European right have already devised their own response to this historic shift in world power. They foresee the necessity for the full integration of the EEC into a strongly capitalist United States of Europe with its own nuclear and conventional military strength capable of rivalling the two existing superpowers. The mechanisms they are using to achieve this are the revived Western European Union and the implementation of the Single European Market in 1992. With the former they are planning the creation of a multinational army with its own nuclear weapons (the Eurobomb so favoured by Dr David Owen). The Eurobomb is already the subject of joint discussions and planning by France and Britain.

With the single European market in 1992, they see the chance of creating a 'fortress Europe' able to use protectionism to exclude the products and peoples of other countries.

The only issue that divides the right within the EEC is the question of how subordinate the new European structure should be to the United States. In contrast to Mrs Thatcher who is taking the most slavishly pro-US position, the West German Christian Democrats and Liberals favour a greater degree of independence which would allow them to negotiate a major expansion of trade with the USSR and Eastern Europe, and perhaps even a separate disarmament deal between the EEC and the USSR.

The problem for the British left is that for nearly thirty years it has reacted against the policies of the pro-marketeers without ever setting an alternative agenda. As our economic integration into the EEC has continued apace, it has seemed increasingly unlikely to the general public that Britain would ever be able to withdraw without major dislocation to industry and employment. Thus at the 1988 Labour Party Conference, when the right wing proposed a motion accepting that Britain was in the EEC for good, even the left-wing constituency activists voted for it by a margin of two to one.

Yet, in the same way that it is absurd for Labour to argue about its defence policy before it has decided where it wishes Britain to stand regarding the present power bloc system, so it is ridiculous for Labour to argue about our position in relation to the EEC before it has considered where it wishes Britain and Europe to stand in relation to the present superpower system which has artificially divided Europe for the last forty years.

It is no good the left complaining about the immorality of the abuse of the Western European economy by the United States. Britain behaved in exactly the same way when it was the predominant world power. Politics is about the application of power and if we don't like the way it is being used against us, we need to assemble an alliance of forces that can change the situation. Fortunately, the changes taking place in the USSR have transformed the popular perception of the motives of the two superpowers, and we must seize this new-found freedom to think afresh.

The Gallup polling organisation conducts regular surveys of public opinion in the main EEC countries and their survey in November 1988 revealed positively seismic upheavals in public perceptions of the cold war. In Britain, only 9 per cent of adults think it is likely that the USSR will attack Western Europe in the next ten years, while 83 per cent reject this idea and fully 58 per cent think that a nuclear war is more likely to be triggered by accident. When asked who is most likely to be responsible for a nuclear attack, 6 per cent suggested the USSR against 27 per cent who expected it to be the USA. Asked which country is the greatest threat to world peace only two per cent nominated the USSR as against 15 per cent who chose the USA. When asked which country is more interested in world domination, 17 per cent pointed a finger at the USSR as against 32 per cent who think this is the objective of the United States, and on the question of who should get the credit for the INF Treaty only 10 per cent nominate the USA as opposed to 24 per cent who give the USSR the credit for this move. These poll figures are similar for all the EEC nations which participated and were, of course, taken before President Gorbachev's speech to the United Nations with its commitment to unilateral conventional force reductions.

Nor is it just these changing perceptions which allow us some freedom to manoeuvre. As explained in the previous chapter, the economy of the USSR needs to double its productive capacity in order to achieve parity with the Western industrialised nations. Even if the USSR could achieve a growth rate 5 per cent greater than the USA or Japan every year, it would still take fifteen years for it to catch up with the most advanced capitalist nations. Whilst I have no doubt that the constitutional reforms of President Gorbachev will succeed, it is impossible that a growth rate of this order can be achieved given the position the USSR is starting from.

This makes it very probable that sometime in the early 1990s Gorbachev or his successor will be looking to pull off a major trade deal to import the new technology and management skills necessary to accelerate the development of the Soviet economy. Given the determination of the United States and Japan to keep the USSR as weak as possible and in particular to exclude it from the economic opportunities opening up in the Pacific basin, it is most likely that it is to the EEC that the USSR will turn.

West Germany's economy is already developing the network of trading links that could rapidly be expanded in just such an eventuality. Nor will the West Germans overlook the fact that anything which reduces tension in Europe aids the continuing development of links between the two Germanies.

The potential for an increase in trade with the 400 million people of Eastern Europe and the USSR is significant. The desire for good quality consumer goods in the USSR, coupled with the needs of the EEC countries for access to the raw materials of the Soviet Union, could give the countries of the EEC the chance to move their economies into top gear and dramatically reduce the present levels of unemployment. It would also provide the economies of the EEC with the opportunity to close the technology gap between themselves and the likely US–Japan axis. Not least it would be a welcome and concrete sign that Western Europe wants to assist the progress of the Gorbachev reform package.

Of course, if trade begins to pick up with the USSR, it would accelerate the progress of nuclear and conventional arms reductions with the corresponding ability to divert the resources thus released into the modernisation of the European and Soviet economies. For both these reasons the United States and, to a lesser extent Japan, will do everything in their power to prevent such events happening. One only has to remember the intense US pressure on the EEC not to cooperate with the USSR in the construction of the gas and oil pipeline a decade ago, or the continuing harassment of EEC companies by the spurious application of the COCOM list in order to prevent increased trade between East and West. These actions reveal the lengths the USA will go to prevent such developments.

In Chapter 7 entitled 'The Vision of Omnipotence', I wrote that before we can understand the real choice now facing the whole of Europe it is necessary to separate the reality from the mythology of 'the benign USA reluctantly dragged from its preferred isolation ... in order to defend European democracy from ... Stalin'. This particular piece of mythology tells us no more about the real economic forces at work over the last hundred years than the story of Helen reveals about the real reasons for the fall of Troy. That city state was destroyed because its control of the straits of the Bosphorus allowed it to tax the ships of the emerging Greek city states which used this vital trade route to the Black Sea. It was these economic realities which made war inevitable between Troy and the Greeks – the abduction of Helen was merely the trigger to a long overdue conflict to determine economic supremacy in the region. Yet the power of mythology is such that school children around the world know only of the beauty of Helen and nothing of the real reasons for this war.

Equally, four generations of US citizens have been raised on the mythology of the brave young republic committed to the destruction of the old European empires in the name of democracy. As these last four chapters have sought to demonstrate, the reality is very different. Having subjugated the indigenous peoples of its own continent, the USA turned outwards to replace the old colonial empires with its unique new concept of the 'Open Door', or neo-colonialism as it became known by the new nations of Asia and Africa. They threw off the chains of Britain, France and Portugal only to find themselves fettered again by US multinationals, military aid and a mountain of debt.

In Western Europe the USA's approach was more subtle. When Woodrow Wilson came to Europe after the First World War he was greeted as a saviour, which in a sense he was because the wealth of the United States had saved Britain and France from defeat at the hands of the economically stronger and more modern Germany. In the years that followed it was US capital that kept Europe afloat. The cheers for the USA were equally genuine in the twenty years following the Second World War as the strength of the US economy directly and indirectly aided the reconstruction of a shattered Europe. But as I have sought to demonstrate, the motivations of the US policy-makers were purely those of enlightened self-interest.

Recognising that it could not enforce its will on the USSR it sought to isolate it and was prepared to divide Europe in order to achieve this. For over forty years the USA has hidden behind the rhetoric that it was here in Europe to defend us from the Russian bear, whereas in reality it was protecting its vital export market. The United States also realised that if a third world war was to be fought it would be better to fight it as far away from home as possible. Thus Western Europe and Britain in particular were turned into the 'unsinkable aircraft carriers' of the USA, and Pentagon planners calculated how long a nuclear war could be confined to Europe in order to minimise the damage and casualties in the USA.

For all this the United States remained massively popular throughout Western Europe – as long as US involvement was directly beneficial to the West European economy. Yet this state of grace ended twenty years ago in the carnage of the Vietnam War and since then the USA has been an aggressive competitor. It has not hesitated to attack and damage the economy of Western Europe during that time, and now that the real profits are to be made in the Pacific basin it is shifting its interest and its priorities to that area. It is not surprising, therefore, that the popularity of the USA has slumped in Western Europe during these last twenty years, but what is amazing is how slowly the political parties of the region have responded to the changed situation. It is almost as though the politicians found the old arrangements so comfortable that they are hoping they can be recreated if we just wait around long enough.

There is no point in wasting time complaining that the USA has abused its superpower status – Britain, France and Spain all did the same in their turn – if one nation acquires such power over others it is almost inevitable that it will abuse its position. What we should complain about is why it has taken the political leadership of Western Europe so long to respond to these events with a new and far-sighted strategy for the future development of our continent.

The outlines of such a strategy are glaringly apparent. The world is moving into a period of regional economic blocs with three main centres of economic power, two of which, the USA and Japan, are increasingly oriented towards the emerging Pacific market. For the third economic bloc of Western Europe there is the obvious attraction of an opening to the east with its huge market of 400 million Eastern European and Soviet citizens.

Not only is the potential for increased trade considerable, but there is also the possibility for the nations of Europe and the USSR to manage the emergence of this new trade grouping of nearly 800 million people in a way that allows all its participants to close the growing technology gap with the USA and Japan.

The defence expenditure implications for such a Euro–Soviet bloc are also enormous. It would be no more imaginable that war could break out amongst the nations of such an economic unit than between France and West Germany today. Participating nations would undoubtedly be able to achieve a major reduction in conventional arms spending, as well as the removal of all nuclear weapons from both Eastern and Western Europe. Indeed, we should already be looking beyond the elimination of all nuclear weapons based in Europe towards the negotiation of a disarmament deal whereby the entire US military presence is removed from Europe, with all armed forces throughout Europe and in the European part of the USSR being scaled down to a purely defensive level.

At the moment, the armed forces of Europe are primarily offensive rather than defensive and as such invite a pre-emptive first strike with 'small' tactical nuclear weapons. British forces in West Germany, for instance, are compacted into less than twenty concentrated deployments and are thus extremely vulnerable to such an attack. Britain's air and sea defences have been neglected in order to provide the capacity to fly bombing raids deep into enemy territory or amphibious landings on the other side of the world, but the structure of both forces is of little use in the defence of the UK from air attack or coastal assault.

Defensive military strategies are by their nature cheaper than offensive ones – offensive military action assumes a three to one advantage on the part of the attacker. The implications of this have been explored by a number of writers – for example, the West German military theorists Horst Afheldt, Lutz Unterseher and General Franz Uhle-Wettler. They argue that we should adopt the Swedish model of decentralised, dispersed forces in thousands of small units armed with precision-guided, anti-tank and anti-aircraft missiles. This pattern of deployment offers no readily identifiable targets and renders tactical nuclear weapons useless, whilst giving the defending nation the capacity to wage a protracted and debilitating war.

There are two other major advantages to this type of defence policy. First, defensive hardware is only about 1 per cent of the cost of invasive weaponry (an anti-tank missile costs £12,000 as against a main battle tank which is a real snip at just £1.5 million), so it would be easy to achieve and even go beyond the 40 per cent reduction in the defence budget spelt out in the chapter on the economy. Second, a purely defensive strategy broadcasts to the whole world that this type of defence force is not a threat to any other nation and would therefore increase the domestic pressures on others for similar defence plans.

The proposal to break the military link between Western Europe and the United States may at first seem inconceivable but military alliances usually follow in the footsteps of economic links. Given that over the last twenty years the USA has become an aggressive competitor against the EEC and that this trend will increase as US interests shift towards the Pacific basin, here again military alliances will begin to reflect the new pattern of economic interests.

Any recession in the future will accelerate the pace of these changes as the USA tries to export the consequences of its military profligacy to the nations of the EEC. In addition to these economic forces, the longer the Gorbachev reforms continue the greater will be their impact in recasting international alliances.

Simply because we have spent the last fifty years in an alliance with the United States does not mean that this must be the case forever. The history of diplomacy is one of constantly shifting alliances and antagonisms. In the past we have entered wars in alliance with one partner only to change sides and swap allies during the course of the war itself!

In looking at what is likely to happen to the balance of power over the next fifty years, we need to realise that we are entering a world in which power will be exercised in a way quite unlike anything we have seen during the last 175 years. The history of the years since the Industrial Revolution has been the history of a world dominated by one superpower after another. The final defeat of Napoleonic France in 1815 ushered in a century of world domination by Britain which, at the height of its power in 1860, controlled at least 25 per cent of total world GNP. By the time that Britain had finally beaten off the German challenge to its supremacy the USA had become the new world superpower. When the United States reached the height of its power in 1945 it controlled 45 per cent of total world GNP and was able to impose its will everywhere outside the Soviet sphere of influence.

What has been amazing about the history of these two superpowers is how quickly each has squandered its predominance in comparison with the great empires from the earlier history of humankind. In *Misalliance*, in 1909, George Bernard Shaw wrote about the wealth and arrogance of the stockbroker towns around London with a very memorable line, 'Rome fell; Babylon fell; Hindhead's turn will come.' In *The Rise and Fall of the Great Powers* (1988), Paul Kennedy substituted Scarsdale for Hindhead to make the point that an era had passed.

Whether we like it or not the world has indeed passed beyond the position of US superpredominance that prevailed from 1945 to the late 1960s. The economic circumstances that allowed the United States to impose its priorities on two-thirds of the world have gone forever and we shall never again in our lifetimes see the world dominated by one nation.

During the 1990s we will see a situation in which the three main economic regions of North America, Western Europe and the Far East will each have about 20 per cent of the world's GNP and the

USSR about 10 per cent. By the middle of the next century China and India will have become major economic forces in their own right and powerful new regional groupings may have emerged based on South America, the Arab nations and possibly Africa.

We are moving into a multipolar world of shifting alliances and in the next twenty-five years the economic forces already at work will produce either a militaristic United States of Western Europe or a purely defensive Euro–Soviet bloc. A Labour government must work for the latter and not get dragged along in the wake of the right towards the former. That means working with progressive forces in both Eastern and Western Europe as well as in the USSR in order to exercise the maximum influence on the future development of the region. Instead of being trapped in arguments about our role in the EEC we must widen the terms of the debate. When we talk of European unity we must mean the 28 per cent of Europe's people who live in Eastern Europe and the 7 per cent who live in the west outside the EEC as well as the 65 per cent in the EEC. We must work with those who advocate a major programme of aid to rescue the East European economies and also with the progressive forces in West Germany and elsewhere who advocate a major expansion of trade with the USSR.

In a world moving towards more protectionist regional blocs there is little attraction in being on the outside of one of those groups. If Britain pursues a path outside Europe, it will inevitably end up in a totally subordinate role to Japan or more likely the USA. It is better that we should fight instead to reform the EEC with a proper programme of democratic and social reforms, as well as seeking its enlargement to include the whole of Europe and become a common trading bloc with the USSR.

Whatever immediate rows we may be having about some aspect of EEC policy, we should not allow these to blind us to the massive shift in international economic forces that is currently under way. Within a generation we may find we are living in a European community of 500 million people in which the present national parliaments have been dissolved. Under such a system the powers of existing nation states could be devolved down to about a hundred regional governments with a European-wide assembly co-ordinating macroeconomic policy, foreign affairs, defence and setting continent-wide minimum standards for the provision of services and environmental protection.

With so much beginning to shift in global politics it is time the left in Britain set an agenda with goals which lift our eyes to the most exciting possibilities, instead of looking backwards to argue about what might have been.

11

'A Thousand Generations'

Sometimes in an election there is one incident or even just a phrase which stays in the memory, remembered long after the issues are forgotten or the candidates have retired or died. In 1964, there was a television advert for President Johnson's campaign against Senator Barry Goldwater (the main issue being peace and whose finger would be on the nuclear button) which showed an angelic little girl in a sunlit field counting the petals on a daisy. Suddenly she froze as her voice was drowned by the harsh, metallic sound of a nuclear countdown. As the camera focused on her shocked eyes the scene was obliterated by a nuclear explosion and faded to black. The advert only needed to be shown once – the scream of protest from the Republicans was proof that it had done its lethal work.

Similarly, the deliciously cruel punchline delivered by Senator Lloyd Bentsen to Senator Dan Quayle, the Republican Vice-Presidential candidate in the 1988 election, will never be forgotten by those who saw it. This eminently forgettable little lightweight had compared himself to the late President Kennedy but was reduced to incoherence by Bentsen's, 'Senator, I knew Jack Kennedy, I served with Jack Kennedy, Jack Kennedy was a friend of mine. Senator, you're no Jack Kennedy.'

British politics has similar memories such as Churchill's warning that if Labour won the 1945 election a Nazi-style Gestapo would be introduced to impose socialism on the unwilling British people. There was also Macmillan's 'You've never had it so good' at the 1959 election (which was not exactly what he said but was so effective that he did not rush to disclaim it either).

Even our political opponents would not disagree that it was Neil Kinnock's 'thousand generations' remark which is the most vivid memory of the otherwise uninspiring 1987 election. It was in the stunning Labour party political broadcast directed by Hugh Hudson that Neil asked, 'Why am I the first of a thousand generations of Kinnocks to go to university?' Few phrases in politics can have said so much with so few words about the terrible waste of talent in the present system or the disadvantages imposed on those born into the working class. So effective was it that no riposte was possible from the Tories and it was taken up as a slogan by one of the candidates for the US presidency.

However, like many other great political slogans that stir our hearts, it was a wildly inaccurate exaggeration. If the Tories or their supporters in the media had had a better grasp of ecological history, they could have turned the slogan to their advantage by pointing out that the reason Neil Kinnock's ancestors were not in university a thousand generations ago was because most of Wales was under a sheet of ice, and Neil Kinnock's relatives were on the Continent gnawing bits of meat off the bones of whatever animal they had been able to catch that day. Unless the early Kinnocks had been prepared to travel to China or the Moslem world, they would have had to wait until the year AD 1100 for the first establishment of universities in Christian Europe – a mere forty-five generations ago.

What is important about this humorous diversion is what it reveals about our lack of perspective on humankind's very recent part in the history of our planet. We were taught at school that if the whole history of the planet could be represented by the time passing in one day with the creation of the Earth taking place at midnight (4,450 billion years ago), then life first appears at 2.20 a.m. (4,000 billion years ago). That primitive, asexual life (such as bacteria and algae) is all that is to be found on the face of our planet until late in the afternoon. With the development of sexual reproduction at 6.30 p.m. the way opened for a massive increase in the rate of evolution and by 8.20 p.m. (670 million years ago) the first simple animals appear to be followed by vertebrates at 9.10 p.m. (510 million years) and reptiles at 10.15 p.m. (313 million years). The rule of the dinosaurs ends at 11.38 p.m. (67 million years) and the apes give rise to the first ancestor of humanity just one and a half minutes before midnight (5 million years). The first species of our genus, Homo habilis, evolves with twenty seconds to spare (2 million years ago) and finally modern humankind, Homo sapiens sapiens, begins to spread out across the world in the last second (40,000 years ago). The progression to civilisation since the first development of agriculture 10,000 years ago would be compacted into the last quarter second of our twenty-four hours.

A more vivid way of getting our species into proper perspective is to look at the few thousand years of human civilisation in terms of the number of generations involved. If we allow twenty years for each generation then the earliest cave art and carvings occur just 1,600 generations ago (30,000 BC). The first use of grind stones took place in Egypt 700 generations ago (12,000 BC) and preceded the development of agriculture by 4,000 years. The first town (Jericho) was established 500 generations ago (8000 BC) and at Sumer, in Mesopotamia, the first urban civilisation arose just 275 generations ago in 3500 BC. The earliest evidence of writing soon followed in the same area by 3100 BC. The initial phase of Greek civilisation started in 1550 BC and reached its peak in 450 BC, a mere 122 generations ago. The first book was printed only twenty-seven generations ago by Gutenberg in AD 1445.

Even more startling is to consider human history in terms of how many lifespans of seventy years (which has been the potential throughout human history although most people have never achieved it) have passed since any particular event. On that basis it is just 143 human lifetimes since the first development of agriculture, seventy-eight since the first urban civilisation at Sumer and just twenty-eight since the birth of Jesus.

Whichever way we choose to estimate it humankind is so recent as to be almost unmeasurable in terms of the history of Earth, yet in our cultural arrogance we imagine a civilised past three or four times longer than the reality. But even in that short space of time we have become the first species out of all the thousands of millions that have preceded us to threaten the destruction of all life on this planet.

Many argue that the major factor behind this threat to the world is the explosive growth of human population and this is certainly a large part of the problem, but it is by no means the only cause. In the *Atlas of World Population History* (1978), Colin McEvedy and Richard Jones estimate that between 100,000 and 10,000 BC, while we were still hunter-gatherers, the human population rose slowly from 1.7 to 4.0 million. Following the advent of agriculture, the total world population reached 100 million by 500 BC and 1 billion by AD 1825. By 1925, the total was 2 billion. The world population is now 5 billion and McEvedy and Jones estimate that it will reach and possibly stabilise at 8 billion by the year 2025 – just thirty-six years away.

Those who think that our destruction of the environment and extinction of other species is a recent phenomenon will be surprised to discover that even at our very beginnings humankind caused the extinction of many other species. It is quite wrong to assume that there was once some idyllic past in which happy hunter-gatherers lived in a state of grace with the rest of nature.

One of the great mysteries of early paleontology was the reason why so many large mammals such as sabre-toothed tigers, cave bears, woolly rhinos, mammoths, steppe bison and Irish elk died out at roughly the same time. When I was at school we were taught that it was all the fault of the last ice age but the truth is that they were hunted to extinction by humankind between 15,000 and 8000 BC. Nor was this a purely European phenomenon, since the first hunter-gatherers who spread throughout the Americas between 9300 and 8500 BC 'burgered' into extinction two-thirds of all the species of mammals they found. In Australia, the same pattern was at work with the destruction of the giant herbivorous marsupials. Only in sub-Saharan Africa, where the population explosion lagged behind the rest of the world, did big mammals survive to modern times in any large numbers.

Having eliminated most of the large animals on the face of the planet humankind then set about obliterating the great forests. Before we rush to condemn the destruction of the Amazonian rain forest we need to remember that the Brazilians are only following a well-trodden path. In Europe, the great forest which stretched unbroken across the Continent from France to Moscow was completely felled, except for a small pocket that remains in Poland on the Soviet border. In Australia, the slash and burn techniques of the Aboriginal peoples devastated the forests and turned vast areas into semi-desert. Long before the Industrial Revolution humankind had already transformed and degraded the world beyond recognition.

The threat that the human race poses to life on the planet is not some recent aberration. It is almost a defining characteristic of our species that we exterminate other species. We should not have been surprised to discover that we have come close to destroying the ozone layer. Such behaviour is wholly in character for a species that is so shortsighted that it destroyed the vast majority of large animals with which it shared the planet. The development of our technology has simply given us the ability to destroy all life on Earth at once instead of working our way through each species one at a time.

In recent years, however, there has been a growing awareness of the risks we are running by continuing with the environmentally destructive practices of the past. When I did my first draft of this chapter it was over 6,000 words longer and consisted of a shopping list of worthy policies to improve the environment. It went into all the details of which chemicals should be banned from pesticides, which hormones should be removed from our foods, the precise form of tougher controls needed to tackle polluters of our air, water and beaches. But in all the detail I realised that I had lost sight of the two most vital environmental issues that should provide the framework for any sound party and government – solving the debt crisis and changing the values by which we live.

This does not mean that it is not important to argue for the environmental shopping list of pollution controls and changes in the tax laws that would make this a cleaner country to live in. Indeed, such a policy is more important here because Britain has the most backward and reactionary government in the whole of Western Europe on issues of the environment. Yes we must

- Develop a complete recycling policy and use the tax system to discourage wasteful packaging
- Switch our transport priorities to favour public transport
- End the pollution of our rivers and coastal waters and stop dumping toxic waste in the sea
- Push for an earlier ban on ozone-destroying CFCs and assist poorer countries with the costs of doing the same
- Completely eliminate pollution from car exhausts and sulphur from our factories (the worst polluters in Europe)
- Phase out nuclear energy and develop the safe alternatives
- Take the lead in declaring that we will protect the natural resources of Antarctica from exploitation
- Shift the burden of taxation on to unearned income, the excessive consumption of natural resources, products with inbuilt obsolescence and the causes of pollution
- Structure taxes so that it becomes cheaper to repair consumer goods rather than replace them
- Use the tax system to encourage energy conservation and the generation of electricity from burning non-recyclable waste

● End the use of dangerous food additives, especially the many questionable antibiotics and hormones used in food production
● Recognise our responsibility towards animals by ending the horrors of factory farming and unnecessary experiments
● Improve our health by a major campaign against tobacco, alcohol and other drugs (including a ban on all advertising)
● Impose much tougher controls on the use of pesticides on our farms and convert surplus farm land back into deciduous forest in order to combat the greenhouse effect
● Ensure that every public and private sector project is subject to an Environmental Impact Analysis by an independent agency before it gets approval.

This list would be a useful programme for a full Parliament but on its own the shopping list approach easily allows politicians to steal the green agenda and squabble amongst themselves about who has the marginally less appalling record on green issues. Given that all politicians now pay lip service to the green cause, now is the time to expand that bridgehead and raise the fundamental point that we cannot just clean up our present act with a few cosmetic changes. Saving the planet involves changing the way we live and our whole system of values.

To start with we must recognise that although humankind has been destructive of the environment for at least the last 17,000 years, the scale of damage is increasing alongside the rise in population, the development of technology and the increasing integration of the world economy. It took early man a full 7,000 years to eat the great mammals to extinction, but on present estimates we will have destroyed a full 25 per cent of all remaining species of plants and animals during the remaining years of this century.

A large part of the problem stems from the very success of the 'Open Door' policy of the USA. Over the last century the United States has been able to enmesh most of the nations of the world in an international financial system based on the dollar and administered by the US controlled IMF and World Bank. One nation after another has been driven to greater and more ruthless exploitation of its natural resources in order to keep up with debt payments to the mainly US-owned banks.

In last year's report the World Bank estimated that Third World debt had reached a total of $1,320 billion – $264 for every person on the face of the planet. The cost of servicing this debt is now so vast that the Third World is repaying $43 billion more a year to the Western world than it is receiving in new lending. The total sum transferred from the poor nations to the rich since the debt crisis started in 1982 is now $143 billion. This means recession and death for Third World nations as they cut health, education and consumer spending in order to switch resources into earning foreign currency. Amongst the fifteen most indebted Third World nations the fall in income for the ordinary citizen between 1980 and 1986 was an annual average of 2.4 per cent.

It is important to remember that these are figures provided by the World Bank which has an interest in hiding the full consequences of its policies. Susan George, writing in *A Fate Worse Than Debt* (1988), estimated that, 'Over $130 billion net – repayments minus new loans – has left Latin America and landed in Northern Banks in the past five years alone.' But as she points out the total Third World debt of $1,320 billion should be compared with the total annual GNP of the twenty-four rich Western nations (members of the OECD) which is more than six times greater than the debt.

Of course, the public debt of the USA is nearly twice as great as that of the Third World. The difference between a Third World debtor and the USA is simply that the United States controls the system and is thus able to force the rest of the world to lend it money on its terms while screwing into the ground those who need to borrow money through its IMF or World Bank agencies.

When we come to look at how Third World debt was accumulated it is obvious that the international banking system has been a bigger culprit than the peoples of the Third World. Many of the original debts were incurred as the newly independent nations were persuaded by Western bankers, governments and economists that they needed to undertake vast development projects on the Western model. No consideration was given to the needs of local people. Instead of aid programmes that developed the rural infrastructure and spread wealth more widely, loans were squandered on huge and environmentally damaging capital projects which tended to benefit small urban élites. The new élites made millions of dollars from bribes which they invested abroad or spent on imported, Western, luxury goods that their countries could ill afford. They then massively expanded military spending in order to keep a resentful peasantry in its place.

For those few countries which have been able to overthrow their corrupt élites, Western banks and governments have usually been happy to provide a refuge for fleeing dictators and whatever part of the national treasury they escaped with.

The banks know exactly what is going on and are happy to cooperate. They make a loan to country 'A' and find that a large part of the money comes back into their bank in the private accounts of corrupt officials. Thus the bank is not only paid interest on the original loan but also gains interest on its handling of the corruptly deposited money. Much of the remaining money is also returned to be invested via Western banks where it produces a quicker profit than if invested in the Third World country concerned. Estimates of the scale of this flight of capital back to the Western banks vary but range from $55 billion between 1977 and 1983 for all Latin American nations (Bank of International Settlements) to 70 per cent of all new loans to Latin America between 1983 and 1985 (Morgan Guaranty). Susan George quotes an unnamed New York banker who explains: 'There is no debate in [my] bank over the dual role of lending money to a country and accommodating flight capital. There is no moral issue. If we don't do it the Swiss will.' Some banks even cooperate in this vast scale of theft by sending their staff, with empty suitcases, to collect the money on behalf of clients. Of course, it is seldom necessary to be so crude as most banks are only too happy to arrange foreign exchange swops, back to back loans, fake investments and offshore trusts. In most major international banks literally hundreds of staff are engaged on this work at any one time.

About a fifth of Third World debt has come from military spending. The Western powers set out quite deliberately to ensnare the newly independent nations in major arms programmes. The USA started by giving arms to the new nations in order to win them as future captive customers unable to switch to alternative suppliers. By 1972 the United States was giving away 40 per cent of all the arms 'required' by Third World countries (worth $2.4 billion). However, once these lucrative markets had been captured the 'freebies' were phased out and within a decade the 'free' arms supplies were reduced from 40 per cent of the total market to just 2 per cent (worth $240 million) of a market that had by then reached $12 billion a year. By then the local military establishments had developed enough political muscle to insist on their governments continuing to purchase modern arms.

The IMF, ever loyal to its US master, always exempts the arms budgets of Third World countries from consideration when demanding that a nation makes public spending cuts as a condition of getting a new loan.

Thus the USA ensnared most Third World nations in a mountain of debt to pay for capital projects (that seldom produced the promised benefits), the luxury lifestyles of local élites and massive arms budgets. In fact if it had not been for the US manipulated rise in oil prices back in 1973 most countries might still have avoided the debt trap. Between 1974 and 1982 the Third World had to pay $345 billion for oil imports and often the only way that they could pay their oil bills was by further borrowing.

Then along came Ronald Reagan with his policy of massive foreign borrowing in order to pay for his own arms expansion, with the result that interest rates exploded. Suddenly, Third World nations found that the cost of interest on their debts had doubled just as the market price of most of the commodities they exported collapsed.

One by one the nations of the Third World were forced to accept the austerity programmes of the IMF and the World Bank as a condition of further loans. First, these nations had to sacrifice their development programmes, then impose massive wage cuts for their already impoverished people followed by huge cutbacks in their health, housing and education budgets. Any nation that refused to accept the cuts or threatened to default was faced with exclusion from the US dominated world trade system.

The results were predictable. One by one the nations of the Third World gave in to the IMF/World Bank austerity programmes and soon the effects were visible in the mounting infant mortality rates. Susan George estimates that the death toll which can be attributed to the consequences of the debt crisis is at least 15 to 20 million a year and possibly more – 'the equivalent of a Hiroshima every two days'.

The respectable grey-suited bankers who sit in the White House, the IMF and the World Bank have become the most successful mass murderers in history. The result of their decisions is that every two years they are responsible for the deaths of more people than the total of all those who died in the Second World War. It took Hitler four years to kill 6 million Jews; these grey-suited infanticides are responsible for a similar total every four or five months.

At the 1985 Havana Debt Conference, Luis Inacio da Silva, the Workers Party Candidate for the Brazilian presidency, put it in the right perspective:

247

the Third World War has already started ... This war is tearing down Brazil, Latin America and practically all the Third World. Instead of soldiers dying there are children, instead of millions of wounded there are millions of unemployed; instead of destruction of bridges there is the tearing down of factories, schools, hospitals, and entire economies ... It is a war by the United States against the Latin American continent and the Third World. It is a war over the foreign debt, one which has as its main weapon interest, a weapon more deadly that the atom bomb, more shattering than a laser beam. (*A Fate Worse Than Debt*, 1988)

The Western banking system has the capacity to reorganise the payment of the debt so that it remains a continuing burden on the nations of the Third World, preventing them from ever successfully challenging the existing world economic order. In such a situation these nations are in a position that is little better than when they were colonies.

The effect of this situation is rapidly to accelerate the destruction of the natural environment as nations strip every asset in order to escape the debt trap. Whilst the bankers will eventually get their money, it is achieved at the risk of a total global disaster such as the greenhouse effect. Of course, the bankers who are primarily responsible for this disaster will have died comfortably in their beds long before their children have to face the disaster they are creating daily.

Not only are these financial policies endangering all life on this planet but they are also depressing world trade. Money spent repaying debt is money not spent on buying useful goods and services. In Britain alone, 250,000 jobs have been lost since 1980 by the loss of trade with Latin America caused by the debt crisis. Once again the needs of industry have been subordinated to the needs of finance capital.

Fidel Castro has proposed that Third World nations should all default together, while President Gorbachev in his speech to the United Nations called for the planned write-off of Third World debt. In contrast, Western governments have done no more than talk about rescheduling the debt.

We need to bring together the interests of the peoples of the Third World who are trying to escape from the debt burden with those of workers and manufacturers in the West who have seen their interests in improved trade smashed by the bankers' short-term greed.

We should gear our aid programme so that it reaches the bulk of the population in the form of developing the local agricultural base and small enterprises, improving health care, education, transport and renewable energy sources. We should not aid dictatorships such as Chile under Pinochet. We should be prepared to accept payment for exports in local currency. Susan George has imaginatively proposed that we should write off Third World debt by converting it into schemes to preserve the environment. Thus in return for saving each acre of rain forest a set proportion of the debt would be abolished. There are almost limitless ways in which the debt could be eliminated whilst preserving the environment.

Equally, the debt could be abolished by converting it into credits which could be used to purchase goods from the country prepared to write off the debt. Thus any loss to the country's financial institutions would be balanced by gains to the productive sector of the economy.

Whichever way we choose to deal with the debt crisis it must involve a transfer of wealth from the rich to the poor nations and from the financial to the industrial sector of the world economy. Bankers will howl but virtually everyone else on the face of the planet will benefit.

Finally, we must democratise the IMF and the World Bank. Instead of the present position whereby the USA effectively runs them as extensions of its own government, they must be brought under the aegis of the United Nations. As an alternative to a voting system in which the IMF/World Bank are controlled by countries on the basis of their economic strength and financial contribution, the votes should reflect the fact that the majority of the world's population are in the Third World.

The most important and immediate task for environmentalists is the resolution of the debt crisis before it leads to the destruction of what remains of the natural world. But more important in the struggle to save life on our planet is the second main task – that of trying to change the value systems that see growth as inevitably good and any form of restraint an infringement of economic liberty.

Clearly growth is required both in our own economy and in the world generally so that each individual can have a satisfying and comfortable life. But if tomorrow the billion inhabitants of China could suddenly have the same lifestyle and patterns of consumption as exists today in the USA, then the world would be polluted to death in a very short space of time. There simply is no way in which we can create a fairer and environmentally safer world without a major redistribution of wealth and power between nations as well as within them. Even that would not be enough to resolve the conflict between our perceived economic needs and the environment. To do that we have to change our value systems.

We evolved over 5 million years as a cooperative animal. Throughout that time the norm was for ten to thirty early humans to live together in extended groups, in much the same way that great apes such as gorillas and chimpanzees do today. As we developed into humans and became the hunter-gatherers who still exist in a few remote areas today, we preserved the cooperative group in which knowledge, food and shelter had to be shared to ensure survival. The whole evolution of our species over 5 million years is thus linked to cooperative groups and values. Therefore, when Mrs Thatcher argues that there is no such thing as society but only the individual, she is denying the very essence of our humanity. If some early Thatcherite hominid hunter-gatherer had suddenly announced, 'Sod this cooperative group, I'm an individual,' and set off to make his fortune on his own, he would merely have starved to death or provided a tasty morsel for a passing sabre-toothed tiger.

The value system that evolved within our cooperative past and still motivates us today would have been one that recognised the worth of each individual as a friend, a lover, a parent, a teacher and a co-worker within the group. But over the last 10,000 years we have seen the development of agriculture, urban society, hierarchies, wealth (which had to be defended from others), professions, slaves, nation states, governments, mass production and alienation. Almost all that has happened to us in these last few thousand years has gone against the grain of our evolved, cooperative humanity. It has substituted a value system in which material possessions have partially displaced the respect and love of those around us. How often we hear someone say, 'I was feeling depressed so I went and bought myself a ...' Yet throughout the millions of years that went into making us what we are, depression or insecurity would have been resolved by seeking the reassurance and love of other members of the tribal group. Therefore, within each of us today there is a conflict between our original value system and the desire for the more recent status symbols of modern civilisation.

If we want to help reassert the original value system we need to redefine the terms by which we judge success. At the present time, when a company opens a factory which pollutes the local river this is registered in our GNP figures as 'good' growth. If the local council pays to clean up the pollution this is a 'bad' addition to public spending. The vast cost of arms production is defined as a contribution to the strength of the economy, whilst the work of women to raise children, care for the home and ageing parents counts for nothing in judging a nation's wealth. An official of the IMF is considered an important and successful person although he or she may be psychosexually incapable of having a loving relationship with another human and instead substitutes the accumulation of personal wealth. The peasant woman who has cared for and enhanced the small plot of land while raising her well-adjusted children in a loving environment is no match for the banker in public esteem. Yet who has made the greater contribution to humanity?

To save our environment we first have to rediscover and cherish our essential and defining humanity. As this runs contrary to much of the conditioning of 'civilization' over the last 10,000 years, it will not be easy. Fortunately, socialism, with its theoretical commitment to planning and the wise use of resources, offers a framework which is not inherently opposed to this task in the way that those who are committed to the freedom of market forces inevitably will be. We are only just beginning to understand the outlines of what such a radically different approach would mean in practice and most of that thinking is taking place in the green movement rather than the Labour Party. Labour will need to develop much stronger links with the greens and approach them with an open mind if we are to ensure that in our quest for economic justice we do not worsen our environmental problems.

12

But Can We Win?

Parties can only win elections when they represent a coalition of social forces large enough to defeat those in power. This is the reason why the trade unions set up the Labour Party in the first place. However, are the unions still a strong enough force to elect a Labour government? If not, what wider alliance does the Labour Party need in order to defeat the Tories? Although much has been written about the weakness of the trade unions under Mrs Thatcher, we must first examine what they are capable of delivering.

The way to form a modernising alliance of social forces to defeat the Tories becomes apparent if we look at the alternative – the society Thatcher is creating. This is sometimes described as a 'two-tier' society in economic literature. It has as one of its primary roles the shattering of the Labour movement and putting the most aggressive sectors of capital in command. It seeks to carry through to a conclusion the processes Thatcher has unleashed – creating in Britain an economy and a society based on those of the United States, with a relatively privileged and secure 'centre' and an increasingly large and oppressed 'periphery'or 'underclass'. In Britain today, this means that each social division is growing. Major pay differentials – between skilled and unskilled, white and black, private sector and public sector, between regions, among teachers, nurses, and white collar workers – are widening. The gap between the employed and unemployed is more entrenched. The political hiatus between the Labour north and the Tory south is widening. Racism is growing at the same time as Black Sections are developing within the Labour Party, and there is more support for British withdrawal from Ireland than ever before. Hysterical campaigns against gays and lesbians, AIDS, and Clause 28 have accompanied the adoption by the Labour movement of its first progressive policy on gay and lesbian rights. The political climate has moved to the right, but we are also seeing the development of radicalised minorities in society. An increasingly open and aggressive right wing in the unions – Hammond in the EETPU, Jordan and Laird in the AEU – is strengthening itself, at the same time as the demands of women and black people for a fair share of power are being felt in the trade unions and the Labour Party. The first substantial split in Labour Party history, that by the SDP, and the first break from the TUC, with the deliberately provoked expulsion of the EETPU, have taken place.

These developments have an economic basis. Big business today is creating an economy with a stable core of skilled, mainly white male, and older workers – the base of the Hammonds, Jordans, Lairds and the Labour right – and a growing number of insecurely employed, mainly female, black, and young workers. The trend is particularly sharp in Britain where the economic effects of the oil revenues permitted average increases in real wages of over 20 per cent for those in employment, at the same time as drastic falls in income took place for those living on low pay, unemployment benefit and pensions. Affluence and poverty have grown rapidly side by side and Britain is an extreme case of the general trend which has developed throughout Western Europe, Japan, and North America.

The long economic depression which has affected the Western European economies since the 1973 oil crisis shows no signs of ending. In those industries hardest hit by unemployment – ship building, mining, steel, textiles, and shoes – there is a combination of declining demand and the impact of new technologies. Secondly, in other sectors of industry, demand and production continue to increase but more slowly than in the past and accompanied by technological innovation which is now having a sharp effect on unemployment. These industries include the motor industry, electrical appliances, construction and public works. Thirdly, there are those high-tech industries enjoying a rapid growth in demand and production, in which the new technologies are having far less impact on employment by virtue of this expansion of demand. These are in the areas of electronics, parts of engineering, the capital goods industry, scientific instruments, medical and pharmaceutical products. Putting these trends together, the obvious development is increased unemployment.

We are at present in the stage of 'semi-automation'. There is no question of manual jobs, or wage labour, being eliminated from industry. In these conditions, the transformation of the working class, the relation between unskilled and skilled workers, and old and new skills, differs according to industries and from plant to plant, depending to what extent new technologies are applied. Any conclusion drawn by generalising about high-tech industries, where robots are often used, assumes something extremely improbable – that in the next ten years all industry is going to be reorganised on this model. The reason it is improbable is simple; when new technology is introduced there are enormous overheads that accompany the changeover because of gigantic sums necessary for investment and the retraining of labour. Plants have to be rebuilt and re-equipped as subsequent stages of the production process are brought into line with the new technology, with corresponding effects on employment. Even more expensive, as Thatcher and Baker are finding out, is the reorganisation of the entire education system needed to supply the new types of labour required. Because the scientific capacity to apply technology is available, it does not follow that big business necessarily has the capital to afford it. It is economic resources, not technological possibilities, which determine what can and cannot be done.

Furthermore, the economic conditions prevalent during the first years of Thatcherism, in particular the massive decline of manufacturing industry, reflected not the general type of economic reorganisation undertaken in other modern capitalist societies, but specific problems caused by an oil boom and fuelled by the extremely high price of oil compared with manufactured goods after 1979. At that time, given the price structure, British finance capital moved its resources out of manufacturing and into oil production. But in the last three years the situation has changed dramatically with the drop in the price of oil and the relative rise in price of manufactured goods. Under these circumstances finance capital will shift resources back into manufacturing where output is now growing significantly more rapidly than the British economy as a whole. Given the pressure on the balance of payments, in a situation where the value of the oil trade surplus has declined, the expansion of manufacturing is likely to continue. The British economy has now entered a phase of reindustrialisation – the 7 per cent increase in manufacturing output in Britain in 1987–8 is rapid by the standards of any country. This may not lead to an expansion of manufacturing employment but to its relative stabilisation; after collapsing by 1.4 million in 1979–82 it has declined by less than 200,000 since 1986.

The error made in many fashionable projections about the future of the economy is that the scale of production is left out of account in discussing new technology. Matters are considered as if new technologies were introduced merely in accordance with technical efficiency and reducing wage costs, without taking note of the fact that they involve not only vast investment but an enormous increase in the volume of production. They therefore require a great expansion of the market. Take one 'famous case: in the manufacture of the Fiat Uno productivity was more than doubled as a result of the use of computers and robots. But this was only 30 per cent of capacity because to run it at 100 per cent Fiat would have to double or treble car sales, and in the last decade car sales have increased at nothing like that rate. Obviously, Fiat could hope to increase its share of the market at the expense of other car manufacturers, but by nothing like enough.

The enormous expansion in the scale of production involved in the most powerful new technologies places major constraints on their introduction outside certain specific sectors of the economy. Furthermore, the support structures these industries and their labour forces require create new employment. This does not mean that in some industries the elimination of jobs has not been vast, but it is wrong to take a single, advanced industry and apply the trends within it to the whole economy. What is vital is the processes taking place in the economy as a whole.

What *is* occurring is that shifts in employment between different sectors of industry are bringing about a reconstitution of the workforce. The most important development is the huge impact on the sexual balance of employment and the creation of a black working class – a shift of unprecedented proportions. Since the onset of the economic crisis in 1973 female employment has risen sharply, accelerating a trend begun during the post-war boom. In contrast, male employment has been declining. In Denmark, the proportion of women of working age in paid work rose from 44 per cent in 1970 to 75 per cent in 1985. In France, the rate rose from 46 per cent in 1960 to 55 per cent in 1985, and in Italy from 35 per cent to 40 per cent. Only in West Germany is the rise slow – from 49 per cent to 50 per cent. A substantial part of this increasing female employment is in the 'periphery' of the two-tier economy – unsteady jobs and part-time work at low pay without security. Between 1973 and 1983 part-time jobs rose from 21 per cent to 24 per cent in Denmark, and from 16 per cent to 19 per cent in Britain. In the rest of Europe women hold more than 80 per cent of such part-time jobs, while in Britain the proportion is lower at 70 per cent for women as against 30 per cent for men. Despite the variations from one country to another, the recomposition of the workforce since the Second World War is dominated by a single fact: *the entire increase in the size of the labour force, and of the working class, in the post-war period is accounted for by the entry of married women and black workers into the labour force*. This shift constitutes the greatest revolution in the structure of the British working class in the twentieth century – as is shown in Tables 12.1 and 12.2.

Prior to the long post-war boom, the proportion of men and women in the workforce remained completely static for a century – with 69 per cent men and 31 per cent women in 1851, and exactly the same

Table 12.1 Sexual and Racial Composition of Employees in Employment, 1851–1951 (millions)

	1851	*1871*	*1891*	*1911*	*1951*	*1973*	*1984*
White men	6.5	8.2	10.1	12.9	15.6	15.4	13.2
Black men						0.4	0.5
Women	2.8	3.6	4.5	5.4	7.0	9.2	9.4

(%)

	1851	*1871*	*1891*	*1911*	*1951*	*1973*	*1984*
White men	69	69	69	70	69	62	57
Black men						2	2
Women	31	31	31	30	31	37	41

Source Calculated from *British Labour Statistics: Historical Abstract, 1886–1968*, HMSO, 1971, p. 195; R. C. O Matthews, C. H. Feinstein and J. C. Odling-Smee, *British Economic Growth, 1856–1973*, Oxford University Press, 1982, p. 563; 'Historical Supplement, no.1', *Employment Gazette*, April 1985; Barber, 'Ethnic Origin and Economic Status', in *Employment Gazette*, December 1985.

Table 12.2 Percentage of Women in the Labour Force in Great Britain, 1881–1983

Year	All women	All women aged 15–64	All married women	All married women aged 15–64
1881	26	39		
1911	26	37	10	9
1921	26	38	9	9
1931	27	37	10	11
1951	27	40	22	24
1973	33	45	43	48
1979	36	52		
1983	36	57	59	

Sources 1881–1973 calculated from Matthews, Feinstein and Odling-Smee, *British Economic Growth, 1856–1973*; 1979–1983, *Historical Statistics, 1960–82*, OECD 1984, and *The Fact About Women Is*, EOC, 1985.

in 1951. But after 1951 the situation began to change drastically. By 1984 the proportion of women in the workforce had risen to 41 per cent – a greater rise in thirty-three years than in the entire preceding century. Simultaneously, 500,000 black male workers entered the paid labour force as well as 400,000 black women workers. The proportion of white men in the workforce fell from 69 per cent to 57 per cent and is continuing to decline.

Even if the higher proportion of women working part time is taken into account – and by 1984 69 per cent of women workers were working at least thirty-six hours a week – then there is no doubt as to the scale of this shift. Its causes and effects are clear. What took place was a process of *proletarianisation* of society and of the social position of women on a large scale – a movement potentially favourable to the Labour movement. A woman doing domestic labour in the home is part of the working-class community but she is not selling her labour power on the market. Drawing married women into the workforce is a process of proletarianisation in the strict sense of the word – women moving into waged work.

The reasons for this social revolution are also clear. In previous waves of expansion capital created a labour force by drawing the population off the land. However, in Britain the proportion of the population in agriculture was extremely low after the Second World War. Capital therefore had to expand the workforce by different means and did so by eating into the traditional family structure. Where capital had previously proletarianised the agricultural population, it now proceeded to draw women into waged work.

There was a second great transformation of the labour force in the post-war period. Following the Second World War capital could not increase the numbers of white male workers because of natural limits in population growth together with the increased numbers of men staying in education and training. Even the numbers of women entering paid work were insufficient to meet the need for an increased labour force. Capital therefore turned to importing black labour. Between 1951 and 1982 the number of black people in Britain increased by immigration and birth from 75,000 to over 2 million – nearly thirtyfold – and a new black working class was created.

These immense shifts in the position of women and black people within the working class accompanied another great change, namely, the increase in the proportion of white collar and public sector workers. Between 1948 and 1979 the number of manual workers declined from 14 to 12 million but the number of white collar workers almost doubled from 6.2 to 11.7 million. The proportion of white collar workers increased from 31 to 49 per cent and the number today probably exceeds that of manual workers.

The extent of workers in the public sector increased from 4.6 million in 1948 to 6.3 million in 1979 – the proportion increasing from 25 to 32 per cent, although it has since decreased due to privatisations.

Seen against the background of these long-term upheavals, the overall setbacks suffered by the trade union movement since 1979 are obvious. Membership fell from 13.4 million in 1979 to 9.5 million in 1986. In 1979–86, the TGWU lost 31 per cent of its members, the NUR 28 per cent, the GMB 23 per cent and the AEU 20 per cent. Only the big public sector unions like NUPE, NALGO and COHSE have maintained their membership, whilst the few major unions to have increased their membership are the Banking, Insurance and Finance Union (BIFU) in the expanding financial services sector and TASS, before its amalgamation with ASTMS to form Manufacturing Science and Finance (MSF).

The right to carry out effective picketing, to boycott goods produced in workplaces in dispute, and to take immediate industrial action after mass meetings have all been removed and the courts have developed the confidence to seize the assets of major unions. The package of measures in the 1987 Tory manifesto enshrines the right to scab, bans the closed shop, bans workplace ballots in union elections and replaces them with postal ballots which usually have a lower turnout. The number of victimisations has increased: more than 800 miners were sacked during the NUM's strike. Derek Robinson and Alan Thornett were victimised in British Leyland and less publicised sackings have taken place in other industries. Entire industrial sectors such as steel have been decimated. Privatisation is a major threat to the unions in health and local government and there is a possibility of the introduction of no-strike laws into the public sector.

Rank and file organisation has decreased. The number of shop stewards in manufacturing fell from 130,000 in 1981 to 80,000 in 1983. The total number of full-time shop stewards in manufacturing dropped from 8,000 to 2,000 in the same period. In some industries, where particularly severe defeats were suffered, the decline in rank and file organisation was greater. At British Leyland's Cowley plant the number of shop stewards fell from 120 to 60 – in part because workers were intimidated into not taking up shop stewards' posts. These trends, together with the defeats suffered in strikes, represent a significant shift against the trade unions. This has been reflected in press headlines such as the *Financial Times*' 'Managerial hawks in search of union prey' and the *Sunday Times*' 'The decline and fall of the trade unions'.

If these defeats were the only developments which had taken place under Thatcher then the situation for trade unionism would indeed be bleak. But beneath the surface important shifts have taken place which although they pose great threats to the Labour and trade union movement may also offer major openings for it. Tied to the development of the two-tier economy, the changes involved are radical and demand a clear strategy from the Labour movement.

To understand the situation facing trade unions today, the first fact which must be grasped is that despite defeats the fall in union membership is still limited compared with historically comparable periods of recession. The scale and length of unemployment now exceeds anything in British history, but the decline in union membership is not nearly as great as the 47 per cent drop in the recession of the 1920s and 1930s. The 27 per cent decline in trade union membership since 1979 is therefore much less than in previous times of recession. The absolute level of union membership is twice that of the interwar period – and, apart from the 1970s, still at the highest level in British history. Shop steward organisation, while weakened, remains significant, whereas it was eliminated between the two world wars. Indeed, 1989 saw a revival of trade union struggles with disputes on the London Underground and buses, in the BBC, and by university lecturers. This reveals the deep discontent against the impact of policies pursued by Mrs Thatcher – discontent which was previously suppressed by the fear of unemployment.

It is the job of the Labour Party to allow people to express their grievances and democratic rights at work as much as in any other sphere of society. This means that Labour must expand trade union and democratic rights in the workplace. Far from seeking to weaken its trade union links Labour should be strengthening them. This means legislating on the right of recognition of trade unions, the establishment of a national minimum wage, the banning of the sacking of workers for participating in strikes, the granting of equal rights to part-time and temporary workers as much as to full-time and permanent workers, and the establishment of specific rights for women workers.

Furthermore, far from being eliminated the trade unions are recasting their role – particularly in the difficult task of linking workers in the 'periphery' with those in the core of the new two-tier economy.

Here the most important developments flow from the restructuring of the capitalist economy. Since the depth of the recession, in 1981, the number of full-time workers has decreased from 16.6 to 15.6 million, whilst the number of part-time and temporary workers has increased from 7.0 to 8.1 million. This two-tier economy with its core and peripheral workforces is the characteristic feature of the recession.

The sex balance of the core and periphery is radically different: of full-time workers 69 per cent are men and 31 per cent women; among part-time and temporary workers 38 per cent are men and 62 per cent women. The economy is being reconstructed around a core of full-time male workers and a periphery of short-term and temporary, mainly female, workers with the periphery increasing in size compared with the core. Outside the periphery is a further 10 per cent of the workforce which is unemployed – on the understated official figures. Within the workforce the number of white collar workers is constantly rising in relation to the number of manual workers.

The differentials affecting these two sectors of the economy are rapidly widening. From 1979 to the end of 1987, the bottom 10 per cent of wage earners have seen an increase of 6 per cent, those on average earnings an increase of 13 per cent, and those in the top 10 per cent an increase of 25 per cent. Two million workers have been forced into poverty through unemployment. In addition to these changes in wages Thatcher has consolidated these divisions through other means – in particular by subsidised sales of council houses and shares. The aim of this has been not only economic but political – to reinforce a prosperous section of the working class that will break from the Labour Party and vote either Tory or SLD/SPD. This strategy, aided by the appalling memory of the last two Labour governments, has been politically successful. Since 1979 3 million workers, the bulk of them skilled or living in the prosperous south of the country, stopped voting Labour and started voting for the Tories or the Alliance.

This developing structure of the workforce, and the increasing divisions inside the working class, pose tremendous strategic problems for the trade unions as well as the Labour Party. The first is how to organise and maintain trade unionism among the 'core', especially in the new industries and those sections of the working class where Thatcher has so far created relatively prosperous conditions. The second problem is how to promote Labour and the unions among the 'periphery' – the new layers of temporary and part-time workers. Finally, and most important of all, is how to recreate the *unity* of the working class that has been broken by the dual economy and the political offensive of Thatcher based on it.

The two-tier economy has provided a base for the development of 'new realism' in the unions. The skilled unions – the EETPU and AEU – with their main support among the 'core' workers are at the centre of this new trend. The social foundation of 'new realism' was accurately described by John Edmonds, general secretary of the GMB, when he contrasted it with developments among the working class as a whole:

> industrial, demographic and technological trends point to a shrinking of . . . well-organised sectors and the growth of a new class of exploited workers . . . New jobs are being created only in private services, and these jobs are primarily for part-time women workers . . . (by 1990) male employment will drop by 600,000 as against a rise in female employment of 400,000 . . . Millions of exploited workers – overwhelmingly women working part-time in service industries or service occupations in other industries – are being removed from trade union protection . . . I cannot . . . see much appeal to these workers in the 'market' or 'business' unionism promoted by some commentators and unions. This model seems geared only to a small part of the workforce (generally on a secure inside track). It also seems to be, in essence, a promotional policy for unions based on an appeal to employers and on 'delivering' a workforce to them as part of a package. (*New Socialist*, June 1986)

Bill Morris, at the conference launching the TGWU's 'link up' campaign – aimed at organising part-time and temporary workers – also condemned the new realist strategy expressed by the EETPU:

> Business unionism is a short step down the path. The single union deals, the sweetheart approach, follow as night follows day, and you end up in a ghastly parody of the old craft unionism, crossing picket lines, selling out the jobs of thousands of your fellow trade unionists to boost your own membership. (*Tribune*, 23 January 1988)

John Edmonds again drew out the implications of this new realism:

> Business unionism is the epitome of . . . sectional trade unionism . . . That kind of approach tends to depress all the social and ideological values the trade union movement is meant to represent in the cause

of narrow, sectional gain. And you might also jeopardise a few civil rights in the meantime, for example, the right to strike or the right to be represented in the way you want to be represented. You are giving up something fundamental in order to achieve a very narrow sectional advantage. (*New Socialist*, June 1986)

New realism is based on a strategy to protect the most privileged sections of the working class, and the unions that contain them. It is prepared to accept the destruction of other sections of the trade union movement – as was shown at Wapping and in the green field site at Dundee, and the membership poaching 'no strike' deals the EETPU signed with big business which led to its expulsion from the TUC. It involves eliminating large numbers of jobs in order to secure high wages for those that remain. In line with this strategy the new realist unions vote against the demands of low-paid workers, women and black people, and workers in the public sector. They are also the unions most prepared to deal with the SLD/SDP.

The need to fight this reactionary drift explains the significance for the trade union movement of the TASS–ASTMS merger to form the MSF. The policies of the new union represent a form of traditional, aggressive trade unionism in the core industrial sectors – an antidote to the policies of the 'new realists' – the MSF having a clear ally in the TGWU in these sectors. The merger of ASTMS and TASS to form the MSF provides an alternative model to that of the EETPU/AEU in the high-tech sector which is why both the Tories and SDP campaigned against it.

The EETPU has decided on a direct confrontation with the MSF by trying to move into the white collar sector. At the end of March 1988, the EETPU launched a campaign to persuade workers promoted to white collar grades to stay in the EETPU rather than join white collar unions. Hammond, general secretary of the EETPU, in launching the campaign warned that 'the union would be entering the eye of a storm in seeking to retain and recruit technicians because of the potential conflicts with white collar unions'. The *Financial Times* noted: 'The EETPU is particularly concerned by the proposed merger of TASS, the manufacturing union, and ASTMS, the white collar union, which would create a powerful union with established roots in the technical area. Mr Hammond predicted that the EETPU would become the main union for technicians as it would provide the natural political home for white collar workers.'

Among the new sections of skilled core workers in the high-tech industries, it is clear that there are only two coherent paths to follow.

The first is open collaboration with the employers by the new realists – no-strike deals, one union deals, political links with the SLD/SDP, and collaboration in eliminating other unions. The second road is dynamic unionism of the MSF/TGWU type.

The second key development is taking place in the 'periphery' where the historical failure of the Labour Party and trade union movement to take up the demands of women and black people is clear. The electoral consequences of this condemned the Labour movement to sixteen years of Tory government between 1951 and 1974 because the Tories appealed over the heads of the male working class to women, to win the elections of 1951, 1955, 1959, and 1970. In the trade union field women were not even allowed to join the AEU until the Second World War. The demand for equal pay was not taken up by Labour until the 1970s and no serious attempt to adapt the structures of unions to the needs of women were made until the 1980s. Even these changes have still not been carried through into the Labour Party.

Some of the implications of the necessity for the unions to start to organise among the 'periphery', where the overwhelming majority of workers are women and/or black, were spelt out by Bill Morris in *Tribune* (23 January 1988):

> First, the trade unions will have to come to terms with their own history; their own failure to represent the very people who are now being pushed into the secondary labour force. Most temporary and part-time workers are women ... child care has in the past been at best a marginal issue for trade unions, as have many of the other central concerns of women workers. That was never right, but now it could be disastrous.

John Edmonds similarly spelt out some of the implications in terms of a strategy for the unions:

> We have got to put together a strategy that does something for all working people ... A system of legal minimum rights, including pay and hours guaranteed, unfair dismissal guarantees on day one for any service, any length of hours. We have got to campaign for such changes, which above all will help the unorganised. This will put the trade union movement on the side of the oppressed and disadvantaged, which is a side of the argument we haven't actually been on for some time. It also puts us on the side of women,

which is good because we have tended to be on the side of men
... Now if we win ... we will establish some legal rights and this
will help us organisationally in these industries very substantially
indeed. Because we can then go to the workers in a particular
establishment and say, 'look, these are your legal rights. Are you
getting them?' And if the answer is 'no', we can say, 'join us, we can
make bloody sure that your employer does what he has to.' (*New
Socialist*, June 1986)

The first decisive step for the future of the Labour movement was
the adoption by the TUC and Labour Party of the policy of a national
minimum wage. Although this policy was ignored by the Labour Party
leadership in the 1987 election, NUPE, the union which has led the
fight to get the minimum wage policy adopted, has shown it is not
going to give up the fight. NUPE's 1987 conference demanded that
a minimum wage be set at two-thirds of average national earnings.
Equally significantly, the conference rejected tying the introduction
of a minimum wage to wage restrictions on higher paid workers –
by voting to oppose any wage restraint measures under a Labour
government. Maintaining *both* positions is vital to unite the working
class. If a minimum wage is tied to support for wage controls, higher
paid workers will simply vote Tory or SLD–SPD and support the new
realists. The policy of the minimum wage is decisive because it affects all
low-paid workers – the entire periphery. These essential policies were
also passed at the 1988 Labour Party Conference despite the opposition
of the party leadership. But to be effective the national minimum wage
must *not* be tied to wage controls on higher paid workers.

The second crucial development for the unions is the shift in their
attitude to the demands of women. The effect of the huge increase in
the number of women in work – up 3 million since 1950 – is working
its way through the unions. In 1987, NUPE became the first major
union to have a female majority on its executive, similarly the GMB
has introduced a system whereby one-quarter of its executive places is
reserved for women. Without developing such systematic policies in
support of women workers it would be quite impossible for unions
to extend their influence in the 'periphery'.

The third development has been the extension of industrial action
into these newly unionised layers. The period before Thatcher's election in 1979 saw an unprecedented wave of conflict by public sector and
health workers – the winter of discontent. Following this, 1982 saw the

longest ever strike in the National Health Service and a year later there was the first nationwide strike in the water and sewage industry. The year 1987 saw the first national strike in telecommunications, followed by strikes by teachers and civil servants – the first serious campaigns of industrial action ever waged by these groups. In addition, the political fund ballots forced under the anti-union laws saw not merely every union voting to retain its political fund but new unions – the IRSF, CPSA and NALGO – voting to establish them also.

In short, while severe setbacks have been suffered in traditional sections of the working class, industrial action and serious trade unionism have been spreading far more widely than previously.

The concentration of industrial action in the public sector is logical. The development of the dual economy has created a highly paid manufacturing base which is maintained by a low-paid service sector – a large part of which is in the public sector. While the government can privatise individual industries such as telecommunications, gas, or steel, it cannot completely dismantle the health service – the largest single employer in the country – the education system, the civil service, or, despite its best efforts, local government. Combine this inability to dismantle large parts of the public sector with constant attempts to undermine spending on it and you have a recipe for prolonged conflict. It is exactly for this reason that the government is considering new anti-union laws banning strikes in the public sector.

The trends of the last eight years are clear. The development of the two-tier economy under the impact of the recession is not just dealing severe blows to the trade union movement, it is also transforming its character. The greatly increased numbers of women in work and the growth of the public sector unions is accompanied by the development of strong right-wing trends in sections of private industry. Such trends have also been seen in other countries, notably Japan, which has the most developed two-tier economy, and where for years the trade union movement has been marked by a division between right-wing, private sector, industrial unions and more militant public sector ones.

When Thatcher came to office in 1979 she had evolved the most sophisticated anti-union policy of any British government this century. Her goal was not to eliminate the trade union movement – no British government could achieve that – but to change its nature. Linked with this was the drive to reorganise the British economy and British politics. It is this which underlies the most significant long-term development British capital is attempting to achieve – the splitting of the TUC.

The reason is clear. The great advantage that US and Japanese capital has compared with their Western European rivals, including Britain, is much greater control by employers over the labour market. Japan was once famous for the 'job for life' contracts, but contrary to the impression given this applied to only a small section of Japanese workers. The protected, privileged position for a minority was accompanied by a far larger casual workforce, with far less rights in employment than Britain.

In the United States, until recently, this clear division of employment did not exist. However, the USA achieved roughly the same effect by having far greater employment fluctuations during booms and slumps than in Western Europe, and also by systematic racism in employment. In recent years, US big business has attempted to establish such divisions through two-tier contracts in which existing workers receive higher wage rates, health protection, employment protection, and so on, whereas new workers are employed at a lower rate, have fewer or no 'fringe benefits' and little or no security of employment. By such means a division is created between employees in the same factory or job.

While Thatcher's plans have not progressed to the level of Japanese or US organisation of the labour market, the direction in which British capital is trying to go is perfectly clear. The conscious restructuring of the workforce into relatively secure, higher paid layers and more marginal and insecure sections lies behind much of Tory government policy.

This economic policy has clear implications for the Tory attitude towards the unions. It does not involve attempting to eliminate the trade unions but to confine them to more privileged and secure groups of workers, and then doing deals with the more right-wing trade unions that will exist in these industries. This overall strategy was spelt out in two of the most important documents the Tory Party drew up when in opposition – the draft proposals on the anti-union laws, and the famous 'Ridley report' which pre-planned the confrontation with the miners. The two complemented each other.

In several respects, the original Tory anti-trade union proposals were simply a copy of the policies adopted by the AEU and EETPU – the key unions the Tories had targeted for winning over. Their key to success was the introduction of compulsory postal ballots, coupled with restrictions on secondary action such as picketing. Mrs Thatcher calculated on, and got, direct collaboration from the leadership of these two big craft unions on certain issues of trade union policy such as government money for ballots.

The second aspect, emphasised in the Ridley report, was that there was an economic basis for collaboration between the Tory government and these right-wing unions – particularly the EETPU. Electricity supply – the key to defeating the miners' strike – was singled out as an industry in which long-term security of employment and high wages should be guaranteed. Confrontation in this sector, Ridley noted, was both avoidable and should be avoided. As regards other higher paid groups of workers, the Tories believed they could gain their support by rejecting incomes policy and wage controls. The strategy succeeded and in 1979 the shift to the Tories among skilled manual workers, 13 per cent, was higher than any other section of the population. The same process that saw an electoral swing to Thatcher among better paid and skilled sections of the working class, concentrated in areas such as South East England, was reflected inside the trade union movement in the seizure of the leadership of the AEU by the right.

As for the low paid and unskilled, Thatcher had an answer for them as well. No economic concessions could be given. On the contrary, they were to bear the main brunt of her attacks. They were to be deprived of the right to fight back through a systematic attempt to weaken or destroy unions such as NUPE. Privatisation policy dovetailed into this approach. If in the areas of relatively more prosperous workers the aim was to create right-wing trade unions, in a whole series of low-paid sectors the aim was to eliminate them.

Such a policy had a tremendous impact at the political level, in terms of the unity and structure of the Labour movement. At the peak of its electoral popularity, in 1945 and 1966, the Labour Party's support was based on an alliance of high-paid and low-paid workers. The unity of the TUC – with its membership stretching from high-paid white collar workers down to low-paid black and women workers – was based on its ability to deliver something for everybody. The move of the Tories to increase differentials sharply within the workforce also meant an attempt to shatter the unity of the Labour Party and the trade union movement.

At the electoral level this process started with a swing of skilled workers' votes away from Labour to the Tories, in 1979. In the Labour Party itself, it was carried through by the split of Owen and Jenkins to form the SDP, in 1981, and then the Alliance. This subsequently captured a substantial part of Labour's 'middle class' and skilled workers' vote in the South and South-East in 1983. The culmination of such a move in the trade unions is to split the TUC into two separate federations. One, organised around the EETPU–AUEW bloc coupled with some white collar and other smaller unions, would be based on the higher paid groups of workers. Such a federation would be 'apolitical' – that is, right wing – and favour cooperation between Labour and the centre parties. The second federation would be based on the unskilled and general unions. This would be more left wing and linked to Labour. The Tories would seek to cooperate with the former and smash the latter. Their aim is to split the Labour movement and they will have the full assistance of the centre parties to do so.

It is therefore totally naive to believe that the EETPU leadership's decision to split from the TUC, in 1988, by engineering their expulsion was purely spontaneous or a one-off reaction. The employers and the 'centre' parties have planned to divide the TUC for at least a decade. Hammond and the EETPU merely served their interests in what was a drive to split the TUC by the same forces that in 1981 split the Labour Party to form the SDP.

The links used to achieve this are relatively easy to identify because when the SDP broke from the Labour Party it took with it continuing strong links to right wing sections of the trade unions. Typical of these was the revelation, in September 1985, that David Steel had held discussions with Len Murray when the latter was still general secretary of the TUC. The most open and spectacular success of the SDP in creating links with the unions came in January 1986, when the SDP gained its first member of the TUC general council through recruiting John Lyons, the general secretary of the Engineers and Managers Association (EMA).

A more concerted and widespread SDP offensive towards the unions was organised through the SDP's trade union officer, Tony Halmos, who was recruited to the post from the policy staff of the TUC.

By September 1983 Shirley Williams claimed at the SDP conference that fifteen trade unions, covering 2 million workers, had responded in one form or other to the proposals put forward by the SDP for trade union 'reform'. In September 1983, the SDP achieved its first success in gaining a formal meeting with a union when the NAS/UWT met Owen. The same month, the NALGO executive voted by a narrow majority to meet the SDP leader. In addition to these official approaches to trade union leaderships, Owen maintained his personal links through his continued membership, after the 1983 election, of the Labour Committee for Transatlantic Understanding. Other members of this committee included Frank Chapple, then the general secretary of the EETPU, Terry Duffy, then president of the AUEW, Bill Sirs, then general secretary of the Iron and Steel Trades Confederation (ISTC), Kate Losinska, ex-president of the CPSA, and Gerry Eastwood, general secretary of the Association of Patternmakers and Allied Craftsmen. The committee also included former Labour foreign secretary Lord Stewart and former Labour leader of the House of Lords, Lord Peart. The Labour Committee for Transatlantic Understanding was set up through Joe Godson, the former labour attaché at the US embassy in London.

A further key link between the SDP and the trade union right wing was through the various organisations campaigning for proportional representation. The SDP Campaign for Fair Votes was launched after the June 1983 election and had the support of Frank Chapple. In October 1983, Gavin Laird, general secretary of the AUEW, assumed the vice-presidency of the committee.

There is no doubt that the SDP tailored its politics specifically towards splitting the TUC and the unions' links with the Labour Party. When the 1984 Trade Union Act became law and voting started on the political funds, the SDP launched a systematic campaign for a 'no' vote – although this failed as lamentably as that of the Tory Party.

A hard line on trade union law was adopted right from the creation of the SDP when, in February 1982, the party issued a 'three point programme' calling for compulsory secret postal ballots for all internal union elections, compulsory strike ballots, and opposition to the political levy. Combined with the legal stick, however, the SDP's overall trade union policy was clearly modelled on the policy adopted by the EETPU and AUEW right wing and it was prepared to make specific adjustments towards individual unions. Thus when the 'Union of Democratic Mineworkers' (UDM) split from the National Union of Mineworkers (NUM) the SDP jumped into local government by-elections in Nottinghamshire with clear declarations of support for the new organisation. The SDP had in fact set out to create links with what became the UDM right from the beginning of the miners' strike.

The relationship with the UDM gave the SDP another connection with the right wing of the unions. Prendergast, the joint leader of the UDM, was vice-chair of Mainstream – the right-wing organisation in the trade unions whose founder was Terry Duffy, the president of the AUEW.

Prendergast kept his position in Mainstream despite the UDM's break from the NUM and the TUC. The EETPU, in January 1986, organised an 'energy conference' with the participation of the UDM, and since its expulsion from the TUC has balloted its members on establishing closer links with the new miners' union.

In addition to these activities, the EETPU has also set about trying to influence dissident TGWU members, railway workers, and the prison service. In short, what is involved is not an individual rogue union but a systematic attempt to create a no-strike organisation linked to political parties other than Labour.

The attitude of the Liberals/SLD is no different from that of the SDP. The Liberals set out consciously to utilise, and intervene in, the crisis in the TUC during 1985–6 over accepting state money for trade union ballots, when David Steel called for a split of the TUC between 'an open minded progressive group ready to talk to the Alliance and the government ... and an old fashioned, socialist group which revolves around Labour politics'. Steel stated that the then Alliance was happy to meet the AEU/EETPU or a new trade union group. Similarly, at its 1985 conference, several SDP leaders stated that they would welcome talks with unions which were 'more democratic and modern' such as the EETPU, AUEW and CPSA.

The most important of all the links, however, continues to be organised by John Grant, an ex-Labour MP who joined the SDP. As press officer of the EETPU Grant directly established a meeting between the union and Eddie Shah's *Messenger* group, via one of its directors, the fellow SDP member Lord Harris, to set up the no-strike deal for the company when it opened its *Today* plant. This was the first inroad of the EETPU into the printing industry which prepared the way for its role at Wapping. The EETPU leadership's direct organisational link to the SDP was paralleled in its political proposals. These were initiated in a centre page article by Frank Chapple in *The Times* immediately following the 1983 general election. Chapple argued that 'the introduction of proportional representation would probably mean a socialist government could never be elected'. He stated: 'I am convinced that it will not be long before some rank-and-file members start suggesting that instead of giving our money to a no-hope Labour party, we should donate it to the cause of proportional representation.' Chapple concluded that 'both wings [of the Labour movement] will have to be more independent of each other', and that, 'if we had not been so completely tied to the [Labour] party's coat tails, we could have urged our members to vote SDP or Liberal if they had a better chance of winning'.

Even before Chapple's article, the Alliance had received backing from the Labour right wing prior to the June 1983 election. In 1982, ISTC general secretary Bill Sirs had stated in the union's journal: 'We cannot write off the SDP, who could well be part of a coalition with Labour if Labour fails to clinch a decisive victory.' Roy Grantham, general secretary of the Association of Professional, Executive, Clerical and Computer Staffs (APEX), called for a vote for the Liberals in certain constituencies. Chapple himself called for a vote for SDP candidate John Grant in Islington.

This then is the choice facing progressives in the Labour movement. We need to form an alliance between those key unions such as the TGWU, NUPE and the GMB (who are committed to representing the growing numbers of women and black people in the rapidly changing labour force), unions such as MSF and the NCU (which are concerned with the high-tech areas in competition with the EEPTU) and with radicals both inside and outside the Labour Party.

So far the Labour leadership has refused to break with the EEPTU and they continue to rely on their votes at conference to control the party and continue the drift to the right. But it is only the progressive alliance that has a chance to mobilise sufficient backing to defeat the Tories. It is therefore vital that the Labour leadership understands that the project of the EETPU and the centre parties is not merely to transform British trade unionism into business unionism as seen in the USA. Together with the Tories and the centre parties the EETPU leadership is fighting to change the entire nature of the British Labour movement, and, by preventing the election of a majority socialist government to institutionalise permanently the changes in British society that have been carried out by Mrs Thatcher. With direct collaboration between the EETPU and the most ruthless bosses of British industry such as Shah and Murdoch, backed by the anti-trade union legislation of the Tories, this is a political assault on the Labour movement of a type which has not been seen this century. Any underestimation of it whatever would be fatal for Labour. The battle is not a foregone conclusion, as is clear from the continuing, underlying strength of progressive trade unions, but the TUC and Labour party leadership must recognise the EETPU and centre parties for what they are: daggers pointed at the heart of the British Labour movement.

13

The Pursuit of Power

For the last ten years the Labour Party has been assailed by a barrage of propaganda predicting its rapid demise. This stream of debilitating nonsense has come from both the left and right of British politics, as everyone from Marxist philosophers to Murdoch's editorial writers have sought to try to explain the massive changes taking place in the social and economic structure of the nation as leading to the inevitable decline of the Labour Party. But as the previous chapter demonstrates the basic strength of the Labour movement is still there in the trade unions, even though it is now irretrievably split. Fortunately for the Labour Party it is the breakaway EETPU-led faction which faces the very real problem of survival – although it will have powerful allies for its 'business unionism' in the media, the government, MI5 and the judiciary, who will do all they can to support the electricians.

The alternative trade union strategy springs from the emerging alliance of the general unions (TGWU/NUPE/GMB) and those in the high technology, white collar sector (MSF/NCU). The success of their strategy will depend on their continuing ability to reflect the changing composition of the workforce. The fortunes of the Labour Party are inextricably linked with these unions because the changes in the labour force have inevitably been followed by similar changes in the electorate.

The differences between Labour's electoral triumph in 1966, when it secured 48 per cent of the vote and a hundred seat majority in the House of Commons, and the present day are shown in Table 13.1. As can be seen there has not, as our opponents claim, been a simple 'decline of the working class' taking place. Contrary to the endless articles spewed out by the Tory press speculating that there has been a change in the class structure of the population, which will make it impossible for Labour ever to win another election, the figures demonstrate quite the reverse. There has been no significant decline in the proportion of unskilled and semi-skilled working-class families in the electorate. In fact these groups have remained an almost constant proportion of the electorate (30 per cent) for more than twenty years. The expansion of white collar sectors, both professional/managerial workers and clerical workers, has been entirely at the expense of *skilled* manual workers with their numbers falling from 39 per cent in 1964 to 27 per cent in 1987. It is this group of voters which has swung most decisively to Mrs Thatcher over the last decade which are in the most dramatic decline as an electoral force. Indeed, there are now more unskilled and semiskilled working class families in the electorate than there are skilled workers.

Table 13.1   Shift in Structure of Electorate, 1964-8

	1964	1966	1974(O)	1983	1987	Change 1966–87
Professional/ Managerial (AB)	10	12	13	17*	19	+ 7
Clerical (C1)	19	22	22	23*	24	+ 2
Skilled manual (C2)	39	37	32	31	27	−10
Semi/Unskilled manual (DE)	31	29	33	29	30	+ 1

* Extrapolated

The significance of these trends for Labour's electoral strategy, and for the trade unions, is evident. The number of skilled manual workers has been squeezed on both sides – by skilled manual workers moving into white collar jobs and by the increased weight within the manual working class of unskilled and semi-skilled workers. This is a deep-seated trend and all the projections suggest that we can anticipate that there will be a continued decline in the number of skilled manual workers.

The important lesson to learn from these figures is that whilst skilled workers *must* be won back to Labour it is absurd for Neil Kinnock to base his entire strategy on pandering to the often reactionary and backward views of a social group which is declining in electoral significance, whilst at the same time being consistently antagonistic to those sections of the population which are increasing in size and influence. The key sectors for the Labour Party's future, and the trade unions', will be the growing white collar sector and the semiskilled and unskilled workers. Both these are groups which have seen radical changes in sexual and racial composition.

If Labour is to be able to assemble the electoral coalition which can deliver a majority Labour government, then our policies must be seen to be both modern and relevant to the component parts of that coalition. Thus, in this book I have ignored vast areas of policy in order to concentrate on the key areas where we have failed in the past, and which it is vital we get right in the future if we are to be able to attract the support we need in order to win.

The first and most vital of these is the economy. It is Labour's past mismanagement of this factor that originally alienated the skilled workers who have swung so decisively towards the Tories. Everything else that we seek to do rests on our ability to succeed in this area, for unless we can demonstrate that the Labour Party has the capacity to lead British society and its economy out of decline we will never win in the first place. Such a policy can only be fashioned in cooperation with the trade unions. First, we must attract the white collar unions in high technology industry – MSF is a prime example together with others such as the NCU. Second, there are the white collar unions in the public 'service' sector such as the teaching unions and NALGO (these unions will not be affiliating to Labour in the short term but this does not prevent us seeking the closest collaboration with them). Third, within the manual sector the key unions are those with large numbers of unskilled and semi-skilled workers – the TGWU, GMB and NUPE which are already adapting themselves to the changing sexual and racial structure of the workforce. These are also the unions that can orient to the area of our greatest weakness – workers in the private service sector.

This is the real electoral base for a Labour Party which wishes to place itself at the head of a dynamic alliance of forces, and it is these unions which are most likely to support the modernising economic policy without which Labour cannot win an election.

The adoption of policies for the modernisation of the British *economy* would give Labour the opportunity to build an alliance which can unite the party, and then, and much more importantly, form a government. I have spelt out earlier in this book what that entails. First, it would mean the redirection of finance capital to increase drastically investment in the British economy and in particular in the high-tech sectors. This must be financed at the expense of foreign investment and not by increased taxes or incomes policies both of which hit at ordinary, middle-income families and individuals. It means a rapid build-up of investment in manufacturing industry. The gains for the workers, and unions, in these industries is obvious and it also creates a basis for Labour to bring together a new social alliance as formidable as that which elected the 1945 or 1966 Labour governments.

A modern economy cannot be run only by investment in factories. It requires a rapid and efficient transport and telecommunications system and massive resources for training, and retraining, its workforce. A modernised British economy would have a far more efficient and larger manufacturing sector, modern railways, and a huge increase in resources for education. The real resources it would release and generate would transform the conditions of the people of this country for the better and give Labour a new base for popularity.

If Labour wishes to make itself not only the party of *caring* but also the party of *production* then these are the policies and alliances it should be creating. This means Labour rebuilding itself not by becoming distanced from those unions which have an interest in the modernisation of the domestic economy but in alliance with them. Indeed without the support of the trade unions it would be impossible to take the drastic measures necessary to modernise the economy. This, therefore, is the basis of a real modernisation of the Labour Party – not in the cosmetic sense of updating its presentation, but in the much more profound intention of transforming Labour to bring it into line with the new social structure of Britain.

The second vital area of policy, linking both economic and social policy, is international. The weakening of the dominance of the United States over Europe is already under way and as the latest trade figures show there is an increasingly determined US assault on the EEC economy taking place. Everyone, particularly the European right, knows that it will continue. The United States cannot any longer bear the cost of its military, economic and political involvement in Europe. Thatcher's hope to maintain a dominant US presence in Europe, which is the core of her foreign policy, is therefore doomed and is rejected even by sections of the European right. The key question is what will replace that US dominance in Europe?

The 'Euro-right', typified in Britain by Paddy Ashdown and Dr David Owen, are determined that United States militarism in Europe must be replaced by EEC militarism. They believe that the EEC must have, or hire, its own nuclear weapons (whether it be the Euro-bomb, Trident or air-launched Cruise missiles) as well as building up conventional forces. They want this organised through the Western European Union.

This policy, shared by Labour's right wing, would be a military and economic disaster for Europe which already lags behind the United States and Japan in economic growth and high technology. If Europe tries to add the burden of increased armaments to its already poor economic performance it faces still deeper economic stagnation.

What makes this policy absurd is the opportunity created by Gorbachev. The majority of the electorate no longer believes the cold war myths that Soviet hordes are poised to invade Western Europe. *The Guardian* found in a poll, in January 1989, that only 4 per cent of the population considered the Soviet Union under Gorbachev a threat. They see the Soviet Union for what it is – a country which wishes to be left to get on with developing its own economy. The voters do not believe it is worth paying the price of wrecked social services, and a stagnant economy, to 'defend' ourselves against a threat which exists only in the minds of right-wing fanatics and the few remaining figures amongst Labour MPs whose primary loyalty is to Washington.

The mutual interest of Western Europe and the USSR is obvious. The USSR wishes to reduce its level of military spending to improve its economy – which will lead to greater freedom and reform inside the USSR itself. Western Europe needs to be able to divert resources from military spending to investment and social services, to speed up economic growth and create a highly trained workforce for tomorrow.

Modernising Labour's international policy means above all seizing the international opportunity to reshape the whole European economy in that direction. We must also break out of the habit of defining Europe as the EEC and recognise that Gorbachev's phrase 'our common European home' has a tremendous resonance with that majority of Europeans who have been born after the Second World War. Instead of spending the next twenty years reacting against the plans of the right to create a new military superpower based on the countries of the EEC we must capture the imagination of the new generation of Europeans with a peaceful and democratic alternative.

This must be based on the principle of a United European Assembly going beyond the EEC to include Eastern Europe. It must be a decentralised and devolved Europe based on the different regions of the continent rather than on the existing nation states. The new Europe must have the closest economic relationship with the USSR and this can only be facilitated by a massive reduction in military spending and the removal of all American and Soviet troops from Western and Eastern Europe respectively. It must reach out to the nations of the Third World, not as yet another centre for the headquarters of damaging and exploitative multinational corporations but as an equal partner with a shared interest in the preservation of the natural world.

The third area of policy that Labour needs to address is that of democracy and the nature of Britain's institutions. One way in which this issue has forced itself on to the political agenda is the concern over the concentration of power around Mrs Thatcher and her government. This led to the creation of Charter 88, yet instead of responding positively and looking for common ground it was the Labour leadership who rushed in to rubbish the ideas of this group. Labour's leaders completely failed to realise that the people behind Charter 88 represented a very large section of concerned middle-class opinion which is a vital part of any anti-Tory majority – not unlike those middle-class voters who gave Labour their support for the first time in 1945. For that wartime generation the swing to Labour had been triggered because they were genuinely shocked by the physical condition of the working-class children who had been billeted with them following evacuation from the inner cities during the war. Now, the seminal issue for humanitarian middle-class opinion is the growing authoritarianism of the state and the rapid erosion of our remaining civil liberties. These people are an absolutely vital part of any coalition of forces to defeat the Tories and Labour will only win their support if it adopts their agenda of concerns.

There is, however, the wider aspect of the new democratic agenda which Charter 88 failed to deal with – that of the rights of workers at work and the rights of consumers of both private and public services. Labour's leaders must recognise that the old paternalism is dead and the redistribution of power is as important to people today as the redistribution of wealth was to our parents.

Finally, there is the way in which we must recast all our policies so that we place their environmental impact as the first item on any agenda about how to proceed with their implementation.

If Labour can have the imagination to set a new agenda based on these areas of policy it will appeal to the concerns of the vast majority of the British people. Once we have accepted the basic commitments to the reconstruction of our economy, a new relationship with Europe and the world, the protection of our environment and the democratisation of Britain, we will find that we have adopted a coherent framework into which all our other policies can easily be integrated. We would also find that for the first time in twenty-five years Labour was unchallenged as the party ready and eager to lead the people into a period of reform and modernisation that would prepare us for the next century.

This then is the agenda for change that can return Labour to government but who in the present party leadership is likely to adopt it? When we look at who is really supporting moves to modernise the Labour Party and its policies, we can see how absurd is the press's characterisation of the difference between 'modernisers' and 'traditionalists' within the party. This issue came to a head around Ron Todd's speech at the Tribune rally at the 1988 party conference. Todd's speech was important not just for the part the press picked up – on unilateralism, but above all for what it said about *modernising* the party. In a key section of the speech, completely unreported by the press, Ron Todd said:

> We know the party needs modernising. We know that you can't work in the old-fashioned way. And we've put our knowledge into practice ... Nor are we slow to respond to political change. We know that this movement must find a new openness, a new willingness to listen to and involve the ethnic minorities and female majority in the country. And we put our votes where our mouths are.

This approach is vital because the brew of public relations gimmicks and right-wing policies which were served up at Blackpool and in the Policy Review are *not* about modernising the party. Nor will they work – any more than brilliant presentation without policy content worked at the 1987 election. To judge who are the real modernisers within the party we should consider how people act and vote rather than what they say.

The attitude of the leadership was made clear on the first day of the 1988 Labour Party Conference when they voted against the inclusion of a woman on every parliamentary shortlist. Women form 52 per cent of the population. They are the only expanding sector of the workforce. They are the most rapidly growing part of the trade union movement, yet they form less than 10 per cent of the PLP. But even the minimal demand that a woman be considered for *possible* selection for Parliament was rejected by the right wing. Those who vote in such a way are not 'modernisers', they are the most deeply reactionary elements in the Labour movement. The same attitude was seen at the 1986 conference when the right wing, led by Neil Kinnock, voted against the proposal that Labour's planned Ministry for Women should have Cabinet status.

What *was* important for Labour's future at the 1988 conference, and what Ron Todd's speech was part of, was the emergence of a truly modernising alliance which can transform the Labour Party. That alliance came together, and defeated the leadership, in the debates on unilateralism, on the minimum wage, on employment training, on women's demands, on black rights, on the reform of the block vote and on international issues such as the plight of the Palestinians. That alliance was expressed in the activity of women during the week. Women in the constituencies and the Labour Women's Action Committee came together with women in trade unions like the TGWU, NUPE and MSF to vote through progressive policies. It demonstrated the reality that it is the left of the party which is the truly modernising force within Labour. Those same unions and socialists which formed the left majorities at Blackpool in 1988 are the unions and socialists with an interest in the modernisation of the economy and the party.

It is because the leadership, behind all its rhetoric, is in reality resisting change that Labour has not made better progress towards defeating Mrs Thatcher and the Tories. Instead, the present leader and deputy leader of the Labour Party have placed themselves four-square in opposition to all the demands of the new social forces currently transforming the workforce. Indeed, they often side with the most reactionary elements such as the EETPU against the demands of women and black people. It was only when opinion polls showed the poor standing of the Labour Party amongst women that some simple gestures were made to try to rectify the situation. Not, of course, to concede any real power to women within the party structure, because that would offend the EETPU and the AEU, but a few public relations gimmicks such as showing more shots of Labour's Shadow Cabinet men surrounded by mothers and children in nurseries.

Not only is the present leadership failing to adopt the modern policies which could galvanise a majority of the electorate, but they also seem to lack the confidence to set our own agenda. Time and time again it merely responds to the agenda set by the Tories and Fleet Street. Whether it was the miners' strike, the Falklands War, 'loony left' councils or the even the Zircon affair with its vital issue of freedom of the press, our leaders seem to accept unquestioningly the agenda and even the parameters of debate set by our political opponents. They are then shocked and surprised when we reach an election and discover that the voters have also accepted the Tories' agenda.

Instead of distancing themselves from the miners' strike, the party leadership should have been at the head of the campaign to raise funds for the miners and their families. Instead of accepting the Tories' agenda about violence, Neil Kinnock should have dispatched a Labour MP to every picket line, so that when the issue of violence was raised we would have been able to produce an eye witness to answer the exaggerations of the media. The presence of a Labour MP would also have helped to restrain some of the more provocative police tactics. Labour's leaders should have exposed how the Tories had deliberately planned and provoked the strike by ignoring the agreed procedures concerning pit closures. They should have exposed the long-term plans to replace coal as an energy source with more expensive and more environmentally damaging nuclear power. In the end, Labour's failure to defend the miners allowed Thatcher to advance and consolidate her position.

The same mistake was made when Norman Tebbit launched his assault on Labour councils. Instead of defending them from Tebbit's racist, sexist and homophobic attack, Labour's leaders could do no more than meekly reply that it was only a small minority of councillors who were behaving badly. Having thus accepted that Tebbit was partly right they legitimised the witch-hunt which the press then redoubled. However, when, following the 1987 election, Goldsmiths College conducted an academic study of the attacks they found that EVERY example of alleged 'looniness' was untrue. They found that Bernie Grant had not banned black dustbin liners because they were racist or instructed staff not to ask for black coffee because to do so would be racist. They found that Islington Council had not banned the use of 'Ba Ba Black Sheep' in its nurseries. And most important of all, they could find no school where homosexuality was being encouraged or promoted. Yet so pervasive was this bit of Fleet Street folklore that it went on to form the basis of legislation in Parliament.

It was quite clear what Tebbit was up to. As Chair of Tory Central Office, he had analysed the polling and local election data which showed that the government's attacks on local councils had rebounded badly on the Tory support in various key areas. In Liverpool, the support for the Labour council in its fight with the government had squeezed the base of the Tories almost to the point of extinction. In Lambeth, the banned and surcharged Labour councillors were replaced by an even bigger Labour majority. In London, popular support for the Labour GLC had surpassed that achieved by Labour in the 1945 and 1966 general elections or in the previous best years for Labour in local government – 1946 and 1971.

In September 1984 the Harris poll recorded support for the Labour GLC at 56 per cent and MORI came up with the almost identical figure of 55 per cent – both agreed that support for the Tories and the Alliance had fallen to 28 and 15 per cent respectively. Had a GLC election gone ahead it would have produced a result of 84 Labour councillors to just 4 Tories and 4 Alliance. The same polls also showed that the Tories could lose up to 33 of the 56 seats they held in London at the next general election. These were figures which Tebbit could not ignore and Tory Central Office began planning its counter-attack.

It was decided to do nothing until after abolition because of the fear that the GLC's public relations machine would have been able to neutralise or at least balance any campaign launched before abolition, but with the GLC out of the way Tebbit, with the full support of the Tory papers, struck. No one borough had the resources to respond, let alone adequate access to the media. The only people who could have come to the help of those Labour councils under fire were the party leaders and they stayed firmly on the sidelines.

What was needed was a calm, rational and humorous response which simply took each charge and presented the facts, in the same way that the Goldsmiths' study did two years later. A party political broadcast in which someone with a bit of authority (Denis Healey would have been ideal) examined the facts and then proceeded to ridicule the charges out of court could have defused the issue. But the party leaders were running scared and, hoping it would all blow over, did nothing.

A typical example of the leadership's attitude came at the height of Brent's notorious McGoldrick case. Merle Amory, the leader of Brent Council, wrote to Neil Kinnock offering to brief him about the council's side of the row but never received a reply. A few days later she opened the papers to read that Brent's policy had been condemned by Neil Kinnock.

By the time of the Greenwich by-election, Tebbit's lies had sunk deep into the public's perception of the Labour Party and played a major part in the loss of that by-election and the rapid demoralisation of the party that followed, continuing right up to the general election itself. On my own canvassing, I still found many people who seriously believed that some schools were giving lessons to children in how to become lesbians!

Another disturbing example of how Labour automatically seems to accept the Tories' parameters was the Zircon affair. When journalist Duncan Campbell exposed that the government had been lying to Parliament and was secretly planning to launch a large spy satellite over the USSR, the police were used to raid his home and the BBC, and pressure was applied to the BBC, to prevent the film about Zircon being shown. In order to minimise the row in Parliament, Neil Kinnock and Denis Healey were summoned to a special briefing by the government at which they were told that the actions taken had been in the interests of national security. Denis and Neil then emerged from the briefing to tell the world that they accepted the government's word and their only complaint was that firmer action should have been taken sooner.

Why it should be in the national interest that the Zircon project remain secret was never made clear. Anyone with two grey cells to rub together would have realised that it was not because Mrs Thatcher wished to keep it secret from the Russian hordes. After all, the USSR has had radar for some time and it would not have been difficult for its leaders to realise that a satellite the size of a small bus, parked over Moscow in a geostationary orbit, with a tight communications beam down to Cheltenham GCHQ was a spy satellite with missile targeting potential.

No, once again it was a case of the government of the day wishing to keep its secret from the British people for fear that they would have been alarmed to discover just what an escalation of the arms race Zircon represented.

Before a missile can be fired into the USSR with any degree of certainty that it will reach its target, the launch computer needs to be programmed with the latest data on many factors such as weather conditions and anti-ballistic missile dispositions. Up until now the UK has had to rely on the USA to provide such information, but if Britain could have acquired its own targeting satellite it would have given Mrs Thatcher a greater degree of independence from the White House concerning any decision to start a nuclear war. Leaving aside the issue of the peace of mind of 56 million Britons faced with the knowledge that Mrs Thatcher had got one step closer to being able to start a nuclear war all on her own, there is the not unimportant question of the impact on Soviet thinking. What would such a changed situation have done to Gorbachev's disarmament proposals, or for the strength of his opponents inside the USSR who wish to revert to a firm cold war posture?

No, the issue was not one of security but the usual sinister nonsense of the British people being excluded from any knowledge of events, let alone having rights to a say in any of them. It was a decision in the great tradition of Attlee's resolve to build the atom bomb without telling the Cabinet, and Wilson's decision to upgrade Polaris into Chevaline whilst also ignoring the Cabinet.

The party leadership should have been able to inflict appalling damage on the government for escalating the arms race, undermining Gorbachev's position, using the police to raid the BBC, applying pressure to the BBC to suppress the Zircon programme, lying to Parliament and doing the whole thing behind the backs of the British people. But it was not to be and Her Majesty's Loyal Opposition chose instead to play the patriot game as trustworthy members of the 'club' who could be relied upon to know their place and play by the established rules. Thatcher had been caught in the act like a burglar climbing out of a window with a bag marked 'swag'. Not only did our leaders not blow the whistle, they actually held the window open and called a cab for her getaway.

The same desire to appear respectable and patriotic underlay Labour's approach to the Falklands War, to exposing the shoot to kill policy in Northern Ireland, and to staying silent in the face of Thatcher's cover-up of the abuses by the security services. This desire for respectability has existed for decades under leaders from both wings of the party, but by thus accepting the Tories' agenda they have invariably strengthened public support for the Tories. To go against these unwritten ground-rules would lead to massive press criticism, but whatever may happen between elections there is always going to be a huge press attack on the Labour Party whenever an election finally arrives.

In fact the Labour leadership only gets a sympathetic hearing in the press when it is accepting the Tories' agenda or attacking socialists inside the Labour Party. The best examples of this in recent times were the periods of highly favourable press coverage that Neil Kinnock received when he attacked Arthur Scargill and Derek Hatton.

Unfortunately, Neil Kinnock's attacks allowed the press to reinforce Mrs Thatcher's claim that socialists were 'the enemy within', thus creating the impression that the ordinary members of the Labour Party and socialism itself were an alien threat to the British people.

Not only did these internal divisions play into Thatcher's hands but they also diverted the efforts of the leadership from the vital task of setting our own political agenda. Because of the legal requirement that the independent radio and television companies should 'balance' the amount of coverage they give to the political parties, the time spent attacking Derek Hatton was time not spent explaining Labour's economic and defence policies. If the vast amount of radio and television time that the leadership wasted attacking Hatton and Scargill had been devoted to explaining our policies, we would have been in a much stronger position when the 1987 election came along.

In retrospect, it seems incredible that so much time was devoted to the leadership's crusade against the left inside the party that they never got around to launching a campaign against the Poll Tax. Both before and during the election Labour, outside Scotland, ignored the issue even though the government had already passed the Scottish Poll Tax Act into law. During the election campaign itself Neil Kinnock's attack on Hatton was shown in two party political broadcasts whilst the Poll Tax was ignored. After the election the leader's office leaked to the press the fact that he was annoyed that the party had not done more on the Poll Tax. But no Labour leader in the history of the party has controlled the party's decision-making processes more tightly than Neil Kinnock and the failure to campaign on the Poll Tax cannot be blamed on anyone else.

Even more surprising was the behaviour of Roy Hattersley. In the run-up to the election he had led a long and divisive campaign to expel two left-wingers from his local party. Their only 'crime' had been to expose the corrupt packing of local party meetings with fictitious members. The charges against these two (Amir Khan and Kevin Scally) were so transparently trumped up that after wasting a vast amount of the national party's time (in the vital run-up to the 1987 election), the local party was forced to readmit the members. Yet when the election campaign was in its last ten days, it became painfully obvious that although Hattersley had found all the time in the world to pursue Khan and Scully, he had not found the time to work out our tax policy in enough detail to avoid the Tories and their supporters in the press from exposing its contradictions. The decline in Labour's support in the polls in that last week of the campaign suggests that the confusion on tax may have lost us a million votes and doubled Thatcher's parliamentary majority.

In contrast to the vigour with which the Labour leadership attacked socialists inside the Labour Party, Thatcher herself was often treated with kid gloves. The one point on which she was vulnerable, and could have been forced to resign, was on the Westland affair when her two closest aids, Charles Powell (Private Secretary) and Bernard Ingham (Press Secretary) authorised Leon Brittan to leak a confidential letter which was damaging to Michael Heseltine.

On the day of the final Commons debate Thatcher herself was telling friends, 'I may not be Prime Minister by six o'clock tonight.' To win, Labour needed to restrict the attack to the area of Thatcher's maximum vulnerability – the use of her closest Downing Street officials to leak the letter. We needed to concentrate on how inconceivable it was that she had not known what her closest officials were doing. But when Labour's attack came the desire to make it respectable, wide ranging and authoritative meant that it failed. The scene was described by *Guardian* columnist Hugo Young:

> Rarely has so inviting a target been so easily missed as when Neil Kinnock failed to pin the Prime Minister to the questions she needed to answer. Bombastic and blustering, he managed the extraordinary feat of making these events sound, after all, almost unimportant. Before he sat down, she could know that she had escaped, as the Tory backbenchers, shaking off their gloom, rejoiced in his discomfort.

It was almost as though Labour's leaders felt that they could not be seen to go straight for the jugular. The Tories knew what was at stake and had no such inhibitions. Throughout Neil Kinnock's speech they behaved like a pack of baying hounds, drowning out his words.

Again and again during the Thatcher years her opponents have seemed uncertain about how to attack her, hesitated, and as a consequence she has got away with things that could have been used to bring down any male Prime Minister such as:

● The business dealings of her son in the Middle East while she was on a trade mission to the area.

● The use of Downing Street headed notepaper by her husband while trying to influence a decision on behalf of a friend.

● Her refusal to investigate the involvement of Airey Neave, her closest friend and campaign manager, in the race against Edward Heath and in the illegal activities of MI5.

● The cover-up over the reason for the decision to sink the *Belgrano*. A decision that was taken because the US Secretary of State, Alexander Haig, had been able to negotiate an agreement with the Argentinian government which would have allowed a peaceful settlement. Whilst this would have saved the lives of hundreds of young British and Argentinian servicemen and guaranteed the rights of the islanders, it would have recognised the Argentinian claim and meant eventual Argentinian control of the islands. At that point in 1982 Thatcher knew that because her economic policies had caused so much pain and dislocation she was already in a weak position within the Parliamentary Tory Party and anything short of an outright military victory would be likely to cause her downfall. For that reason the decision was taken to sink the *Belgrano*, although it was moving away from the islands, knowing that such an action would destroy Haig's negotiated settlement and allow Thatcher the chance to retake the islands by military force and survive as Prime Minister.

On all these issues a male Prime Minister would have been mercilessly hounded but her critics both inside and outside the Tory Party have time and again simply failed to go in for the kill. Perhaps they are prisoners of their own sexism but whatever the cause she has exploited it ruthlessly and survived. Her critics have been defeated or replaced and she has been allowed to wrap herself in the flag.

It is perhaps the greatest irony of all that she should be allowed to use patriotism so blatantly when one considers the meagre nature of her own commitment to Britain during its hour of need. When young Margaret Roberts finished her schooling Britain was fighting for survival against the Nazis in the midst of the Second World War. But the value of enlisting in the armed forces, working on the munitions lines, helping on the farms, or in any of the other ways that civilians were able to assist in the war effort, was not immediately obvious to the future Iron Maiden. At that point in time when she could have demonstrated her own patriotism and courage, she chose instead to scuttle off to Oxford University and left the fight to others. The leader who would one day wrap herself in the flag as she sent young men off to die in the Falklands, saving her own political career in the process, chose to get herself a degree in chemistry rather than throw herself into the war effort. Of course, this did mean that after the war she was ready to do vital research into discovering how much air could be added to ice cream.

Instead of attacking Thatcher or assembling a coherent package of ideas, Labour's leaders relied on a slick advertising campaign to win them the 1987 election. What they failed to realise was that Thatcher had won in 1979 because she had spent the previous four years campaigning to win the ideological battle against traditional labourism, and until Labour can regain the upper hand in the field of policy they will not be able to win an election. In this book I have tried to spell out what I believe that coherent package of ideas should include. We can never defeat the Tories by accommodating their ideas or moving on to their terrain because voters will always realise that the Tories are the best party to carry out Tory policies. If we take just one example from the many where Labour has made concessions to the Tories, we should take the issue of race. For all Labour's concessions to the racists, it has still not defused the issues of immigration or racism and clearly demonstrates the pointlessness of conceding ground to our opponents. When the Macmillan government introduced racist immigration controls for the first time, in 1962, Gaitskell opposed them on principle, but with Gaitskell dead and the less principled Wilson in the party leadership it took just nine months for Wilson to change the policy. In November 1963, he told the Commons, 'We do not contest the need for the control of Commonwealth immigration into this country.' A year later Labour lost three seats in the 1964 election due to a racist backlash. The badly shaken Labour government did not have the courage to fight to change racist attitudes amongst its own supporters. Instead it produced its own White Paper proposing further restrictions on black immigration. The Cabinet Committee on Immigration spelt out the motive force behind these new proposals: 'it has been quite clear that immigration can be the greatest potential vote-loser for the Labour party if we are seen as permitting a flood of immigrants to come in and blight the central areas in all our cities'. Labour Home Secretary Frank Soskice did not mince words 'If we do not have strict immigration rules, our people will soon all be coffee-coloured.'

Of course, these concessions did not placate the racists. Many Tory MPs and the National Front continued to agitate for a total ban and even repatriation. In October 1967, the then Home Secretary, Roy Jenkins, warned that as many as 50,000 Kenyan Asians might exercise their rights to come to Britain each year because of increasing hostility from the Kenyan government. Although these people had been given full British citizenship as part of the deal on Kenyan independence, they were simply stripped of their rights to come to Britain because the Labour government feared another racist backlash. Had the UK had a written constitution or a Bill of Rights this would have been illegal and unconstitutional, but lacking these safeguards it was possible for the Labour government to push the law through in just three days. The formula used introduced the patrial concept whereby the right of British passport holders to enter Britain was restricted to those who had one parent or grandparent who had been born in the UK. This meant that virtually anyone from the old white Commonwealth could get in but not black people. This legislation would not have been out of place in the first years of Hitler's government, but only thirty-five Labour MPs broke the three-line whip and voted against it.

Labour having introduced the concept of patriality, the Heath government extended it further and although Labour voted against the new legislation its opposition seemed hollow, and when returned to government in 1974 the party made no effort to repeal the measure. Even worse was the decision in 1976 of Labour Prime Minister Callaghan to sack Alex Lyons, the minister in charge of immigration, on the grounds that he had been letting too many black people into the country.

The failure to tackle the issue of racism head on and defeat the racists' propaganda that black people were a problem meant that support for the National Front continued to grow, and in the 1977 GLC elections they won 5.3 per cent of the vote in London. Whilst the Labour government seemed paralysed and did nothing, leadership passed to the extra-parliamentary left who began the fight against the NF on the streets. Mrs Thatcher also moved decisively. Realising that the NF vote was a vital, potential part of her own coalition to defeat the Labour government, she made a direct and blatant appeal for the white racist vote. Appearing on television at the start of the 1978 council election campaign, she pandered to the racists with the statement that she understood the fears of ordinary people who felt that British culture was being swamped by an alien tide. The effect of her shift to the right was immediate. NF support collapsed as their voters switched to the Tories. Many NF activists soon joined the Tory party and rose to occupy positions in the local Tory associations, were selected as Tory candidates for seats on local councils, and in one case even for a winnable parliamentary seat.

The Thatcher government repaid its racist support with the introduction of vicious immigration controls which have split families and caused untold human misery. Throughout it all, the occupants of Labour's front bench have wrung their hands on the sidelines whilst promising to replace Thatcher's racist controls with 'fair' ones.

This despicable record of appeasement to racism should be a warning that Labour cannot defeat the Tories by shifting to accommodate their policies. As soon as Labour moves, the Tories simply take another step to the right and the same will happen on the defence issue. If Neil Kinnock eventually succeeds in persuading the trade union leaderships to abandon our policy of unilateral nuclear disarmament, Thatcher will not turn around and say this is no longer an issue between the parties. She will demand we commit a Labour government to the 'first use' of nuclear weapons or increase the rate of modernisation of NATO's nuclear strike force.

We are lucky that Mrs Thatcher has no sense of humour or she might follow the logic of her policies on wider home ownership and wider share ownership and extend it to wider bomb ownership. 'A nuclear bomb for the nuclear family' – 'every owner-occupier equipped with their own tactical nuclear weapon so they can stand on their own two feet and fight the Russians without having to rely on the state to do it for them'!

Yet for all our past experience of the disasters which follow when Labour attempts to steal the Tories' policies, we still seem to be intent on trying it. Instead of putting Thatcher under massive pressure to respond to Gorbachev's unilateral peace initiatives, Labour's leaders have often sounded as cautious and anti-Soviet as Thatcher herself. Instead of questioning NATO's obstructive attitude to the Soviet proposals for reducing the NATO and Warsaw Pact forces, Labour's leadership has committed itself loyally to accept even those NATO decisions which are contrary to our existing policy, such as our opposition to the 'first use' of nuclear weapons. Indeed, in going out of his way to emphasise his commitment to NATO, Labour's Shadow Foreign Secretary, Gerald Kaufman, has disappeared so far up NATO's fundament that only the soles of his feet remain visible.

A similar desire for respectability has prevented Labour gaining the full benefit it should have received from the growing public concern for the environment. Labour's leaders have for years kept the environmentalists at arm's length for fear that they would alienate workers in the nuclear and other environmentally damaging industries, who feared that tough policies on the environment could lead to job losses. Even when we adopted good policies they seldom featured in the leader's speeches. Thus when Thatcher made her totally cynical bid for the green vote Labour appeared to be struggling to keep up, and an area of policy which should have been Labour terrain fell to Thatcher.

Instead of trying to con the British people with a watered-down version of the Tories' policies, we should remember that Mrs Thatcher's three election victories have been achieved with just 44, 43 and 42 per cent of the votes, and when the high rate of abstention is taken into account it reveals that at the 1987 election only 32 per cent of the British people voted for the Tories. Mrs Thatcher has won because traditional labourism was an exhausted, unimaginative and spent force which had degenerated into corporatism and insensitive bureaucracy. She was then the main beneficiary when the most pro-US section of the Labour Party split away and gave her the advantage of a divided opposition. Finally, she has been the luckiest Premier of the twentieth century with a bonus of £120 billion from North Sea oil which has allowed her to bribe the electorate on a scale Wilson and Macmillan could only dream about.

Labour MPs should not be bewailing the fact that we cannot win and wondering aloud about the need for pacts with the centre parties. When we examine the opinion surveys it becomes quite clear that there is a massive anti-Tory majority in Britain and our problem is simply how to mobilise that majority behind the Labour Party. On virtually all her most contentious policies Mrs Thatcher has faced and continues to face overwhelming opposition from the public. From the 2 million unemployed created by her recession between 1979 and 1981, through the abolition of the GLC to the present day policies of the Poll Tax and water privatisation, there has been overwhelming public opposition to her policies which she has contemptuously ignored.

There is no doubt that at the end of the Callaghan government the majority of people were in favour of rolling back the state, curbing trade unions and cutting taxes. But this was a reaction against the incompetence and drift of the Labour government rather than a sea change in the popular will. Within two years, as Thatcher's policies began to bite, public opinion had turned around and has stayed that way ever since. It is not just that there is a vast majority in favour of retaining a completely free health service, but on the underlying values that lie at the core of people's beliefs a majority of the population is committed to some form of socialist society.

A detailed and exhaustive poll was conducted by MORI in 1988 after nine years of the Thatcher experiment. It showed that when asked to define an ideal society 49 per cent opted for socialism and a controlled economy, as opposed to the 43 per cent who chose capitalism. Asked to choose between the collective provision of welfare services or self-sufficiency, 55 per cent wanted collectivism and 79 per cent said they would prefer a society which valued caring above wealth creation.

These impressive figures show that it would be possible to elect a socialist government if people could only be convinced that the Labour Party was fit and ready to govern with a coherent package of policies that were capable of modernising Britain.

If instead we lose our nerve and try to do a deal with the other anti-Tory parties in order to defeat Thatcher, such a strategy is bound to fail. Even if the opposition parties could agree to stand a single anti-Thatcher candidate (committed to proportional representation) in each constituency, there is no evidence to suggest that the whole anti-Thatcher vote could be delivered to such a candidate. The vast majority of the electorate would not vote for a coalition of forces whose only agreed programme was to get rid of Thatcher and introduce PR. They would want to know what economic policies the new government would follow and how would they defend or improve the standard of living. If the economic policies did not seem adequate for the task then the majority of voters would put the Tories back for a fourth term.

It is when we come to consider the sort of economic policies that a Kinnock–Owen–Ashdown pact could agree on that the whole project falls apart. Both Owen and Ashdown are completely committed to the free movement of finance capital and would not support any deal with Kinnock if it involved any controls in this respect. Even if they could be persuaded to accept the intellectual case for controls, they would never be prepared to allow the bitter fight with the EEC which will be necessary because controls on capital could be interpreted as a breach of the Treaty of Rome.

We could only do a deal with the centre parties on grounds which would involve dropping the very policies which are essential to the modernisation of Britain. On the other hand, those who advocate the well trodden path of watering down our policies and scuttling into the centre ground ignore the fact that the centre ground is already crowded with the SDP, the SLD and the rebels from the old Liberal Party. It also overlooks the fact that Labour wins elections when it is radical, as in 1945, 1964 and 1974, and loses them when we are cautious and respectable as in 1951, 1970 and 1979.

There is no short cut to power.

But I am not pessimistic about Labour's chances. With so many of Thatcher's economic chickens now coming home to roost and with Gorbachev making our defence policy more relevant than ever before, we have every chance to win. As things go wrong in the economy and the trade deficit widens, it will become glaringly obvious that the Thatcher years really are the years the locusts consumed, and it will require bold and imaginative socialist policies to build in the wasteland they have left. Yet although the coming election is Labour's best chance to win since 1974, throughout the party ordinary rank and file members can be heard doubting that our leaders will ever show the necessary boldness or imagination required. But this is not a new situation, the sad truth is that our leaders never did. I sometimes hear socialists speak as though there was some long lost golden age of socialism when fiery radicals led us to great victories. They never did. What has occasionally happened in the past is that amongst ordinary people a massive desire for change has built up and developed into an irresistible force. When, finally, it becomes obvious that the demand for change can no longer be held off, it is then that the grey and respectable little men who perch on the green leather opposition benches in the Palace of Westminster wake up and rush off to place themselves at the head of that irresistible force. Having won power they dutifully carry out a package of reforms, the crisis passes, the irresistible force ebbs, and then the grey little men begin to talk of 'consolidation' (as Attlee did) or of being the 'natural party of government' (as Wilson did). They let the demand for change flicker out and as a consequence they are then thrown out and the Tories return.

This is exactly what happened with the Labour government of 1945. The demands for change that built up in the 1930s, as Britain declined under the complacent rule of Baldwin and Chamberlain, came from outside Parliament. They came from radical Labour councils which were fighting to establish local welfare states, from trade unionists struggling for better wages and conditions, and from the radical academics and intellectuals who debated the possible ways to create full employment and a welfare state. Some of this percolated through to Parliament but when the 1945 election finally arrived no one on Labour's front bench thought they would win. Indeed, because the votes of servicemen and women had to be brought back from overseas for the count, there was a three-week delay between the polling day and the count. For those three weeks Labour's Shadow Cabinet wandered around speculating whether Mr Churchill had got a majority of 150 or, if they were really optimistic, only 50. They had just lived through the greatest Labour victory of all time and they did not have a clue as to what had happened outside their isolated little parliamentary world. When they recovered from the shock of having won they did indeed respond to the demand for change and created both full employment and a welfare state.

Nor is it just Labour Party leaders who respond to pressure from outside. The most unlikely figures in the trade union movement can end up leading highly political strikes when their rank and file members demand it. There is no better example of this than dear old Len Murray, the greyest and most respectable man to lead the TUC in living memory.

When six dockers were imprisoned in 1973 for breaking the Heath government's anti-union laws, there was a tidal wave of anger from workers all over the country demanding an immediate general strike. Murray moved like lightning to place himself at the head of this angry reaction for fear that it would sweep, out of control, past the official trade union structure. He warned the government that he would call an official general strike unless the men were released at once. Recognising the strength of the forces mobilised against them, the government complied, the anger dissipated and Len Murray returned to a life of legal and constitutional propriety.

Trotsky once used an interesting analogy to describe this process of grass-roots pressure. He likened the economic and social forces which lead to great change to the rising wind in a gathering storm, depicting society as a tree buffeted by those elemental and uncontrollable forces. It was the newest and most distant leaves that first began to stir – the students and intellectuals. As the storm gathered force the great branches of the tree begin to move – the trade unions and organised workers. If this analogy is true then the leadership of the Labour Party is somewhere in the tap root, buried deep underground, and the first they know of what is happening is when the tree is torn out of the ground and they are exposed to the full force of the hurricane.

That is why Labour should devote the bulk of its energy to the struggles outside Parliament. Of course, Labour MPs need to be there for those few occasions when a Tory rebellion gives us the possibility of defeating a government measure, and also when there is an issue of great principle, but for the rest of the time we should be out in the country organising, educating and agitating against the government. We should go into the factories and offices, the colleges and the community centres, meeting students and pensioners, the workers and the carers and build a Labour party that is part of every struggle being waged against this government and for a better world.

If instead of organising the Labour Party only in wards and constituencies we built a Labour Party branch in every workplace, it would create the space in which millions of workers could discuss and plan what a Labour government could and should do to modernise their particular industry or profession. It would arm ordinary women and men with the knowledge and confidence to challenge the accountants and the economists and create the conditions for an extension of democracy to the workplace.

It is in the workplace that the Thatcher experiment has done its best to reduce the rights of workers – to use the fear of unemployment to break the will and confidence of workers and recreate the obedience and insecurity of the Victorian era.

Fifty-seven years ago Franklin Roosevelt was elected President of the USA in the depths of the greatest depression the world has ever known. On the day he took office the economy was collapsing around him. Unemployment was worse than anything we have known even under Thatcher and the banking system was just hours away from complete disintegration. Whatever differences a socialist would have about the policies that Roosevelt introduced, no one can deny that he correctly understood that the first step he had to take was to restore the confidence of ordinary people that it was still possible to impose their will on the economic forces that had devastated their way of life. In his first address as President, Roosevelt told the American people 'the only thing we have to fear is fear itself'.

That assertion is relevant to us today because this government has used fear to achieve its ends. It has used fear against its own people

– the fear of unemployment to undermine their confidence and independence. The first step on the route to a just and democratic society is to offer hope and confidence in place of that fear. And the best place to begin building that confidence is in the workplace itself. It is there that we can show what could be possible if our society recognised that every individual has the right to make a contribution to how that workplace should be run.

After ten years of Thatcher this may seem an impossible dream but the evidence of British history shows that the periods of great change and reform come suddenly and unexpectedly after long periods of Tory rule. We have had two such periods in this century – the Liberal government of 1906 and the 1945 Labour government. Their task was to respond to the poverty they saw around them and create new economic and social institutions which would bring that misery to an end. That had been the dream of trade unionists, socialists, academics and reformers for generations, and when those governments were elected they were responding to an agenda which had been created outside Parliament. The Liberals started and Labour finished that great task of creating a welfare state and full employment.

Similar struggles took place in most of the industrialised countries of the world over much the same period, but with the completion of the bulk of that task the parties of the left have seemed uncertain of their role.

Two days after the defeat of the Labour government in 1951 Attlee invited Hugh Dalton to join him for a last lunch at Chequers. They reminisced about the achievements of their government and concluded: 'We've done all that now; written the first chapter of the Socialist story, in law and administration. What next? The younger people must write the second chapter.' Certainly, here in Britain, Labour never seemed clear what that second chapter was to contain and following Labour governments lacked the surety of purpose that fired their predecessors.

The next Labour government will find that the task of repairing the welfare state awaits it, as does the relief of unemployment. But difficult though these tasks will be they are no more than the revision of the first chapter of the socialist story.

When we look at the theme of the next chapter it may seem as much of a dream to us as the creation of a welfare state was to those who fought the poverty of the Victorian era.

If the first chapter was about the redistribution of wealth then logically the next chapter is about the redistribution of power. It must feature the breaking up of the great, unaccountable concentrations of power that exist both here and internationally and passing that power down to the people; not creating great new bureaucracies to hold that power on behalf of the people but placing it in their own hands. To achieve this we must entwine democracy and socialism so that they become inseparable. In doing this we will change the nature and potential of both in ways that we can only just begin to glimpse. Once such a process starts it will be irreversible. Without such a process I doubt it will be possible for humankind to survive on this planet for much more than another lifetime.

Bibliography

The list that follows is my own arbitrary selection from the many hundreds of books which I believe most influenced my thinking as I worked on *Livingstone's Labour*. This does not mean to say that all the books listed reflect my own beliefs – for example, John Ranelagh views the history of the CIA from a political perspective completely at odds with my own, yet that does not prevent it being an excellent source of information on which I have drawn. I should also acknowledge seven journals which have provided much of the information that has contributed to my perspective on events, although, once again, I need to emphasise that I turn to them for information rather than political guidance. They are: *The Economist, The Guardian*, the *Wall Street Journal*, the *New York Times, The Independent*, the *New Statesman* and *New Left Review*.

Adams, Gerry, *The Politics of Irish Freedom*, Brandon, 1986.

Adams, Gerry, *A Pathway to Peace*, Mercier Press, 1988.

Andropov, Yuri V., *Speeches and Writings*, Pergamon Press, 1983.

Bailey, Geoffrey (ed.), *Hunter-gatherer Economy in Prehistory*, Cambridge University Press, 1983.

Beckman, Robert, *Into the Upwave: How to Prosper from Slump to Boom*, Milestone, 1988.

Bell, Geoffrey, *Troublesome Business: The Labour Party and the Irish Question*, Pluto Press, 1982.

Benn, Tony, *Office Without Power*, Hutchinson, 1988.

Bloch, Jonathan and Fitzgerald, Patrick, *British Intelligence and Covert Action*, Junction Books, 1983.

Blum, William, *The CIA: A Forgotten History*, Zed Books, 1986.

Butler, David and Kavanagh, Dennis, *The British General Election of 1987*, Macmillan, 1988.

Calder, Nigel, *Timescale*, Chatto & Windus, 1983.

Coates, David and Hillard, John (eds.), *The Economic Decline of Modern Britain*, Harvester Press, 1986.

Crankshaw, Edward, *Kruschchev*, Collins, 1966.

Dimbleby, David and Reynolds, David, *An Ocean Apart*, Hodder & Stoughton, 1988.

Dworkin, Andrea, *Our Blood: Prophecies and Discourses on Sexual Politics*, The Women's Press, 1982.

Dworkin, Andrea, *Letters from a War Zone*, Secker & Warburg, 1988.

Eisenstein, Zillah R. (ed.), *Capitalist Patriarchy and the Case for Socialist Feminism*, Monthly Review Press, 1979.

Ekins, Paul (ed.), *The Living Economy: A New Economics in the Making*, Routledge & Kegan Paul, 1986.

Farb, Peter, *Man's Rise to Civilisation as Shown by the Indians of North America from Primeval Times to the Coming of the Industrial State*, Paladin, 1971.

Farb, Peter, *Humankind*, Paladin, 1978.

Foot, Paul, *Who Framed Colin Wallace?*, Macmillan, 1989.

George, Susan, *A Fate Worse Than Debt*, Penguin Books, 1988.

Gorbachev, Mikhail, *Perestroika*, Collins, 1987.

Greider, William, *Secrets of the Temple: How the Federal Reserve Runs the Country*, Simon & Schuster, 1987.

Griffin, John (ed.), *Socialism in a Cold Climate*, Unwin Hyman, 1983.

Halliday, Fred, *The Making of the Second Cold War*, Verso, 1986.

Ham, Adrian, *Treasury Rules: Recurrent Themes in British Economic Policy*, Quartet Books, 1981.

Harrington, Michael, *The Next Left: The History of a Future*, vol. I, B. Tauris, 1987.

Hill, Jeremy and Scannell, Hilary, *Due South: Socialists and World Development*, Pluto Press, 1983.

Horowitz, David, *From Yalta to Vietnam*, Penguin Books, 1967.

Jackson, Thomas Alfred, *Ireland Her Own*, Lawrence & Wishart, 1976.

Kee, Robert, *The Most Distressful Country*, Quartet Books, 1976.

Kee, Robert, *Ireland: A History*, Abacus, 1982.

Kennedy, Paul, *The Rise and Fall of the Great Powers*, Unwin Hyman, 1988.

Lappe, Frances Moore and Collins, Joseph, *World Hunger – 12 Myths*, Earthscan Publications, 1988.

Leakey, Richard E., *The Making of Mankind*, Michael Joseph, 1981.

Leigh, David, *The Wilson Plot*, Heinemann, 1988.

Lewin, Moshe, *The Gorbachev Phenomenon*, Hutchinson Radius, 1988.

Mackintosh, Maureen and Wainwright, Hilary, *A Taste of Power: The Politics of Local Economics*, Verso, 1987.

McEvedy, Colin and Jones, Richard, *Atlas of World Population History*, Penguin Books, 1978.

McRae, Hamish and Cairncross, Frances, *Capital City: London as a Financial Centre*, Methuen, 1985.

Malinowski, Bronislaw, *Magic, Science and Religion*, Doubleday, 1954.

Miles, Rosalind, *The Women's History of the World*, Michael Joseph, 1988.

Nove, Alec, *The Economies of Feasible Socialism*, Allen & Unwin, 1983.

Palmer, John, *Europe Without America*, Oxford University Press, 1987.

Palmer, John, *Trading Places: The Future of the European Community*, Radius, 1988.

Pijl, Kees van der, *The Making of an Atlantic Ruling Class*, Verso, 1984.

Ponting, Clive, *Breach of Promise: Labour in Power, 1964–1970*, Hamish Hamilton, 1989.

Porritt, Jonathon and Winner, David, *The Coming of the Greens*, Fontana, 1988.

Ranelagh, John, *The Agency: The Rise and Decline of the CIA*, Sceptre, 1986.

Rentoul, John, *The Rich Get Richer*, Unwin Hyman, 1987.

Rowbotham, Sheila, *Dreams and Dilemmas*, Virago, 1983.

Rowbotham, Sheila, *The Past Is Before Us: Feminism in Action Since the 1960s*, Pandora, 1989.

Rowthorn, Bob and Wayne, Naomi, *Northern Ireland: The Political Economy of Conflict*, Polity Press, 1988.

Shorter, Edward, *A History of Women's Bodies*, Penguin Books, 1983.

Wainwright, Hilary, *Labour: A Tale Of Two Parties*, Hogarth Press, 1987.

Waring, Marilyn, *A New Feminist Economics*, Macmillan, 1989.

Williams, William Appleman, *The Tragedy of American Diplomacy*, W. W. Norton, 1988.

Wright, J. F., *Britain in the Age of Economic Management*, Oxford University Press, 1979.

Wright, Peter, *Spycatcher*, Viking, 1987.

Index

Abbott, Diane 124
abortion 96–7, 100, 103–4, 110
accountability
    civil service 79
    local 82
    MPs 23
Acheson, Dean 161, 180
ACTT 118–19
Adenauer, Konrad 170, 179, 182
AEU 109, 117, 258, 263, 270, 279
    'new realism' 261–2
    right-wing union 253, 266–7
AEUW 268–9
Afghanistan 200
Afheldt, Horst 235
Aganbegyan, Abel 200, 204–6, 209
aid programmes, Third World 245, 249
'Aims and Values' 34, 151
Alaska 153
Albania 196
Alliance 10, 109, 268
    proportional representation 81–2
    and unions 270–1
    women's vote 98
    working-class vote 260
    see also Liberal Party; SDP; SLD
Alternative Economic Strategy 23
American Federation of Labour (AFL) 184
Amory, Merle 281
Andropov, Yuri 198, 200–2, 209
Angleton, James Jesus 51, 53, 56
animal rights 244
Antarctica 243
anti-colonialism, US 151
    see also colonialism
anti-trade union legislation 4, 72, 81, 258, 265–7,
    271, 293
APEX 119, 271
Arab–Israeli War (1973) 219
Archangel 190
Argentina 286
armed forces, Europe 234–5
arms race 195–8
Arnold, G.L. 191
Ashdown, Paddy 80, 275, 291
Ashe, Thomas 146
Asquith, Herbert 145
ASTMS 118–19, 258, 262
Atkin, Sharon 113, 122
Atlantic Charter 176
atom bomb 283
    US 165–6, 175, 195
    USSR 168, 196–7
Attlee, Clement 175, 283, 292, 295
Attlee government (1945) 19, 48 292–3
Australia 46, 53, 242
Austria 186
authoritarianism, state 277

'B' Specials 147
Baker, Albert 126–33
Baker, James 222
Baker, Kenneth 38, 75, 208, 254
Bakers' Union 117, 119
balance of payments 225
    UK 18, 29–30, 37, 54, 162, 227, 254
    US 214, 216–17, 221–2, 224–5
Ball Major Joseph 48
Baltic States 190

banking system 31
    and Third World debt 245–6, 248
Barbie, Klaus 172
BBC (British Broadcasting Corporation) 48,
    282–3
Belgium 164, 175, 179
    Communist Party 184
    Socialist Party 187
Belgrano 286
benefits, state 29, 103
Benn, Tony 22–3, 47, 57, 67
Bentsen, Lloyd 239
Beria, Lavrenti 199
Bevin, Ernest 48–9, 186–7
BIFU 119, 258
Bill of Rights 70–2, 76, 83, 288
biotechnology 39–45
Black and Asian Advisory Committee
    (BAAC) 122
Black and Tans 146
Black and White Britain (PSI) 114
black people 112–24, 253, 279
    in Britain 120–1
    self-organisation 115–16, 118–20, 123
    and trade unions 113–20, 263
    in workforce 113, 256–7
Black Sections 112–13, 120–4, 252
Black Workers' Charter (TUC) 116, 119
Blaine, James 153
Blessing, Karl 215
block vote 55, 279
Blum, Leon 164
Blunkett, David 90
Blunt, Sir Anthony 50, 60–1
Borah, Senator 156, 190
borrowing 23, 25–6, 29
    US 220, 247
BOSS (Bureau of State Security) 48, 52
Brandt, Willy 51, 53, 188
Braunthal, Julius 182
Brent Council 281
Brent East constituency 2–3, 54
Brest Litovsk, Treaty of 183
Bretton Woods agreement 161–2, 214–16
Brezhnev, Leonid 198-200, 202
Brian Boru 135
British Aerospace 30
British Intelligence 128, 131–2, 134
    see also MI5; MI6; security services
British Leyland 258
British Telecom 35–6, 39
Brittan, Leon 285
Brookeborough, Lord 147
Brown, George 50
Brussels Pact 173
Bulganin, Nikolai 199
bureaucracy 70–1, 74
Bush, George 228
business unionism 261, 271–2
Byrnes, James F. 165, 195–6

Cabinet 70, 77
Callaghan, James 20, 23, 67, 79
    and defence policy 2
    and immigration 288
    and security services 57, 65
Callaghan government 22, 290
Camden Council 91
Campaign Against Racial Discrimination 121